Michèle Bald
Editor

D0148100

Second Edition

*Pre-publication
REVIEWS,
COMMENTARIES,
EVALUATIONS . . .*

" *The Use of Self in Therapy* is a remarkable book. With a delightful variety of voices and methodologies, its chapters seek to document and then resolve the historical tension between the intimate touch of healing and the detachment of modern clinical science. Speaking to clinicians of all medical disciplines, it invites us to integrate our professional and personal selves, to step out from behind the mask of our professional roles in order to be more personally present to our patients or clients (and ultimately to ourselves, as well). Its message is uplifting and meaningful: more than any particular clinical theory or methodology, it is human contact that heals. The self of the therapist is a tool to be applied with studied skill and artistry (for it is also capable of harm if applied injudiciously). And conversely, as David Keith writes in his chapter, 'if the therapist cannot be a self, neither can the patient.' "

Anthony L. Suchman, MD
CEO/Chief Medical Officer,
Strong Health MCO,
Rochester, NY;
Associate Professor
of Medicine and Psychiatry,
University of Rochester

" Virginia Satir was a pioneer in training therapists in the use of self in therapy. Now the concept and practice has become mainstream thinking in the therapeutic community. The book goes far beyond the earlier idea of a positive relationship between therapist and client. The various chapters encourage therapists to develop a state of being that is congruent, authentic, wholesome, loving, and, possibly, spiritual. Within that state of being, therapists are encouraged to connect with their clients and help them develop their inner resources to grow and become more responsible for their lives.

The contributors have presented their ideas, understandings, and wisdom in clear, theoretical, and practical ways. Of course, chapters by Satir and Rogers are a must. So are the chapters on 'Revealing Our Selves,' 'The Self in Family Therapy,' and 'The Person and Practice of the Therapist.'

This book needs to be read and studied by professors, therapists, and students of all therapeutic orientations. *The Use of Self in Therapy* has a convincing message of being and using our self."

Dr. John Banmen, R.Psych
Adjunct Professor,
University of British Columbia;
Co-author, *The Satir Model:
Family Therapy and Beyond*

More pre-publication
REVIEWS, COMMENTARIES, EVALUATIONS . . .

"**T**he therapist, inescapably, is a critical element in the effectiveness of therapeutic relationships. Yet during their professional education, few therapists have adequate opportunities to reflect on who they are and how they can use themselves effectively in their work with clients. Each of the thirteen chapters of *The Use of Self in Therapy* is written by a psychotherapist who addresses aspects of these issues and examines the impact of the person of the therapist on the process and outcomes of therapeutic relationships. The authors come from a variety of theoretical orientations and have different styles of practice and writing. They have all, however, been influenced by Virginia Satir and Carl Rogers, the insightful clinician-educators whose chapters appear in both the previous and this new edition of the book.

In this edition, which is dedicated to the memory of Virginia Satir, Michèle Baldwin nicely summarizes the special ways in which Satir contributed to the use of self in therapy. Two other excellent new contributions to this edition are chapters by Judith A. Bula, who writes both about the use of the 'multicultural self' for effective practice and the use of self by therapists following their own trauma experiences, and Charles Kramer, who challenges some of the traditional cautions about therapists revealing themselves to clients. Kramer goes on to describe how self-disclosure can actually enhance therapy.

The Use of Self in Therapy provides an array of useful perspectives and ideas for therapists, other health professionals, and educators who want to reflect on who they are and how they can most effectively use themselves in their efforts to be helpful to others."

Jane Westberg, PhD
Clinical Professor
of Family Medicine,
University of Colorado
Health Sciences Center;
Associate Editor,
*Education for Health:
Change in Learning and Practice*

The Haworth Press, Inc.

The Use of Self in Therapy

Second Edition

THE HAWORTH PRESS
Additional Titles of Related Interest

The Use of Self in Therapy

Second Edition

Michèle Baldwin, MSSW, PhD
Editor

The Haworth Press
New York • London • Oxford

The Haworth Press, Inc., 10 Alice Street, Binghamton, NY 13904-1580

Cover design by Monica L. Seifert.

Library of Congress Cataloging-in-Publication Data

The use of self in therapy / Michèle Baldwin, editor. — 2nd ed.
    p. cm.
  Includes bibliographical references and index.
  ISBN 0-7890-0744-4 (hc. : alk. paper). — ISBN 0-7890-0745-2 (pbk. : alk. paper).
  1. Self. 2. Psychotherapy. I. Baldwin, Michèle. [DNLM: 1. Psychotherapy—methods. 2. Professional-Patient Relations. WM 420 U84 1999]
RC489.S43U87 1999
616.89′14—dc21
DNLM/DLC
for Library of Congress   99-36719
                                                                                         CIP

This book is dedicated to the memory of Virginia Satir,
teacher, colleague, and friend,
with gratitude and love

CONTENTS

ABOUT THE EDITOR

Michèle Baldwin, MSSW, PhD, is a faculty member of the Family Institute at Northwestern University and a faculty member of the Chicago Center for Family Health. She also conducts a limited practice of marriage and family therapy and is a master teacher and trainer of PAIRS (Practical Application of Intimate Relationship Skills). Dr. Baldwin has been certified by the Academy of Certified Social Workers and by the American Association of Marriage and Family Therapists, where she is also an approved supervisor. She became a student of Virginia Satir's in 1969 and learned from her the importance of the person of the therapist in psychotherapy. She later worked with Virginia Satir for part of each year until the latter's death in 1988. She co-authored two books with Dr. Satir, *Satir Step by Step* and *The Use of Self in Therapy* (The Haworth Press, Inc.). Dr. Baldwin is also the author of a number of articles that have appeared in professional and lay journals.

CONTRIBUTORS

Harry J. Aponte, MSW, is Director of the Family Therapy Training Program of Philadelphia, Philadelphia, Pennsylvania.

DeWitt C. Baldwin Jr., MD, is Professor Emeritus, Department of Psychiatry and Behavioral Sciences at the University of Nevada School of Medicine, Reno, Nevada; and Senior Associate, Institute for Ethics, and Scholar in Residence, American Medical Association, Chicago, Illinois.

Judith F. Bula, PhD, is an Associate Professor at the Graduate School of Social Work, University of Denver, Denver, Colorado.

Helen V. Collier, EdD, is a licensed Counseling Psychologist and Marriage and Family Therapist, and a member of the American Psychological Association. After thirty years as a therapist, she now specializes in working with family systems, small work units, and the management of large organizations, both private and public. She is the author of *Counseling Women: A Guide for Therapists* (1982), *Freeing Ourselves* (1981), and numerous book chapters and articles.

Bunny S. Duhl, EdD, is currently Clinical Instructor in Psychology in the Department of Psychiatry of Harvard University Medical School. She teaches at Cambridge Hospital in the Couples and Family Therapy Training Program.

David V. Keith, MD, is Professor of Psychiatry, Pediatrics, and Family Medicine, and Director of Family Therapy, SUNY Health Science Center, Syracuse, New York.

Charles H. Kramer, MD, is Professor Emeritus, Psychiatry and Behavioral Sciences, Northwestern University Medical School, and founder of the Family Institute.

Grant D. Miller, MD, is Professor and Residency Director, Department of Psychiatry and Behavioral Sciences, University of Nevada School of Medicine, Reno, Nevada.

Carl Rogers, PhD (1902-1987), was a psychotherapist born in Oak Park, Illinois. He received his doctorate in psychology at Columbia University in 1931, and published his first book, *Clinical Treatment of Problem Children,* in 1939. He taught at the University of Chicago (1945-1957), where his research on the one-to-one relationship in therapy resulted in the book *Client-Centered Therapy* (1951). This nondirective approach rejected doctrinaire interpretations of the patient's symptoms and fostered the development of encounter groups in which the therapist acted primarily as a moderator. By the 1960s, Rogers' method was being widely adopted, from drug treatment centers to business organizations, and he himself became one of the best-known professionals in his field. Some of his other publications include *Psychotherapy and Personality Change* (1954) and *On Becoming a Person* (1961).

Virginia Satir, ACSW (1916-1988), was an educator and psychotherapist born in Neillsville, Wisconsin. She studied at the University of Chicago, and pioneered the development of family therapy by conducting workshops in the United States and many foreign countries. She helped found the Mental Research Institute at Palo Alto, California, and established the International Human Learning Resource Network, as well as the Avanta Network. Her publications include *Conjoint Family Therapy* and *Peoplemaking,* as well as many articles.

Meri L. Shadley, PhD, is an Associate Professor in the Counseling and Educational Psychology Department, University of Nevada, Reno, Nevada. She has been in private practice as a Marriage and Family Therapist for over twenty years.

Joan E. Winter, LCSW, PhD, is Director of the Family Institute of Virginia, Richmond, Virginia.

Foreword

When former patients are asked, "What was most helpful in the course of your therapy?" they almost never name a technique, interpretation, or theory. New therapists are shocked to find that these "important" topics are seldom mentioned. It turns out that effective therapy is a matter of the personality of the therapist. Former patients typically describe qualities such as these:

- No matter what I did or said, I never got clobbered.
- All was accepted, yet I was led to see where I had gotten on the wrong track, and helped to find a better way.
- It was really great to be able to say anything at all, no matter how shameful, and not be rejected.
- I became more courageous about my life after I heard about hers.
- Sometimes he had more trust and confidence in me than I had. That helped bridge me over to confidence in myself. By the time I finally got there, I was ready to quit.

These comments are not proof that people's descriptions are necessarily the true reasons for success. We never completely know the "true" reasons. Good therapy is the outcome of an intricate concatenation of factors, many intangible, a mystery. But one thing we can be certain of is the importance of the person of the therapist.

On the other hand, when patients have been in what they consider unsuccessful therapy, their most common complaints are about poor emotional connectedness to the therapist:

- I never felt like I was with a real person.
- Going three times a week for three years, I never heard my therapist give a single comment or opinion about *me*.
- She seemed mechanical, like she was working from a book.

- I didn't get either encouragement or criticism for what I did, which was okay at first, but eventually I wanted to know how I came across to him. I never found out, so I quit.

Our humanity is essential for therapeutic chemistry. Being fully present conveys the powerful message of listening without an axe to grind. Relaxed attentiveness increases the magic and decreases the misery. Shaping therapy so that it works is an art that generates from our creativity. And art that inspires, as good therapy does, is deeply spiritual, transcendent. I'm sure you have those moments.

Our consulting rooms are sanctuaries where the spirit of the process blossoms, where safety, intimacy, and deep emotion transform lives. The space and time wherein people are exclusively and seriously devoted to the work has the feel of a sacred quest.

Therapy proceeds simultaneously in two interpenetrating worlds, outer and inner. They are so closely intertwined that we seldom think of them as different. Yet for learning and doing therapy, and for evolving as an ever-more-competent therapist, temporarily separating the two is valuable.

The *outer* world of therapy is our everyday domain, which is taught and practiced everywhere, fills our professional journals, makes up the majority of training programs, and dominates our conferences. It is the world of many theories, many methods, many techniques for doing therapy. It has to do with diagnosis, treatment, outcome, grants, reimbursement, managed care, organizations, standards, credentials, and so on. This is the bread-and-butter world that every therapist must be knowledgeable about. For some it is the *only* world.

But there is another world, the *inner* world of therapy—your subjective realm: thoughts, feelings, attitudes, behavior, emotions, therapeutic experience, memories, life history, level of evolution toward mastery, inner cast of characters, style, opinions, personal story, family life, spiritual inclinations, philosophical beliefs, and more. Students get little help developing their inner worlds. Usually they are simply advised to enter therapy, thus sequestering personal growth from teaching and supervision. They are seldom shown how to integrate their maturation, seasoning, and self-mastery in the consultation room.

This book is about your inner world of therapy. There is an abundance of resources about the outer world. The dearth of help in evolving our inner world is the compelling motivation of the various authors, each contributing an aspect of how they use themselves in therapy. They make it clear that, ultimately, what we have to offer is not a technique, not a theory, but who we are.

Charles H. Kramer, MD
Professor Emeritus
Northwestern University Medical School

Preface

I feel the sadness of the loss of Virginia Satir as I begin writing this preface without her. I remember how pleased we both were when Charles Figley asked us in the fall of 1985 to put together a collection of articles about the use of *self** in therapy for the *Journal of Family and Psychotherapy*. We had for a long time bemoaned the fact that this very important topic, which had been discussed by individual and group therapists (Buber, 1970; Kopp, 1972; Yalom, 1980), was not considered very central to the concerns of family therapists.

Indeed, the field of family therapy, which had started in the 1960s as a movement questioning conventional patterns of therapy, initially focused on the development of theories and models in order to make this new form of therapy appear scientific, and thus valid. With the exception of Virginia Satir, Carl Whitaker, Murray Bowen, and a few others, most theorists and clinicians avoided dealing with the self of the therapist, which did not seem a valid topic of scientific inquiry. What is somewhat puzzling is that the concern about scientific objectivity was arising at a time when scientists in basic disciplines such as physics, chemistry, and molecular genetics had begun to question the validity of a purely technological approach to life. They stated that pure objectivity is an illusion, that objects are changed by the very process of observation (Heisenberg's uncertainty principle, 1927), and that not everything that exists is observable (Lynch, 1977).

Why did we believe that the self of the therapist was such an important topic? Because we believed that the importance of therapeutic techniques should not overshadow the fact that the self of the therapist is the funnel through which theories and techniques be-

---

*Whenever the term *self* is first employed in a chapter as part of the concept of the use of self in therapy, it is italicized to call attention to its special use.

come manifest. In most instances, individuals who enter therapy are in pain and feel isolated, and unless the therapist makes a real contact with the individual and/or the family members, no real therapy can take place, since they will not take the risk of exposing their vulnerabilities.

This can only happen if the therapist knows how to use himself or herself to make contact (read "The Therapist Story," Chapter 1). As Yalom points out along with many others, "it is the relationship that heals. Every therapist observes over and over in clinical work that the encounter itself is healing for the patient in a way that transcends the therapist's theoretical orientation" (1980, p. 401).

The request from Charles Figley came when the pendulum had begun to swing away from the preoccupation with models, putting emphasis back on the person. As Richard Simon (1986) expressed it: ". . . an increasing number of critics within the field have charged that our preoccupation with analyzing systems has led to a coldly mechanistic view of human relationships . . . we have grown strangely distant from the struggle of individuals to find purposes in their lives" (p. 34). Although this criticism still seemed to address the person of the client, who was supposed to have the experience of a human relationship, and did not say anything about the other party to the interaction, the opening was there to introduce the importance of the therapist-patient relationship.

We believed that the journal issue of *The Use of Self in Therapy* and the book, which came out simultaneously, marked the beginning of a new wave in which the person of the therapist would become the focus of much interest. The continuing sales of the original book and recent request by the publisher to produce a second edition seems to confirm this belief.

Most family therapists would agree that, of course, the self of the therapist is important. However, if the subject was seriously considered, it would not be treated casually, but researched and written about, and this did not happen. As Meri Shadley points out in her revised chapter in this second edition, "Although articles about models and theories have decreased in number, Naden et al. (1997) found that 61 percent of all writings in the field between 1980 and 1995 centered on clinical issues. Sprenkle and Bailey (1996) reported that clinical manuscript submissions to the *Journal of Marital and Fam-*

ily Therapy between 1993 and 1996 had increased by approximately 50 percent, but submissions about training had decreased by 60 percent. . . . Fewer than 10 percent of the training and professional issues articles encountered by Naden et al. (1997) were about the self of the therapist" (Chapter 9, p. 192). It is of interest, however, that at the 1999 Family Therapy Network Symposium, seven presentations featured aspects of the use of self.

What are the reasons for which this important topic has taken so long to get the attention it merits? One reason has to do with the changes in the field. Indeed, in the past decade, with the advent of managed care, expedience in clinical work has become a necessity, demanding that the focus remain on assessment, intervention, and problem solving, thus keeping the attention primarily on client change.

I do believe, however, that the greater resistance is at another level: As several authors in this book point out, if we believe that the relationship between therapist and client(s) is essential to the therapeutic process, using the self means that the therapist has to be willing to face his or her pain, finiteness, and vulnerability, in addition to possessing and using all the other therapeutic skills. Moreover (according to the sociologist Hans Mauksch, personal communication), scientific literature has failed to acknowledge ambiguity as an integral condition of human functioning. Scientific inquiry looks for certainty, instructions, and specificity, when in fact the self as process makes no sense unless you accept that its effectiveness is positively correlated with openness and imprecision.

Since this second edition is dedicated to the memory of Virginia Satir, I would like to address some of the very special ways in which she contributed to the use of self in therapy. It is important to remember that although she was one of the early contributors to the field, many considered her as a largely charismatic exception, whose unique ability to connect and communicate enabled people to make positive changes in their lives. Although her book *Conjoint Family Therapy*, written in 1967, was one of the first in the field, she did not in further writings contribute an explicit model that would have allowed a school to develop. In the absence of an easily identifiable system, her work was difficult for mainstream family therapists to understand.

She insisted that it was essential for the therapist to be able to use herself or himself effectively. Many other skills were needed to be an effective therapist, but they could only be used through the means of an authentic self. For Satir, "One of the characteristics of the dysfunctional family system is a lack of constructive feedback between family members regarding the impact of their behavior on each other. When the therapist does not allow his or her own self to be present with a family, the therapist operates under the same system as the family. When, however, the therapist uses his or her own reactions as a therapeutic tool, by sharing with the family how she or he is impacted by what is happening, and asking how his or her actions are impacting the family, a new way of operating is modeled which can effectively change the family system" (oral communication from Virginia Satir, November 1985).

Through the years Satir was able to attract followers who resonated with her message and who helped her to make explicit what seemed to be only "Satir magic." Some of her colleagues later helped to make explicit the model that she had implicitly developed and used over the years, thus dispelling the idea of her "magic," if that word meant that her methods were unique and could not be replicated. Essential to her model is an educated self. This education, which Satir called "Education to Become More Fully Human," was basic for therapists trained in her method. This meant that the therapist needed to learn mature and wise ways of being and behaving, in a way that very few people learn in their family or through their education.

One of the basic qualities necessary to be "more fully human" is congruence. Congruence is the ability to see and say things as they are, while respecting the Self, the Other, and the Context. This is an essential quality a therapist needs to make wise and honest decisions regarding the use of self with another person in a given context. In the state of congruence, the self of the therapist is fully present, nondefensive, and thus vulnerable, aware of the needs, vulnerabilities, and possible defensiveness of the other, within the context of the situation, in this case the therapeutic situation. A more fully developed discussion of the need for congruence on the part of the therapist is given by Judith Bula in her chapter, "Differential Use of Self by Therapists Following Their Own Trauma Experiences," in this book.

Another important consideration for Satir has to do with the three contexts in which a self functions and how to function in each congruently: First, in the monad, the self, through introspection, meditation, therapy, and other individual quests, learns to know itself better, learns self-acceptance, the foundation of self-esteem, realizes the many layers of the self, and develops the values that will guide him or her in the conduct of therapy. Second, in the dyad, the basic issue for the self becomes: "Does any self have the right to tell another self what to do?" which is the issue of power in any personal or professional relationship. In the context of therapy, the power should not be in the person of the therapist, but in the process of empowering the client or family to take charge of their lives. The third way of being in this world is in a triad or multiple, in which the self needs to learn the complexity of being at times a bystander and an observer, comfortable in that role, but possessing the skills necessary for intervention when needed. Knowing how to operate in a triad is a particularly essential skill for the family therapist.

Another way in which the Satir training focused on the self of the therapist was there all along, but was only fully developed and made explicit in *The Satir Model: Family Therapy and Beyond,* written in collaboration with John Banmen, Jane Gerber, and Maria Gomori (Satir et al., 1991). There she compared the person to an iceberg, in that only a small part of him or her was observable or apparent, while the largest part was invisible, hidden under water. When we do not know a person, we are only aware of the visible part, while the most important aspects of knowing a person deal with understanding the hidden layers, where each of us spends most of our time. We need to understand the yearnings, expectations, feelings, perceptions, and coping mechanisms of a person to have access to his or her self. Each person's uniqueness comes from his or her personal history, which affects the way we process internally. This is true for all human beings, but since "in the area of building relationships and intimacy, a therapist cannot take people where he has not been" (Luthman and Kirschenbaum, 1974, p. 62), the therapist's training needs to focus on the way in which the different layers of his or her personal iceberg interact. This, then, enables him or her to connect with clients.

One important note needs to be made regarding the content of this book. All the contributing authors have had training in couple and family systems in addition to engaging in individual psychotherapy. In the absence of specific guidelines, they were left free to decide from what perspective they would write. I do not believe that this is a major problem. Although the therapist is much more active in family than in individual therapy, the way the therapist uses himself or herself in relationship to the context appears to reflect differences in form rather than in function.

Also, it is important to state that, although this book concerns the use of self in therapy, many of the issues that are being raised here apply to other fields as well, such as teaching, parenting, or any other helping activity.

Finally, I would like to thank Bill Palmer, vice president and managing editor of the book division at The Haworth Press, for inviting me to put together this second edition; Patricia Brown, production manager, for her advice and support; Melissa Devendorf, administrative assistant; Andrew R. Roy, production editor; Peg Marr, senior production editor; Karen Fisher, copy editor; Dawn Krisko, production editor; and Donna Biesecker, typesetter. I have much appreciation for The Haworth Press. I would also like to express my appreciation to the authors of the first edition who agreed to review and revise their earlier contributions and to the new authors who responded to my invitation. I was very grateful for their timely responses in sending in their manuscripts. My deepest appreciation goes to Charles Kramer, whose friendship and mentorship has meant much to me through the years and who agreed to review the manuscripts and write a foreword. Last, but not least, is my husband, who pushed me to accept this assignment knowing fully that he would have to listen to my complaints and excitements as well as review my own contributions.

Michèle Baldwin

REFERENCES

Buber, M. (1970). *I and Thou.* New York: Charles Scribners.
Kopp, S.B. (1972). *If You Meet the Buddha on the Road, Kill Him.* Ben Lomond, CA: Science and Behavior Books.

Luthman, S.G. and Kirschenbaum, M. (1974). The Dynamic Family. Palo Alto, CA: Science and Behavior Books.

Lynch, J.J. (1977). *The Broken Heart.* New York: Basic Books, Inc.

Satir, V., Banmen, J., Gerber, J., and Gomori, M. (1991). *The Satir Model: Family Therapy and Beyond.* Palo Alto, CA: Science and Behavior Books.

Simon, R. (1986). Our Quarterbacks and Coaches. *Family Therapy Networker,* March-April, 30-34.

Yalom, I.D. (1980). *Existential Psychotherapy.* New York: Basic Books, Inc.

Introduction

Michèle Baldwin

This book includes thirteen chapters written by psychotherapists with varying theoretical orientations, all concerned with the impact of the person of the therapist on therapeutic process and outcome. Excluding Virginia Satir and Carl Rogers, who have since died, contributors to the first edition were asked to participate in this second edition. With the exception of one, they all agreed, and two authors were added.

The two lead chapters, the first written by Satir and the second an interview with Rogers, were not changed from the first edition. The work of these two seminal thinkers and clinicians forced the field of psychotherapy to open itself to new possibilities, and their ideas had an impact on all the other contributors to this book. The third chapter, written by DeWitt C. Baldwin Jr., gives historical perspective to this collection. Chapters 4 through 6 are written by three therapists, Charles H. Kramer (new to this second edition), Helen V. Collier, and Bunny S. Duhl, all of whom describe the way in which they use, or have used themselves in their clinical practice. By looking at the implications that her model has for the training of therapists, Bunny Duhl's writing provides a bridge to the next two chapters, which deal with education of the *self*.* Chapter 7, written by Harry J. Aponte and Joan E. Winter, focuses on developing the competency of the person of the therapist, while Chapter 8, written by Judith F. Bula, another new contributor to this edition, focuses on the development of the self from a multicultural perspective. Chapter 9, written by Meri L. Shadley, describes research done on the use of self across different schools of family therapy. In Chapter 10, Judith Bula fo-

---

*Whenever the term *self* is first employed in a chapter as part of the concept of the use of self in therapy, it is italicized to call attention to its special use.

cuses her research on the use of self by therapists following their own trauma experiences. The topic of her research on the "wounded" therapist segues into Chapter 11, co-authored by Grant D. Miller and DeWitt C. Baldwin Jr., on the relationship between the wounded-healer paradigm and the use of self in therapy. In the last two chapters, we follow David V. Keith in his musing thoughts and reflections as he looks at the way in which the relationship between a community of selves and the "I" affects psychotherapy.

Virginia Satir, in "The Therapist Story" (Chapter 1), takes an overview based on her experience and observations in forty years as clinician and teacher. She starts by acknowledging the revolutionary contribution of Freud to mental health practice, then points out how, since the 1960s, the model of therapy has been expanded from the authoritarian doctor-patient relationship to include the patient as a partner. Next, Satir indicates the need to take into account the self of the therapist. Freud advocated that for the protection of the patient, the self of the analyst should remain neutral, and, to achieve this goal, mandated that he or she submit to a training analysis. Pointing out the damage that can be done by a therapist who is not aware of how he or she uses the self, Satir focuses on specific aspects of the therapist's behavior, such as the use of power, dealing with personal vulnerability, and congruence. Having thus alerted the reader to the dangers of the unaware self, especially in the misuse of power, she then states that the self of the therapist can and must be used to achieve positive therapeutic results. She views therapy as providing the context for empowering patients and opening up their healing potential, and states that this goal can only be obtained through the meeting of the deepest self of the therapist with the deepest self of the client. In concluding, she makes a plea that the self of the therapist be considered an essential factor in the therapeutic process.

Carl Rogers' career spanned over half a century of tremendous change in the field of psychotherapy, and his perspective on his evolution as a therapist seemed essential for an understanding of our topic. When initially approached, Carl Rogers stated that he was unable to take on an additional writing commitment at that time. Because of his interest in the subject, however, he suggested the alternative of an interview. We were faced with the choice of foregoing his participation or accepting his contribution in the form he proposed, and decided to present this interview in the form of an essay (Chapter 2). Rogers starts by pointing out his increased awareness of the use of self over time, and his own experience with the use of self, including some of the risks involved. He then states his view about related topics such as the therapist as a model, self-determination, transference, what constitutes appropriate goals for the therapist, and the importance of maturity in the therapist. The middle section of the essay reviews the major turning points of Rogers' career and his evolution from a traditional therapist and academician, through person-centered therapy, to an increasing awareness of the spiritual potential and dimension of the therapeutic relationship. This leads him to review the qualities of the authentic therapist, who, as a person, is both secure and aware of the flaws that make him or her vulnerable. He then briefly comments on his views about the training of person-centered therapists, and concludes with a few words about what he believes his impact—or lack of it—has been in the field of psychology, psychiatry, medicine, nursing, and counseling.

DeWitt C. Baldwin Jr., in "Some Philosophical and Psychological Contributions to the Use of Self in Therapy" (Chapter 3), writes a scholarly chapter in which he gives historical perspective to this collection, making only some minor changes to his writings for the first edition. After a brief discussion of reasons why the concept of the use of self in therapy has emerged at this time, the author looks retrospectively at the fascination concepts of self have held for writers and philosophers through the ages. He develops the view that it was not until Kierkegaard and the existential philosophers called attention to the world of subjective experience that the concept of the human being as both subject and object—as a self—emerged.

Conceptualization of self excited the attention of philosophers such as Heidegger, clinicians such as Carl Rogers, sociologists such as George Herbert Mead, and theologians such as Tillich. This led to the renewed interest in the "I/Thou" relationship, as posited by Buber, as well as in client-centered therapy as proposed by Rogers, both of whom place emphasis on mutual respect between patient and therapist.

After briefly reviewing the evolution of the concept of self in the works of Freud, Sullivan, Horney, Kohut, and Arieti, Baldwin examines how psychiatry has been affected by changing views of the neuroses since Freud, and by the emergence of existential philosophy. In this context, he examines the works of Victor Frankl, R. D. Laing, and Carl Rogers. He concludes by giving a description of the characteristics of the existential therapist for whom the use of self is an essential element in therapy, whether it be with individuals, groups, or families.

In "Revealing Our Selves" (Chapter 4), Charles Kramer starts by pointing out that as therapists we cannot *not* reveal ourselves and that we are *models* for patients, whether we like it or not. The question is how this is best done and to determine what sort of a person the therapist should be with patients. He points out how self-disclosure is essential to good therapy and gives guidelines and suggestions necessary for self-disclosure. He describes how self-disclosure enhances therapy, giving many examples based on his own experience.

Next he explores the risks inherent in this process, either saying too much—bad disclosure—or saying little—avoiding disclosure. Because errors of omission are less obvious than errors of commission, most beginners are taught to say nothing personal as a safer way "to establish a professional boundary." They do not learn how to create an optimal boundary by the appropriate self-disclosure that would facilitate the client's trust and openness. Kramer then points out that the most important benefit of self-disclosure is to diminish transference. He compares the process of analysis, where minimizing personal information is aimed at building the transference, to the very different process of face-to-face therapy, in which a regressive, dependent transference is not desirable. Another benefit of openness is that it teaches therapists to take the risks and make the mistakes necessary for becoming an authentic therapist. By disclosing his or her inner process, the therapist helps patients and students to do the same. In addition, beyond the enhancement of therapy, self-disclosure has the benefit of enabling the therapist to become more open in other areas of life, especially with his or her own family.

Kramer debunks the concern about slippery boundaries by observing that the fear of overinvolvement in order to maintain professionalism seems to have been ineffective in preventing 5 to 10 percent of physicians from having ill-advised sex with their patients. Self-disclosure is also effective because it demonstrates empathy, which people often do not learn in their family relationships. It can also be helpful in cotherapy situations as patients become aware of how therapists deal with their disagreements, thus offering them corrective experiences on how to deal with negativity. Kramer offers specific information about dealing with therapist illness and "other distractions," suggesting that we overestimate the negative impact of a simple explanation, which has a calming effect, whereas "stonewalling" or ignoring the issue is often upsetting. Seeing people as needing protection is disempowering and has more to do with avoidance of the discomfort of self-revelation than with the patient's benefit.

Finally, Kramer examines the process of giving and receiving, pointing out that it is usually a one-way street, in which only the patient is supposed to self-disclose and where the giving only goes in the direction of the patient. This undermines the process of health, which requires the ability to both give and receive. A list of suggestions and ground rules is given on how to self-disclose. The chapter ends with the author's evolution of self-disclosure styles through the several phases of his career.

In "The Differing Selves" (Chapter 5), Helen Collier examines the use of self from a woman's perspective. She begins by stating her position regarding the myth of objectivity and reliance on scientifically replicable techniques in therapy. Although these techniques are useful, only the personal presence of the therapist is central to the therapeutic process.

This personal presence needs to be carefully monitored, however, because an unaware self can be dangerous for the therapeutic process. Indeed, if the therapist's ego becomes central or dominant, the therapeutic process is derailed and the therapy will be unsuccessful. The awareness of how to use the self may be the most valuable technique a therapist can have because clear choices can be made as to which role to play in a given situation. Collier sees this steady awareness, which she calls "healthy energy," as the normal human experience of total presence in the world. This healthy energy is essential to being a good therapist. She points out that we cannot hope to increase the degree of consciousness and responsiveness to the interaction between organism and environment and the sense of aliveness in the client if we do not have it in ourselves.

The next section of this chapter deals with the differing selves of men and women, in that they experience reality differently, the differences centering around experiences of attachment and separation. Males hold tight boundaries for the exercise of exclusion and believe that there is one right way to live, while females have loose boundaries for the process of interconnection and believe that there are many right ways to live, their task being to find the right one for now. Inevitably they speak in different voices. Of course, one must beware of creating rigid stereotypes, but more recent empirical research shows that certain values, attitudes, and behaviors are related to gender. Collier advocates an expansion of each sex into the virtues of the other, resulting in the enrichment of everyone's professional skills. She proceeds by giving a summary of how she brings herself into the therapeutic process. Essentially, she helps her clients to decide whether autonomy or detachment would be a better choice for them in a particular situation, fully respecting the different female and male voices. She ends her chapter with the observation that for many years men used to enter therapy with her because they felt confusion and frustration with regard to women. They now seem to come with the hope that they can love and live with women more effectively, embracing the ethic of caring and attachment. They seem to understand that what we share as humans is much greater than what separates us as women and men. She concludes that if her assumptions are correct, the important choice for the client is to find the therapist who will offer the widest and most flexible response as an individual to the dilemmas he or she presents. Thus it is essential for the therapist to learn to use the self with the flexibility, integrity, and range that each and every client merits.

In "Uses of the Self in Integrated Contextual Systems Therapy" (Chapter 6), Bunny Duhl explores the many ways in which she uses herself in therapy. She starts by giving a brief description of the therapy model which was developed at the Boston Family Institute, a model that derives from general systems and learning theory. To facilitate change in such a model, the therapist helps people to internally update the way in which they hold beliefs, meanings, and information and externally experience and enact alternate ways of behaving and relating. The task of the therapist is to tune people into their untapped resources and offer them tools with which to use these resources in daily life and problem solving. Duhl then briefly reviews the implications that such a model has for the training of therapists. The second half of her chapter consists of problem-solving anecdotes from her own life, which she has used successfully with her clients.

In "The Person and Practice of the Therapist: Treatment and Training" (Chapter 7), Harry J. Aponte and Joan E. Winter focus on the development of the competency of the "person of the therapist." They begin by examining the four essential skills that a clinician needs to effect a positive therapeutic outcome in the authors' training model: external skills (technical behavior), internal skills (integration of personal experience), and theoretical and collaborative skills. The authors point out that although theoretical and collaborative skills are generally viewed as requisite for the clinical practitioner of any school of training, a major division exists between schools of training which focus on the technical and behavioral skills of the therapist, such as Haley, Minuchin, and Falloon, and those which stress the personal integration of the clinician, such as Bowen and Satir. Although Bowen and Satir were very different, they both believed that the therapist needed to be personally integrated in order to work effectively with their clients. Because few programs offer an integration of both personal and technical skills, trainees are often faced with making an "either/or" choice: to develop expertise in technical or in personal skills. In contrast, the "Person and Practice of the Therapist" training model does not depend on a specific clinical framework, and utilizes a generic teaching method that can accommodate a variety of clinical models. The theoretical framework in this approach is designed to elicit all participants' development of their own theories, technical and collaborative skills, and how they use themselves to attain positive outcomes with clients. The authors then give us a historical perspective by comparing Freud's psychoanalytic model of training, with its emphasis on the analyst's needs to provide a blank screen for clients, with that of the family therapist, who plays an active role in creating family change.

Further clarification of the connection between the clinician and treatment is made by looking at the therapeutic relationship from the perspectives of both the client family members and the therapist. Although treatment is for the benefit of the client family members, therapists' lives are also affected by the process. Within the Person-Practice framework, the practitioner must be aware of interface issues and how they are affected by the therapy. Indeed, successful therapists learn how to employ their strengths and problems as resources for their clients' growth and change, converting the pain of their flaws into life wisdom to better help their clients. To do this successfully they need training.

The Person-Practice model recognizes that when therapists engage in clinical work with family systems, their own personal issues are jostled in a way that few encounters do. Therefore, in this model, training becomes an occasion for clinicians to obtain an intervention for themselves within the context of their work. Also, the authors believe that providing treatment acts as a potent stimulus to personal growth and possibilities for change in the practitioner. They continue this section by pointing out the catalytic forces inherent in the conduct of therapy that provide this opportunity in a way that may not have happened in the therapist's personal or family treatment.

Next, the authors give an overview of predominant models of training, emphasizing those which focus on the person of the therapist, specifically Bowen and Satir. The Person-Practice model differs from them in one major respect by focusing primarily on the *bridge* between the therapist's personal life and the actual conduct of treatment. The training model utilizes and selects among a variety of contexts to affect the therapist, including the contexts of clinical practice, supervisory relationship, marital relationship, nuclear and family of origin, practice setting, collegial relationships, and personal therapy.

The goals in training the person of the therapist are then described: the primary purpose of the training is on the therapist's clinical work; the second complementary goal is to assist the therapist toward improved individual functioning and personal development. After describing the actual format of the training, the chapter ends by illustrating the training process with a transcript of a training session and the trainee's written reaction to this intervention, followed by the transcript of a live therapy interview conducted by the trainee one month later.

In "Use of the Multicultural Self for Effective Practice" (Chapter 8), Judith Bula looks at the long-overdue emergence of multicultural awareness in the helping professions, putting special emphasis on the use of the multicultural self. In addition to her own clear thinking on the subject, she offers a good review of important literature.

According to Bula it is essential for the counselor to be aware of his or her own assumptions, values, and biases as a first step before attempting to understand the worldview of a culturally different client. The first section of this chapter offers a definition of the "multicultural self" as implying a "sense of simultaneous loyalty to and embracing of more than one culture," and identifying the eight following multicultural factors: ethnicity, gender, age, religion, socioeconomic status, sexual orientation, differing abilities, and language. To become familiar with one's self-identification with these factors, an assessment is necessary both in terms of content and affect, followed by learning more about one's beliefs, attitudes, and knowledge related to each factor. One must be willing to experience empathy for this self, which may experience inner conflicts when different parts are at odds with one another. A couple of self-assessment tools are offered that can serve as helpful exercises for knowing one's multicultural self.

Having ascertained that the first step for a helper is to be aware of the multicultural self, Bula looks at the ways the helper can use that information to better understand and assist those with whom he or she works. The essential quality required to truly embrace differences is the ability to experience empathy. The next step is to have a way for the helper to assess his or her cross-cultural competencies. This includes having to be sensitive to the need to use techniques and methods that fulfill the service needs of ethnic minority persons. Multiculturalists recommend the development of the process of *conscientizacao*, meaning "the development of critical consciousness." Specific guidelines are then offered for counselor self-assessment of cross-cultural counseling competencies, followed by the identification of the skills necessary for developing appropriate intervention strategies and techniques. Bula stresses the necessity of defining interventions that are systemic and provide a "good fit" for the various needs of each client. She then points out how the verbal and nonverbal communication skills of the counselor can promote or block the further development of the connection with the client. In the last part of the chapter, a case example is given of a skilled counselor using himself sensitively in the therapeutic setting, providing us with an interesting interweaving of multicultural factors of ethnicity, religion, age, and gender with family of origin dynamics.

In "Are All Therapists Alike? Revisiting Research About the Use of Self in Therapy" (Chapter 9), Meri Shadley starts by reporting the results of her original study (1987). The chief result was that the manner in which a therapist makes use of himself or herself in therapy has less to do with a therapist's theoretical stance than with personal realities such as gender, developmental stage, and personal attitudes. Discussions and writings since this original research support the validity of these findings in 1999.

Shadley conducted a multidimensional investigation into family therapists' use of self as part of broad part research on the professional development process. The thematic analysis of her investigation was derived from semistructured interviews with thirty therapists. The themes about the therapist's use of self broke down into four general areas.

The first area dealt with the therapists' definition and awareness of self. This question of what is the self of the family therapist was the most difficult for the subjects of the research to answer, but seemed to indicate that the professional and personal selves are intricately interwoven. This confirmed the researcher's premise that the professional self is a constantly evolving system that is changed by the conscious and unconscious interplay affecting the clinician.

In the second area, dealing with the personal qualities described as critical to therapeutic relationships, nine categories emerged, with each therapist finding two or three categories particularly valuable to the use of self. The most important result in this section of the study was that therapists from all orientations found genuineness to be one of the most important qualities for the effective use of self.

In the third area, interviewees indicated that their own personal characteristics were a vital part of their professional way of relating to client families. Many saw that certain personal traits could be simultaneously a strength and a weakness in their professional work.

Finally, Shadley examined the dimensions related to the use of self. One dimension continually referenced was verbal versus non-verbal disclosures of who the therapist was as a "real" person. A number of dimensions emerged as important to the interviewees' comfort with being self-disclosive. Although most felt that paralleling their own life with the client's family was useful, they varied in what and how to self-disclose, and Shadley delineated a continuum of self-disclosure styles, illustrated by many examples. The most disclosive style is *intimate interaction*, followed by the *reactive response*, and then the *controlled response*. Finally, the least personal self-disclosure is exhibited in the *reflective feedback* style. She found that all styles were fairly equally distributed among therapists in terms of program attended, degree, marital status, and parenting status, but that specific differences were found in viewing the styles across therapeutic orientation, gender, birth order, and clinical experience. Personal transitions such as having children, or tragedies such as losing a parent, were the most frequently mentioned events likely to induce therapeutic style changes in the direction of more openness and emotional intimacy with clients. An excellent summary of Shadley's research findings concludes this chapter.

Judith Bula, in "Differential Use of Self by Therapists Following Their Own Trauma Experiences" (Chapter 10), notes that there is little focus in the literature on the helping professional's use of self when they face their own trauma responses. She goes on to research the way in which a therapist uses herself or himself differently as a professional helper when that self has experienced a trauma. This topic is important, since there is evidence that the impact of personal trauma is a large factor in inducing therapeutic style changes in therapists. In approaching this inquiry, Judith Bula decided to use the qualitative research method of narrative analysis, and selected fifteen therapists who agreed to be interviewed. They had experienced a variety of trauma situations, and with one exception were at least one year beyond the traumatic incident.

A description of the content of the research follows. Therapists' responses to the traumatic event were similar to those of nonprofessionals in that they experienced a disconnection with their past selves. However, because of their academic and professional training they had a "head knowledge" that was sometimes helpful, but did not necessarily help in living through the experience. Therapists working with therapists who have recently suffered trauma must avoid the easy assumption that the latter will know how to respond to the trauma because of their intellectual understanding.

Since working with clients could reactivate their own trauma, therapists have to make some important choices following a traumatic experience: Should they continue to work after the experience, should they tell or not tell clients of their trauma, and would it be helpful for the client to know? A variety of responses emerged from Bula's subjects and it is important to look at how the therapists who decided to continue working used self-disclosure with their clients while also facing their own trauma. The concerns these therapists voiced included the relationship with the self, the relationship to their clients, and the context. This is the stance of congruence, as defined by Virginia Satir, when Self, Other, and Context are considered, allowing wise decisions to be made. Although therapists seem to be very aware of their clients' needs and of the differential context of family and workplace, they need to be careful to attend to the needs of their own traumatized selves and are responsible for seeking their own therapy.

In the last section of this chapter, Bula examines the deep, usually positive impact of the experience of trauma on the therapist's effectiveness. What seems to emerge from the variety of experiences described is an increased empathic recognition of the needs of the other resulting from a deep shift in perception through an experience of one's own. It also helped these therapists to move away from a disease model of posttraumatic experience to a more natural reaction, as part of a restorative process, rather than as abnormal behavior. Many of the therapists who were part of the study described a wholeness of experience that went beyond an intellectual approach to helping others.

Chapter 11, "Implications of the Wounded-Healer Paradigm for the Use of Self in Therapy," by Grant Miller and DeWitt Baldwin, again reminds us of the way in which our human frailties and vulnerabilities play a role in our effectiveness as healers. For them, the helping relationship embodies the basic polarities inherent in the paradigm of the wounded-healer, polarities that ultimately relate to the vulnerabilities and healing power of both the healer and the patient. It is their belief that only through appropriate recognition and use of the helper's own vulnerability can healing power effectively be realized in the therapeutic relationship.

They start with a historical perspective on the concept of the wounded healer, dating back to Greek mythology. They also provide a diagrammatic model to help analyze the interactional dynamics of the patient-healer encounter. They continue by describing the factors that facilitate healing. In addition to altruistic factors, such as trust, warmth, and empathy, conscious inner attention to oneself as a therapist must be present as well for a therapist to be an effective healer. Such inner attention can be developed either in personal therapy, during which unconscious elements emerge or are encouraged to be investigated, or through a conscious attention to the sense of vulnerability emerging from the therapist's own pain and suffering. Miller and Baldwin assert that this makes possible an unconscious connection, which activates the patient's healing power. In the process both patient and therapist can experience a sense of wholeness. This chapter concludes by suggesting that attention to one's vulnerabilities is not only indispensable to the healing process, but also decreases the likelihood of professional burnout through the energizing experience of creativity by the therapist.

The last two chapters of this book include some wide-ranging thoughts by David Keith about the complexities of the self. Although Keith wrote a new essay for this second edition, I decided to include the essay he originally wrote in 1987, because it makes clearer the evolution of his thinking on the topic.

In the 1987 essay, "The Self in Family Therapy: A Field Guide" (Chapter 12), David Keith started with the hypothesis that many enter the profession of psychotherapy in an effort to deepen their own connections with the self. Too often, however, professional training patterns take over and the self becomes dormant. The therapist may even become a prisoner of a model, with damaging results for the patient. Indeed, for Keith, the dynamics of therapy are in the person of the therapist. If he cannot be a self, neither can the patient. Social change may take place, but there will be no gain in spontaneity. It is therefore essential that the therapist knows his or her self in order to use it appropriately in therapy. Keith also points out that what applies to the self in family therapy does not automatically apply to individual therapy.

Next, Keith discusses the difficulty in knowing the self. Relating his personal experience in dealing with the self, which is in fact a community of selves, he suggests that the term "familiarity" with the self is a more accurate descriptor than the term "knowledge" of the self. The chapter then gives us glimpses of the self, collected over the previous eight years, and describes manifestations of the self as it appears in therapy. He includes the issues of power, integrity, a sense of the absurd and the use of humor, freedom for anger and "creative hatred," metaphorical reality, the influence of outside experience, the development of peer relationships, and the ability to let patients know that we love them. Keith concludes by stating that the patient's self will only appear if invited by the therapist's self.

In his new chapter, "I Look for I: The Self of the Therapist—Part II" (Chapter 13), David Keith starts by creating "A Bridge Over Nonlogical Waters" and points out that this more fundamental chapter logically should have preceded his original contribution. He explains that in both essays there is a lack of clarity, due to the abstract fluid reality of the I, the self, and the social self. Whereas in his first essay he wrote as an observer of the self, he now sees himself more as trying to give the I a voice. He begins by stating the difficulty of knowing oneself, and the constant dialogue between the self who knows he is Dave, and the I who is Dave's unknown daemon and has little to do with the practical aspects of living.

He points out that the difference between the I and the social self is unclear. The difference can emerge in therapy, in intimate relationships, in existential situations such as death, and in encounters with madness, confusion, and depression. In the confusing labyrinth of the I, categories are not clearly distinguished, but trying to avoid the madness of the I prevents us from becoming aware of what we don't know that we don't know.

In looking at the self in psychotherapy, he believes that, for him, it is most available in the multipersonal context of family therapy, as the self appears to be activated by ambiguity and intimacy. This self, however, makes our social self become anxious because it is spontaneous and unstructured, thus undermining social values and structure. Keith believes that family therapy started as a movement which questioned conventional patterns of living and healing. As it became more popular, it became a culture-supporting institution, which meant that it needed to conform to the forces of the mass culture, which requested conformity and scientifically proven results.

Keith draws a distinction between a psychotherapy that acknowledges and nurtures the I, and a psychotherapy which helps toward social adaptation. In life, we all play games of social adaptation, and Keith describes some of his adult roles. But there is more to him than a tricky social game player. He is a printout of early programming by his family, the strongest programming in terms of self-esteem happening at a preverbal time virtually inaccessible to reason-based language. Most psychotherapy does not focus on this period, focusing instead on the social adaptation that begins around age two and a half. Keith refers to this early programming as the "software" of the self, which is not changeable, but accessible through therapy. He sees learning to use the computer as a model for accessing the self, in that hesitations, frustrations, and mistakes ultimately lead to learning. This way of thinking was stimulated by working with families with schizophrenia, which can be understood as a desperate, forced immersion in the I.

In his concluding paragraph, Keith shares his perspective that the search for the I is a crucial counterbalance to mass culture. Unfortunately, when psychotherapy is taken over by the culture, it is unable to descend with the eyes of a searcher into the labyrinth of meaninglessness, a descent that is necessary to deepen the meaning of life and relationships.

Chapter 1

The Therapist Story

Virginia Satir

One hundred years ago, as today, we were nearing a new century. Then as now, people strongly felt that they lived in a period of great change. America was moving from a predominantly rural, agricultural way of life to an urban, industrial culture. The battle for human rights was emerging. Unions were forming to protect the rights of workers. Concerned citizens were lobbying for protection of children through child labor laws. Social reformers were mounting campaigns for women's suffrage. In the sciences, foundations were being laid for today's nuclear weaponry, space travel, and electronic communications. In that same period, a new psychology was being formulated that would change the way we think about ourselves. I would like to think that the advent of another new century will bring with it another change of consciousness about ourselves—one that places a high value on humanness. The therapist who makes *self** an essential factor in the therapeutic process is a herald of that new consciousness.

Sigmund Freud opened his practice 100 years ago in Vienna. In 1921, he visited the United States, bringing with him the new form of psychotherapy that he called psychoanalysis. His main thesis was that human beings carry the seeds of their construction as well as their destruction within them. This was a radical idea that eventually initiated a revolutionary breakthrough in mental health practice.

This chapter originally appeared in *The Journal of Psychotherapy & the Family*, Volume 3, Number 1. © 1987 by The Haworth Press. Used with permission.

*Whenever the term *self* is first employed in a chapter as part of the concept of the use of self in therapy, it is italicized to call attention to its special use.

Up to that time, the prevailing reasons for deviant and other unacceptable forms of behavior were thought to be bad environment, personal unworthiness, and "genetic taint." The cure was usually isolation, punishment, abandonment, or death.

Freud's views also offered a new way of understanding human behavior. By 1940, psychoanalytic concepts underlay almost all psychological thinking and treatment and it continued that way until the appearance of existential and holistic thinking in the 1960s. In some ways, I compare the impact of Freudian concepts with the work of Jellinek (1960), who advanced the idea that alcoholism was a disease and not the result of perversity or weakness. That, too, changed society's way of thinking and eventually led to new methods of treatment which offered hope to those who previously had no hope.

Originally, psychoanalytic treatment was administered by a trained psychotherapist (usually a physician) who, by "analyzing" the emotional experience and process of the patient, hoped to clear the way for the growth of health within the troubled individual. The early treatment model was that of the traditional doctor-patient relationship. The aim of treatment then, as it is today, was the eradication of symptoms, although the nature and meaning of symptoms have been greatly expanded over the years. The basic elements of psychotherapy remain the same, namely: a therapist, a patient, a context, the interaction between the therapist and patient, and a model for approaching treatment. However, the definitions of these elements have also expanded and changed through additions and deletions over time. For example, the patient now is sometimes known as the client, and may represent an individual, a group, or a family (Rogers, 1951). The therapist may also be called a counselor, and can include one, two, or even more persons. The therapist may be drawn from a variety of disciplines in addition to medicine and psychiatry, such as psychology, social work, education, or theology. The context now includes the office, the home, the hospital, and the school.

The therapeutic interaction is also seen as a relationship between therapist and patient and may be characterized by a variety of treatment approaches, such as psychoanalysis, psychodrama, Gestalt therapy, transactional analysis, the various body therapies, family therapy, and a host of others. The model of therapy has been ex-

panded from the traditional, authoritarian doctor-patient relationship to include the patient as a partner (Hollender and Szasz, 1956).

We have all observed that two people using the same approach
have come out with quite different results. We have also seen that
two other people using quite different approaches can come out
with similarly successful results. Yet very few training programs
really deal with the person of the therapist. Those that do are usually
in psychoanalytic and Jungian institutes where training in psychoanalysis is required or in some family training programs.

THE ROLE OF SELF IN THERAPY

Common sense dictates that the therapist and the patient must
inevitably affect each other as human beings. This involvement of
the therapist's "self," or "personhood," occurs regardless of, and in
addition to, the treatment philosophy or the approach. Techniques
and approaches are tools. They come out differently in different
hands. Because the nature of the relationship between therapist and
patient makes the latter extremely vulnerable, it is incumbent upon
the therapist to keep that relationship from being an exercise in the
negative use of power, or of developing dependency, both of which
ultimately defeat therapeutic ends.

Freud recognized the power of the therapist. He maintained that
the successful therapist had to handle his or her personal life in such
a way as to avoid becoming entangled in the personal life of the
patient. This led to the neutral, nonpersonal format of the psychoanalytic couch, with the therapist out of sight and relatively nonactive;
this despite the fact that Freud is reported to have given massage at
times to his patients and to have become actively involved in their
lives. Needleman (1985) claims that the secret of Freud's great
success and creativity was due to the great force of his personal
attention to his patients, which enabled him to project a quality of
compassion and insight that radiated a healing influence.

Perhaps doubting his own capacity and that of others not to
negatively influence patients, Freud developed the idea of mandato-
ry training analysis for all psychotherapists, during which the trainees were supposed to understand and master their own conflicts and

neuroses. This requirement was aimed at protecting the patient and creating the optimum conditions for change.

These ideas clearly stood on two basic principles: that therapists have the power to damage patients, and that they are there to serve patients, not the other way around. Most therapists today would agree that they would not consciously want to harm their patients. On the contrary, they would claim that they try to create treatment contexts that are beneficial to their patients. Most therapists would also say that they are there to serve their patients. However, the words "harm" and "serve" are open to many interpretations.

Furthermore, there was, and is, the idea that unconsciously, without malice or intent, therapists can harm patients through their own unresolved problems (Langs, 1985). One manifestation is reflected in what Freud called countertransference. Briefly, this means that therapists mistakenly and unconsciously see patients as sons, daughters, mothers, or fathers, thereby projecting onto their patients something which does not belong—a real case of mistaken identity. This is a trap, well recognized by many therapists. However, unless therapists are very clear and aware, they may be caught in the trap without knowing it. Unless one knows what is going on, it is tempting to blame the patient for a feeling of being "stuck" as a therapist. A further manifestation of this phenomenon is rescuing or protecting, taking sides, or rejecting a patient and, again, putting the responsibility on the patient.

When the prevailing model of therapeutic transaction, the authoritarian doctor-patient relationship, is experienced as one of dominance and submission, the patient and therapist can easily move into a power play that tends to reinforce childhood learning experiences. Throughout the therapeutic experience, the therapist may unwittingly replicate the negative learning experiences of the patient's childhood and call it treatment. For instance, when therapists maintain that they know, when they actually do not know, they are modeling behavior similar to that of the patient's parent. The dominance and submission model increases chances for therapists to live out their own ego needs for control. Manifestations of this control can appear to be benevolent, as in "I am the one who helps you; therefore, you should be grateful," or malevolent, as in "You'd better do what I tell you, or I won't treat you." These, of course, are shades of childhood past. When they are present in therapy, treatment aims will be defeated.

POWER AND THERAPY

The above are all disguised power issues. But power has two faces: one controls the other; the second empowers the other. The use of power is a function of the self of the therapist. It is related to the therapist's self-worth, which governs the way in which the therapist handles his or her ego needs. Use of power is quite independent of any therapeutic technique or approach, although some therapeutic approaches are actually based on the therapist maintaining a superior position (Dreikurs, 1960). There also are cases where there is outright and conscious exploitation by the therapist, and some even justify their aggressive, sexual, or other unprofessional behavior on the grounds that it is beneficial to the patient (Langs, 1985). Once, a man came to my office with a bullwhip in his hand and asked me to beat him with it so he could become sexually potent. While I believed that it was possible that his method would work for him, I rejected it on the basis that it did not fit my values. I offered to help him in other ways and he accepted.

Using patients for one's own ego needs or getting them mixed up with one's own life is ethically unsound. However, the therapist can be in the same position as the patient, denying, distorting, or projecting needs. It is possible for a patient or a client to activate something within the therapist of which the latter is unaware. It is easy to respond to a patient as though he or she is someone else in one's past or present, and if one is not aware that this is going on it will needlessly complicate the situation. If one is a family therapist, it is likely that somewhere, at least once, one will see a family that duplicates some aspects of one's own family. When this happens and the therapist has not yet worked out the difficulties with his or her own family, the client may be stranded or misled because the therapist also is lost. Therapists should recognize that they are just as vulnerable as patients.

While therapists facilitate and enhance patients' ability and need to grow, they should at the same time be aware that they have the same ability and need. One way to avoid burnout is to keep growing and learning. A great part of our behavior is learned from modeling, and therapists can model ways of learning and growing. It is also important to model congruence. An oversimplified definition of congruence is that one looks like one feels, says what one feels and means, and acts in accordance with what one says. Such congruence develops trust. This is the basis for the emotional honesty between therapist and patient, which is the key to healing. When a therapist says one thing and feels another, or demonstrates something that he or she denies, the therapist is creating an atmosphere of emotional dishonesty which makes it an unsafe environment for the patient. I find that there is a level of communication beyond words and feelings, in which life communicates with life and understands incongruence. Young children show this awareness more easily. In adults, this level of communication usually presents itself in hunches or in vague feelings of uneasiness, or sensing. If I, as a therapist, am denying, distorting, projecting, or engaging in any other form of masking, and am unaware of my own inner stirrings, I am communicating them to those around me no matter how well I think I am disguising them.

If patients feel that they are at risk because they feel "one down" in relation to the therapist, they will not report their distressed feelings and will develop defenses against the therapist. The therapist, in turn, not knowing about this, can easily misunderstand the patient's response as resistance, instead of legitimate self-protection against the therapist's incongruence. Therapy is an intimate experience. For people to grow and change they need to be able to allow themselves to become open, which makes them vulnerable. When they are vulnerable, they need protection. It is the therapist's responsibility to create a context in which people feel and are safe, and this requires sensitivity to one's own state. For example, it is quite possible for a therapist who is focusing on a technique or a theoretical construct to be unaware that her own facial features and voice tone are conveying the messages to which the patient is responding.

The presence of resistance is a manifestation of fear and calls for the utmost in honesty, congruence, and trust on the part of the therapist. The only times that I have experienced difficulty with people were when I was incongruent. I either tried to be something I was not, or to withhold something I knew, or to say something I did not mean. I have great respect for that deep level of communication where one really knows when and whom one can trust. I think it comes close to what Martin Buber called the "I-Thou" relationship (Buber, 1970).

Very little change goes on without the patient and therapist becoming vulnerable. Therapists know that they have to go beyond patient defenses, so they can help them to become more open and vulnerable. Defenses are ways patients try to protect themselves when they feel unsafe. When the therapist acts to break down defenses, the therapeutic interaction becomes an experience which is characterized by "who has the right to tell whom what to do, or who wins." In this struggle, the therapist, like the parent, has to win and the patient loses.

When the patient is somehow thought of as a trophy on the therapist's success ladder, this is another repetition of the way in which many children experience their parents—where they were expected to be a showcase for family values. Sometimes the therapist puts the patient in a position of being a pawn between two opposing authorities—as when a therapist puts a child between the parents, or between the parents and an institutional staff.

When the therapist sets out to help someone and leaves no doubt that he or she knows what is best for the patient, the therapist is subjecting the patient to repetition of another childhood experience. There are therapists who feel challenged to make something of the patient, "even if it kills you." These are often therapists who want to give messages of validation, although the outcomes are often very different.

THE POSITIVE USE OF THE SELF

If therapists can influence therapeutic results negatively through their use of self, then it must be possible to use the self for positive results. Therapists have that power by virtue of their role and status and person. We know that this power can be misused and misdirected. However, therapists also have the choice to use their power for empowering. Because patients are vulnerable, therapists can use their power to empower patients toward their own growth.

In the new model of treatment that emerged in the 1950s and 1960s, the therapist began to form a partnership with the patient. Patient and therapist could work together utilizing their respective actions, reactions, and interactions. The therapist was encouraged to model congruent behavior, and the focus of the therapeutic partnership was on developing health through working with the whole person. Eradication of the symptom was achieved by the development of a healthy state, which no longer required the symptom. In the traditional, authoritarian doctor-patient model, the emphasis was first on eradicating the symptom, with the hope that health would follow.

When the emphasis is totally on empowering the patient, the therapist will tend to choose methods that serve that purpose. When therapists work at empowering, the patient is more likely to have opportunities to experience old attitudes in new contexts (Rogers, 1961a). They have the experience of literally interacting with their therapists, of getting and giving feedback. The treatment context becomes a life-learning and life-giving context between the patient and a therapist, who responds personally and humanly. The therapist is clearly identified as a self interacting with another self. Within this context the therapist's use of self is the main tool for change. Using self, the therapist builds trust and rapport so more risks can be taken. Use of the self by the therapist is an integral part of the therapeutic process and it should be used consciously for treatment purposes.

MY USE OF MY SELF

I have learned that when I am fully present with the patient or family, I can move therapeutically with much greater ease. I can simultaneously reach the depths to which I need to go, and at the same time honor the fragility, the power, and the sacredness of life in the other. When I am in touch with myself, my feelings, my thoughts, with what I see and hear, I am growing toward becoming a more integrated self. I am more congruent, I am more "whole," and I am able to make greater contact with the other person. When I have spoken of these concepts in workshops, people thank me for speaking out, legitimizing what they have been feeling themselves. In a nutshell, what I have been describing are therapists who put their personhood and that of their patients first. It is the positive people-contact which paves the way for the risks that have to be taken. Many adults have reported they did not feel they were in contact with their parents and the others who brought them up. They did not feel like persons, but were treated as roles or expectations. If the therapeutic situation cannot bring out the people contact, then what chance does it have for really making it possible for people to feel differently themselves?

The metaphor of a musical instrument comes to mind when I think of the therapist's use of the self. How it is made, how it is cared for, its fine tuning, and the ability, experience, sensitivity, and creativity of the player will determine how the music will sound. Neither the player nor the instrument writes the music. A competent player with a fine instrument can play well almost any music designed for that instrument. An incompetent player with an out-of-tune instrument will vilify any music, indicating that the player has an insensitive, untrained ear. I think of the instrument as the self of the therapist: how complete one is as a person, how well one cares for oneself, how well one is tuned in to oneself, and how competent one is at one's craft. I think of the music as the presentation of the patient. How that music is heard and understood by the therapist is a large factor in determining the outcome of the therapy.

I give myself permission to be totally clear and in touch with myself. I also give myself full permission to share my views, as well as permission to see if my views have validity for the people with whom I am working. The person of the therapist is the center point around which successful therapy revolves. The theories and techniques are important. I have developed many of them. But I see them as tools to be used in a fully human context. I further believe that therapists are responsible for the initiation and continuation of the therapy process. They are not in charge of the patients within that process.

The whole therapeutic process must be aimed at opening up the healing potential within the patient or client. Nothing really changes until that healing potential is opened. The way is through the meeting of the deepest self of the therapist with the deepest self of the person, patient, or client. When this occurs, it creates a context of vulnerability—of openness to change.

This clearly brings in the spiritual dimension. People already have what they need to grow and the therapist's task is to enable patients to utilize their own resources. If I believe that human beings are sacred, then when I look at their behavior, I will attempt to help them to live up to their own sacredness. If I believe that human beings are things to be manipulated, then I will develop ways to manipulate them. If I believe that patients are victims, then I will try to rescue them. In other words, there is a close relationship between what I believe and how I act. The more in touch I am with my beliefs, and acknowledge them, the more I give myself freedom to choose how to use those beliefs.

What started as a radical idea 100 years ago has become part of a recognized psychology predicated upon the belief that human beings have capacity for their own growth and healing. In this century, more research and attention has been given to the nature of the human being than ever before. As we approach the twenty-first century, we know a great deal about how the body and brain work and how we learn. We can transplant organs, we can create artificial intelligence, we can go to the moon and other planets. We can communicate anywhere in the world instantly by satellite. We can fly across the Atlantic in three hours—a trip that took several weeks, 100 years ago. We have also created the biggest monster of all time—the nuclear bomb. We still have not learned to accept a positive way of dealing with conflict.

Amid these changes is the growing conviction that human beings must evolve a new consciousness that places a high value on being human, that leads toward cooperation, that enables positive conflict resolution, and that recognizes our spiritual foundations. Can we accept as a given that the self of the therapist is an essential factor in the therapeutic process? If this turns out to be true, it will alter our way of teaching therapists as well as treating patients.

We started out knowing that the person of the therapist could be harmful to the patient. We concentrated on ways to avoid that. Now, we need to concentrate on ways in which the use of self can be of positive value in treatment.

REFERENCES

Buber, M. (1970). *I and Thou.* New York: Charles Scribners.
Dreikurs, R. (1960). The Current Dilemma in Psychotherapy. *Journal of Existential Psychology* 1:187.

Freud, S. (1959). *Collected Papers,* Volume II. New York: Basic Books.

Hollender, M.H. and Szasz, T.S. (1956). A Contribution to the Philosophy of Medicine. *Archives of Internal Medicine* 97:585-592.

Jellinek, E.M. (1960). *The Disease Concept of Alcoholism.* New Haven, CT: College and University Press.

Langs, R. (1985). *Madness and Cure.* Emerson, NJ: Newconcept Press.

Maslow, A. (1962). *Toward a Psychology of Being,* Second Edition. New York: Van Nostrand Reinhold.

Needleman, J. (1985). *The Way of the Physician.* New York: Harper and Row.

Rogers, C. (1951). *Client-Centered Therapy.* Boston: Houghton-Mifflin.

Rogers, C. (1961a). The Process Equation of Psychotherapy. *American Journal of Psychotherapy* 15:27-45.

Rogers, C. (1961b). *On Becoming a Person.* Boston: Houghton-Mifflin.

Yalom, I. (1980). *Existential Psychotherapy.* New York: Basic Books.

Chapter 2

Interview with Carl Rogers
On the Use of the Self in Therapy

Michèle Baldwin

Carl Rogers, on account of his leading role in the field of humanistic psychology, was the first psychotherapist whom we asked to be a contributor to this volume. He felt that his busy schedule did not allow him to contribute a chapter at this time. Because of his interest in this area, however, he suggested as an alternative that he be interviewed on this topic. These words were spoken during a relaxed morning in his living room.

Over time, I think that I have become more aware of the fact that in therapy I do use my *self*.* I recognize that when I am intensely focused on a client, just my presence seems to be healing, and I think this is probably true of any good therapist. I recall once I was working with a schizophrenic man in Wisconsin whom I had dealt with over a period of a year or two and there were many long pauses. The crucial turning point was when he had given up, did not care whether he lived or died, and was going to run away from the institution. And I said, "I realize that you don't care about yourself, but I want you to know that I care about you, and I care what happens to you." He broke into sobs for ten or fifteen minutes. That

---

This chapter originally appeared in *The Journal of Psychotherapy & the Family*, Volume 3, Number 1. © 1987 by The Haworth Press. Used with permission.
*Whenever the term *self* is first employed in a chapter as part of the concept of the use of self in therapy, it is italicized to call attention to its special use.

was the turning point of the therapy. I had responded to his feelings and accepted them, but it was when I came to him as a person and expressed my feelings for him that it really got to him. That interested me, because I am inclined to think that in my writing perhaps I have stressed too much the three basic conditions (congruence, unconditional positive regard, and empathic understanding). Perhaps it is something around the edges of those conditions that is really the most important element of therapy—when my self is very clearly, obviously present.

When I am working, I know that a lot of active energy flows from me to the client, and I am now aware that it probably was present to some degree from the first. I remember a client whose case I have written up, who said toward the end of therapy: "I don't know a thing about you, and yet, I have never known anyone so well." I think that is an important element, that even though a client did not know my age or my family or other details of my life, I became well known to her as a person.

In using myself, I include my intuition and the essence of myself, whatever that is. It is something very subtle, because myself as a person has a lot of specific characteristics that do not enter in as much as just the essential elements of myself. I also include my caring, and my ability to really listen acceptantly. I used to think that was easy. It has taken me a long time to realize that for me, for most people, this is extremely hard. To listen acceptantly, no matter what is being voiced, is a rare thing and is something I try to do.

When I am with a client, I like to be aware of my feelings, and if feelings run contrary to the conditions of therapy and occur persistently, then I am sure I want to express them. But there are also other feelings. For instance, sometimes, with a woman client, I feel: "This woman is sexually attractive, I feel attracted to her." I would not express that unless it comes up as an issue in therapy. But, if I felt annoyed by the fact that she was always complaining, let us say, and I kept feeling annoyed, then I would express it.

The important thing is to be aware of this feeling, and then you can decide whether it needs to be expressed or is appropriate to express. Sometimes, it is amusing. I know in one demonstration interview, I suddenly was aware of something about the recording. I believe they had not turned on the recorder or something like that. It was just a flash and then I was back with the client. In discussing it afterward, I said, "There was one moment when I really was not with you." And he replied, "Yes, I knew that." It is very evident when there is a break in a relationship like that. I did not express that concern because it seemed irrelevant and yet, it was relevant. It would have been better had I said, "For a moment there, I was thinking about the machine, and now I am back with you."

I think that the therapist has a right to his or her own life. One of the worst things is for a therapist to permit the client to take over, or to be a governing influence in the therapist's life. It happened to me once, and was nearly disastrous. It was with a schizophrenic client of whom I got tired, I guess. I had done some good work with her—and sometimes not—and she sort of clung to me, which I resented, but did not express. Gradually she came to know me well enough to know just how to press my buttons, and she kept me very upset. In fact, I began to feel that she knew me better than I knew myself, and that obviously is nontherapeutic and disastrous to the therapist. It helped me to realize that one of the first requirements for being a therapist is that there be a live therapist. I think it is important to realize that one has a need and a right to preserve and protect oneself. A therapist has a right to give, but not to get worn out trying to be giving. I think different therapists have different kinds of boundaries: Some can give a great deal and really not harm themselves, and others find it difficult to do that.

A number of years ago, I would have said that the therapist should not be a model to the client—that the client should develop his or her own models, and I still feel that to some degree. But, in one respect, the therapist is a model. By listening acceptantly to every aspect of the client's experience, the therapist is modeling the notion of listening to oneself. And, by being accepting and non-judgmental of the feelings within the client, the therapist is modeling a nonjudgmental self-acceptance in the client. By being real and congruent and genuine, the therapist is modeling that kind of behavior for the client. In these ways, the therapist does serve as a useful model.

The way I am perceived by the client also makes a difference, but not in the therapeutic process. If I am seen as a father figure, for example, then that makes a difference in the therapy; it makes a difference in the client's feelings. But, since the whole purpose of therapy, as I see it, is to hear and accept and recognize the feelings that the client is having, it does not make much fundamental difference whether the client sees me as a young person or a lover, or as a father figure, as long as the client is able to express some of those feelings. The process is the same regardless of which feelings are being experienced.

This is why I differ so fundamentally with the psychoanalysts on this business of transference. I think it is quite natural that a client might feel positive feelings toward the therapist. There is no reason to make a big deal out of it. It can be handled in the same way as the fact that the client might be afraid of the therapist, or of his or her father. Any feelings are grist for the mill as far as therapy is concerned, providing the client can express them and providing the therapist is able to listen acceptantly. I think the whole concept of transference got started because the therapist got scared when the client began to feel strong positive or negative feelings toward the therapist.

The whole process of therapy is a process of self-exploration, of getting acquainted with one's own feelings and coming to accept them as a part of the self. So, whether the feelings are in regard to the parents, or in regard to the therapist, or in regard to some situation, it really makes no difference. The client is getting better acquainted with and becoming more accepting of his or her self and that can be true with regard to the transference feelings. When the client realizes: "Yes, I do love him very much," or whatever, and accepts those as a real part of self, the process of therapy advances.

I think that therapy is most effective when the therapist's goals are limited to the process of therapy and not the outcome. I think that if the therapist feels, "I want to be as present to this person as possible. I want to really listen to what is going on. I want to be real in this relationship," then these are suitable goals for the therapist. If the therapist is feeling, "I want this person to get over this neurotic behavior, I want this person to change in such and such a way," I think that stands in the way of good therapy. The goal has to be within myself, with the way I am. Once therapy is under way, another goal of the therapist is to question: "Am I really with this person in this moment? Not where they were a little while ago, or where are they going to be, but am I really with this client in this moment?" This is the most important thing.

Another important element is the maturity of the therapist. I recall that in Chicago, a graduate student did some research that seemed to indicate that the more psychologically mature the therapist, the more effective the therapy was likely to be. It was not a definitive research, but I suspect that there is a lot of truth in it. Not only experience in living, but what one has done with that experience in living makes a difference in therapy. It ties in with another feeling I have—that perhaps I am good at helping people to recognize their own capacities, because I have come to value and represent the notion of self-empowerment. However, somebody else may be good at helping them in another way, because they have achieved maturity in another realm. What I am saying is that different therapists have different characteristics of their mature personality and probably these different elements help clients move in those directions.

The mature person is always open to all of the evidence coming in, and that means open to continuing change. Often people ask me, "How have you changed over the years?" And I can see from the way they phrase their question that they are asking, "What have I rejected, what have I thrown away?" Well, I haven't rejected much of anything, abut I have been astonished at the fact that those ideas which started in individual therapy could have such very wide implications and applications.

My career as a therapist has gone through a number of phases. One of the earliest and most important was when I gave up on a mother and her son. My staff was handling the boy and I was dealing with the mother, trying to get across to her the fact that her problem was her rejection of the boy. We went through a number of interviews and I had learned to be quite attentive and gentle. I had been trying to get this point of view across but I was not succeeding, so I said, "I think we both have tried, but this is not working, so we might as well call it quits. Do you agree?" She indicated that she thought so, too. She said "goodbye" and walked to the door. Then she turned and said, "Do you ever take adults for counseling here?" I said "yes," and with that she came back and began to pour out her story of problems with her husband, which was so different from the nice case history I had been taking that I could hardly recognize it. I did not know quite what to do with it, and I look back at this as being the first real therapy case that I ever handled. She kept in touch with me for a long time. The problems with the boy cleared up. I felt it was successful therapy, but did not quite know how it came about.

Later, another change occurred. I had been impressed by Rankian thinking. We had him in for a two-day workshop and I liked it. So I decided to hire a social worker who was a product of the Philadelphia School of Social Work, Elizabeth Davis. It was from her that I first got the idea of responding to feelings, of respecting feelings—whether she used that terminology or not I am not sure. I don't think she learned very much from me, but I learned a lot from her.

Then, another stepping-stone. I had long been interested in recording interviews, but it was very difficult to do in those days. The equipment required that somebody be in another room, recording three minutes on the face of a record and then brushing off the shavings of glass, since we could not get metal during the war. Then, they had to turn the record over and continue. Anyway, it was really difficult. But when we began to analyze these interviews—and we gradually got better equipment—it was astounding what we learned from these microscopic examinations of the interviews. One could clearly see where an interview had been going along smoothly—the process flowing—and then one response on the part of the counselor just switched things off for a while, or perhaps for the whole interview. We also began to see that some of the people in my practicum came to be called "blitz" therapists, because they would seem to have a couple of very good interviews with their clients, and then the client never came back. It was not until we examined the recordings that we realized that the therapist had been too good, had gone too far, revealed too much of the client's inner self to them and scared the hell out of them. Another important development in my career was the writing of a very rigorous theory of the client-centered approach. I was very excited that what had gradually been developing quite experientially could be put into tight cognitive terms which could be tested. This gave me a great deal of confidence, and a great deal of satisfaction. Another change in my career occurred when I moved out to California. Having had the opportunity to realize the power of relatively brief intensive group experiences, I directed my energy to the development of intensive encounter groups. I also developed the applications of my theories to education, and then to large groups.

Finally, early in life I acquired a strong belief in a democratic point of view, and that belief has impacted my therapy. I became convinced that the final authority lies with the individual and that there is no real external authority that can be depended upon. It comes down to one's internal choice, made with all the evidence that one can get and the best possible way that one can cope.

I have always been able to rely on the fact that if I can get through the shell, if I can get through to the person there will be a positive and constructive inner core. That is why I hold a different point of view from Rollo May. He seems to feel that there is a lot of essential evil in the individual, but I have never been able to pin him down as to whether it is genetic or not. I feel that if people were evil, I would be shocked or horrified at what I found if I was able to get through to the core of that person. I have never had that experience—just the opposite. If I can get through to a person, even those whose behavior has a lot of destructive elements, I believe he or she would want to do the right thing. So I do not believe that people are genetically evil. Something must have happened after birth to warp them. It has often been said that I could not work with psychopaths, because they have no social conscience. Well, my feeling is: yes, it would be difficult and I don't think they would come easily into one-to-one psychotherapy. But if they could be part of a group for a long period of time, then I think they could probably be gotten to.

Recently my views have broadened into a new area about which I would like to comment. A friend, who is a minister, always kids me about the fact that I am one of the most spiritual people he knows, but I won't admit it. Another time, a group of young priests were trying to pin me to the wall, saying that I must be religious. I finally said to them and it is something I still stand by—"I am too religious to be religious," and that has quite a lot of meaning for me. I have my own definition of spirituality. I would put it that the best of therapy sometimes leads to a dimension that is spiritual, rather than saying that the spiritual is having an impact on therapy. But it depends on your definition of spiritual. There are certainly times in therapy and in the experience I have had with groups where I feel that there is something going on that is larger than what is evident. I have described this in various ways. Sometimes I feel much as the physicists, who do not really split atoms; they simply align themselves up in accordance with the natural way in which the atoms split themselves. In the same way, I feel that sometimes in interpersonal relationships power and energy get released which transcend what we thought was involved.

As I recently said, I find that when I am the closest to my inner, intuitive self—when perhaps I am somehow in touch with the unknown in me—when perhaps I am in a slightly altered state of consciousness in the relationship, then whatever I do seems to be full of healing. Then simply my presence is releasing and helpful. At those moments, it seems that my inner spirit has reached out and touched the inner spirit of the other. Our relationship transcends itself, and has become part of something larger. Profound growth and healing and energy are present.

To be a fully authentic therapist, I think that you have to feel entirely secure as a person. This allows you to let go of yourself, knowing confidently that you can come back. Especially when you work with a group, you have to surrender yourself to a process of which you are a part and admit you can't have a complete understanding. And then when you get to dealing with a group of 500 or 600, you surrender any hope of understanding what is going on, and yet, by surrendering yourself to the process, certain things happen.

The therapist needs to recognize very clearly the fact that he or she is an imperfect person with flaws which make him vulnerable. I think it is only as the therapist views himself as imperfect and flawed that he can see himself as helping another person. Some people who call themselves therapists are not healers, because they are too busy defending themselves.

The self I use in therapy does not include all my personal characteristics. Many people are not aware that I am a tease and that I can be very tenacious and tough, almost obstinate. I have often said that those who think I am always gentle should get into a fight with me, because they would find out quite differently. I guess that all of us have many different facets, which come into play in different situations. I am just as real when I am understanding and accepting as when I am being tough. To me being congruent means that I am aware of and willing to represent the feelings I have at the moment. It is being real and authentic in the moment.

I am frequently asked what kind of training is necessary to become a person-centered therapist. I know some very good person-centered therapists who have had no training at all! I think that one could go to small remote villages and find out who people turn to for help—what are the characteristics of these people they turn to? I think to be a good person-centered therapist, one needs to experience a person-centered approach either in an intensive group for some period of time, or in individual therapy, or whatever. I don't, however, believe in requiring such an experience. I feel that the opportunity should be available, but not required.

Then, in addition to that, I think that breadth of learning is perhaps the most important. I'd rather have someone who read widely and deeply in literature or in physics, than to have someone who has always majored in psychology in order to become a therapist. I think that breadth of learning along with breadth of life experience are essential to becoming a good therapist. Another thing: the importance of recording interviews cannot be overestimated. Videotaping is even better, although I have not had much experience with that. But to have the opportunity to listen to what went on, be it right after the interview or one year later, to try to understand the process of what went on, should be a tremendous learning experience. I think that one should let the beginning therapist do whatever he wants in therapy, provided that he records the sessions and listens to them afterward, so that he can see the effects on the process. I think that the careful review of recorded interviews is essential.

I think that my present viewpoints are difficult to admit in academic circles. In the past, I could be understood at a purely cognitive level. However, as I became clearer as to what I was doing, academicians had to allow room for experiential learning, which is quite threatening, because then the instructor might have to become a learner, which is not popular in such circles. I think it is much easier to accept me as someone who had some ideas in the 1940s that can be described, than try to understand what has been happening since. I know very few people in major universities who have any real or deep understanding of my work. In some of the external degree institutions, yes, and outside of institutions there are a number of such people. It is interesting that the degree of understanding does not depend on the degree of contact with me. When people are philosophically ready for that part of me, they can pick it up entirely from reading. If they are not philosophically ready, they can do an awful lot of reading and still not get the point. Basically, it is a way of being, and universities are not interested in ways of being. They are more interested in ideas and ways of thinking.

People have asked me what effect I think my work has had on other professions. I think that my most important impact has been on education. I don't feel that I have had much influence on medicine or psychiatry or even on psychology. I have had much more influence in counseling, but not on the mainstream of psychology. I think I have had some impact on nursing. Nurses don't need to defend themselves against change and new ideas. I am also intrigued with the thought that the idea of leaving a human being free to follow his own choices is gradually extending into business.

Finally, I have been interested to see an evolution in the practice of medicine, where the idea of empowering the patient has brought medicine "back" to the idea that patients can heal themselves. I am also pleased to see the development of personal responsibility in health. One of the most important things is that we have opened up psychotherapy and substituted the growth model for the medical model.

Chapter 3

Some Philosophical and Psychological Contributions to the Use of Self in Therapy

DeWitt C. Baldwin Jr.

INTRODUCTION

It is always interesting to speculate why certain ideas emerge at a particular time. It is especially intriguing to review the reasons why attention should be called at this time to the use of *self** in therapy. According to systems theory, therapists are unavoidably part of the treatment situation, both as therapists (change agents) and as themselves. They do not choose to be in or out, they can only choose to be aware or not. That this role can operate along a continuum from activity to passivity has been alluded to by a number of authors (Hollender and Szasz, 1956). Indeed, a major development of the past several decades has been the increasingly active and participatory role in such transactions accorded to the patient. In this particular evolution, the seminal work of Carl Rogers must be noted, in that he saw the potential for self-direction in patients, whom he began to refer to as clients, viewing the therapist as assisting rather than promoting the process of self-determination and development.

It is not surprising that the movement toward a more humanistic psychology which emerged after World War II was accepted by many therapists, who found the determinism and reductionism of the

---

*Whenever the term *self* is first employed in a chapter as part of the concept of the use of self in therapy, it is italicized to call attention to its special use.

Freudian view unsatisfactory from a personal and professional stand-point. This resulted in an outpouring of interest in the uniqueness and authenticity of human experience. Belief in the self-actualizing abili-ty of people led to the formation of the human potential movement of the 1960s and 1970s (Maslow, 1962). Unfortunately, proponents of this movement often carried the idea of personal growth to the limits of personal license and failed to develop a disciplined and systematic examination of its assumptions and implications. Each person's ex-perience was considered valid in itself and, in the place of the rigid-ities of traditional psychiatry and psychology, there emerged a pleth-ora of therapeutic systems and approaches, based on individual style, inclination, and popularity. Indeed, the field of therapy appeared to move from an excessive dependence upon rigid theories and formats to an equally excessive emphasis on idiosyncratic techniques and therapeutic stratagems, that, often as not, were more artificial and manipulative than the traditional approaches.

Recent attempts to bring order out of such confusion have been based on the finding that the differences between patients/clients treated with different approaches and techniques tend to be rather minimal (Wolpe, 1961; Strupp, 1963, 1973). Indeed, Yalom (1980) cites research that attempted to correlate client and therapist percep-tions of key moments of change or growth in therapy, only to find that what the therapist imagined was critical or insightful was fre-quently not so perceived by the client or patient (Standal and Corsini, 1959). Thus, there appears to be increasing acceptance among thera-pists of all persuasions that there is something in the unique nature of the therapeutic relationship and the person of the therapist that plays a critical role in the process of therapy (Rogers, 1961a, 1987; Truax et al., 1966a, 1966b). Since this awareness comes close to what Martin Buber (1923) referred to in the early part of the century as the essential quality of the I-Thou relationship, a brief look at a defini-tion of the self and at some of the philosophical and psychological developments that have contributed to this concept is in order.

THE CONCEPT OF THE SELF

The concept of the self has intrigued writers and philosophers throughout the ages. Its very definition comes close to overwhelming the *Oxford English Dictionary,* with some five pages devoted to attempting to define the word itself in its many senses and forms, and yet another fourteen pages to its many modifications.

For the ancients, the idea of self was usually implicit in the concept of the soul, which was conceived of as the vital, immaterial, life-principle, or "essence" of humans (Roccatagliata, 1986). Primitive religions saw the soul as directing or controlling both mental and physical processes. The cessation of these, as in death, inevitably posed the unanswerable question of immortality—a question that has occupied a central place in all subsequent religious thought. While Hinduism and Buddhism do not admit the existence of the individual soul, the doctrine of reincarnation provides a vehicle for persons to obtain progressively higher levels of virtue and piety. For Islam and later Judaism, the soul comes from God and, thus, is independent of the body; but, for the pious, it is rejoined with the body on the Day of Judgment. Influenced by the Neoplatonists, many medieval and later Christians believed that the God-given soul existed in a dualistic relation with an inferior and earthbound body.

The nature of the soul also has intrigued philosophers. Plato believed in the immortality of the soul, which he saw as separate and distinct from the body, from which it was released by death for full expression. Aristotle began as a Platonist, viewing the soul as immaterial, but in *De Anima* (*On the Soul,* 1957) he later described the soul as the inseparable, substantial form of the living organism, guiding and directing it. He further defined the soul in terms of vegetative, animal, and rational functions, thereby setting the stage for later preoccupation with the mind/body relationship.

This view reached its acme in Descartes' famous statement "cogito, ergo sum" (I think, therefore, I am), and the subsequent dualism of body and mind with which he is identified. This position, of course, served to draw the battle lines between a concern with the external, objective, natural world of objects and the less accessible, more subjective, inner world. Despite its limitations, and the criticisms currently directed toward Cartesian dualism by biobehavioral research, this concept enabled the development of critical inquiry in the physical sciences in a way that has made possible much of today's progress in science and technology. Because of this emphasis, however, the objective and materialistic side of life achieved a commanding lead over that of the subjective and nonconscious, and it was not until philosophers such as Kierkegaard and Husserl, writers such as Dostoevski and Tolstoy, and clinicians such as Freud, Jung, and Adler, that the subjective world began to be explored in terms more appropriate to its understanding.

Freud's theories initiated a renewed attack upon the established lines of Cartesian dualism by adding the elusive concept of the unconscious to confuse the comfortable physical terms to which the domain of the mental and conscious had been assigned. In his 1915 paper "The Unconscious," Freud (1934) differentiated between unconscious ideas, which continue to exist as formations after repression, and unconscious affects, which are discharged. He and his followers went on to describe a whole continuum of the unconscious, from lack of awareness of vegetative and neurological processes to fantasy and dreams. Although his emphasis on psychic determinism confused the philosophers, it served to stimulate a new and fruitful discussion of the concept of the self, among both his followers and those in other disciplines. At the same time, it must be remembered that Freud basically was a scientist and did not, himself, directly challenge the heavy investment which science had in Cartesian dualism. Thus, despite the efforts of William James, John Dewey, and others to examine the self on an empirical basis, the concept of a self, complete with philosophical, social, and religious connotations, was largely ignored by an emerging psychology seeking to establish itself as a scientific discipline.

It was the writers and philosophers, primarily from the existential school, who continued to explore the world of subjective phenomenology. Still, it remained for George Herbert Mead (1934) to reintroduce the concept of the self as a basic unit of personality into scientific thought, along with the roles that the self learns to take in the course of its socialization. He saw the self as a process rather than a structure, and maintained that self and the consciousness of self emerged from social interaction—the interaction of the human organism with its social environment. He believed that what made humans unique was their capacity to be both subject and object at the same time. Since they could even be an object of their own thought and action, self-interaction, they stood in a markedly different relation to their environment than the then-prevailing view of behavior as resulting from external factors or internal drives. Mead's work, while not theoretically explicit, laid the groundwork for the later development of symbolic interactionism, a field that has greatly influenced modern sociological and psychological thought. Indeed, the revival of interest in the self has been so widespread that it is difficult to find a modern personality theory that does not place the self in a central position (Arieti, 1967; Kohut, 1971, 1985).

Special note must be made of the contributions of the developmentalists, such as Erikson and Greenacre, who described the emerging self in terms of the psychosexual and ego development of the child. They noted the fundamental absence of a distinction between the self and the not-self as a basic characteristic of newborns, who, partly as a result of their perceptions, begin to differentiate various aspects of their body image from objects in the external world. Multiple self-presentations gradually lead to the formation of a concept of the self, which becomes more stable and permanent as a result of the achievement of object constancy.

Closely related is the concept of identity (Greenacre, 1958; Erikson, 1950, 1959), which constitutes an awareness of separateness and distinction from all others, in which the borders of the self are hypercathected by the early experience of separation from the mother. Thus, the distinction of the I from the not-I is reinforced by a variety of internal and external experiences. Indeed, the mechanism of projection is based on the primal lack of distinction between the self and the not-self. These contributions have allowed Spiegel (1959) to define the "self as a frame of reference or zero point to which representations of specific mental and physical states are referred, and against which they are perceived and judged" (p. 96).

It is clear, however, that Cartesian dualism still plays an influential role in modern life and thought. As Buber (1955, 1965, 1970) points out, most of our transactions with our fellow human beings and our environment are in the nature of subject-object or I-It relationships. In calling attention to our essential need to participate in reciprocal I-Thou relationships, in which each person fully regards and accepts the subject and object both in self and other, Buber pleads for a reunification of our subjective and objective parts. Far from being merely the absence of an infantile distinction between the subjective and objective, or the self and not-self, this is the achievement of a new unity which, while existing in both conscious and unconscious spheres, is available and accessible to the dedicated searcher.

The use of self in therapy, then, as a subject of theoretical and practical psychotherapeutic importance, emerges at this time in history, largely because of the reemergence of a concern with the uniqueness of human experience and relationship over the past century.

THE CONTRIBUTIONS OF EXISTENTIAL PHILOSOPHY

Perhaps the most important influence on the twentieth-century view of humanity and on the emerging concept of the use of self in therapy comes from the existential philosophers, who take their lead from the seminal work of Søren Kierkegaard (1959). Writing out of the depths of his own personal concerns, Kierkegaard objected to Hegel's efforts to unite the ambiguities of life in an abstract fashion through positing of a higher synthesis. He insisted that the dichotomies of life—good and evil, life and death, God and humans—could not be mediated, but that we were called upon to make decisions between these polarities. He asked us to turn from the world of thought to that of existence as it is actually lived, believing that only through an examination of human experience in all its complexity could one approach the basic question: What is the meaning of life?

Kierkegaard believed that meaning is to be found in the decisions between such polarities and that these decisions must be based on one's own closely examined experience, rather than on any authority or abstract concept. Such an act, of course, is frightening, in that one is asked to abandon the usual sources of support and to leap into the unknown. It was his belief that each individual must, of necessity, make fully conscious, responsible choices among the alternatives that life offers. His works, "Sickness Unto Death" and "The Concept of Dread," are classics of early depth psychology. The former alludes to the role of the unconscious in depression, while the latter makes a clear distinction between "angst" (dread), which he defines as a feeling that has no definite object, and the fear and terror that derive from an objective threat.

It was not until some time after his death that the philosophical and psychological implications of Kierkegaard's work began to be fully appreciated. Indeed, existentialism is generally viewed as a twentieth-century phenomenon and has profoundly affected the development of philosophy, religion, and psychology in this century. Within this century, seminal thinkers in the development of existentialism have included the religious thinkers Bultmann, Marcel, and Tillich, as well as those who have clearly disassociated themselves from the religious view, such as Sartre and Camus. Of note in this development is the work of Edmund Husserl (1965), who introduced the phenomenological method in philosophy, calling upon us to examine our own experience. Of special importance was his insistence on "intentionality," the idea that every meaningful word must be rooted in the experience of which it is only a name, stating, "Consciousness is always consciousness of something."

Although he rejected the existential label, Heidegger (1962) is usually regarded as the figurehead of twentieth-century existentialism. He believed that we can learn something about the fundamental nature of human beings—our "being-in-the-world"—through an analysis of our anxieties, particularly, our fear of death. He accepted life as fundamentally contingent, stating that the only way to live authentically is to accept our own finitude and to develop a capacity to care (Sorge). This includes not just "solicitude" for others, as suggested by the later existential psychologists, but also an ontological caring for, or custodianship, of Being.

Tillich (1952) differed from Heidegger in believing that it is in "the boundary situation"—that situation in which one is denied the supports of authority and intellectualism, and even the traditional concept of God is found wanting—that one finds the unconditional certainty of the "Ground of Being," the "Being—itself," which appears when all else has been dissolved in anxiety and doubt. He believed that we are all aware of the contrast between the ideals that we hold and the lives we live, calling this the difference between "essence" and "existence." He maintained that we can resolve this difference only in the boundary situation, defining authenticity as "the courage to be and, thus, to escape 'non-being.'"

Perhaps the most radical of the modern existentialists was Jean-Paul Sartre (1950). He concluded that one is not only "en-soi" (in oneself)—a passive recipient of fate—but also "pour-soi" (for oneself), transcending the present. Thus, we are free from the limitations imposed by the world of experience. Indeed, we are forced to be free. To live authentically means to accept this dreadful freedom and to see that values are merely projections of our decisions. Such a position suggests a radical nihilism and individualism that has strongly influenced the development of the field.

The Influence of Martin Buber

Although he rejected the label during his lifetime, Buber's thought was profoundly influenced by existentialism (1923, 1955, 1965, 1970). He believed that our access to being is neither through the ideal forms of Plato, nor through the "existent" as in Heidegger, but, rather, through our capacity to enter into dialogue or relationship with the existent, or "the between." He rejected the traditional idea of reason as the distinctive characteristic of human beings, but, rather, defined a human as a "creature capable of entering into living relation with the world and things, with men both as individuals and as the many, and with the 'mystery of being'—which is dimly apparent through all this but infinitely transcends it" (Friedman, 1965, p. 16). Thus, we are unique in our capacity to participate in both finitude and infinity. Human beings, Buber states, are "the crystallized potentiality of existence."

Starting from a concern with humanity's three vital relationships, with God, with other human beings, and with nature, Buber's views were elaborated in *Ich und Du* (1923), in which he states that our relation to God, the Great Thou, enables us to participate in I-Thou relationships with other humans. For Buber, I-Thou establishes the world of relation, "into which both parties enter in the fullness of their being, with a sense of and appreciation for the subject and object in each." It is a relationship "characterized by mutuality, directness, presentness, intensity, and ineffability" (Friedman, 1965, p. 12).

This is contrasted with the I-It, or subject-object, relationship, in which others are regarded as mere tools or conveniences. I-It is the medium of exchange in the world of things and ideas, dealing with categories and connections, with experiencing and using. Indeed, the scientific method is our most highly perfected development of the I-It, or subject-object, way of knowing. It is qualified to compare object with object, even humans with humans, but not to know their wholeness or their uniqueness.

The I-Thou relationship, on the other hand, is immediate and unmediated. There is no intervening purpose. It is an end and not a means. It is enduring—"always there in potentiality, waiting to be touched—released, known." It is not fixed in time or space. It is only in the now, the moment. However, Buber warns, "one cannot live in the pure present: it would consume us" (Buber, 1970, p. 85).

It also is responsibility—in the sense of one's ability to respond to another. "There is a reciprocity of giving: you say You to it and give yourself to it; it says You to you and gives itself to you" (Buber, 1970, p. 84). It is through this relation that one becomes known to oneself and to others as a self. "Man becomes an I through a You" (p. 80). Self-realization, thus, is the by-product, rather than the goal, as is often assumed.

For Buber, the highest expression of the I-Thou relationship lies in the act of confirming the other. He sees mutual confirmation as the key element in the definition of the self. One realizes one's uniqueness only in relation to another who reciprocally defines oneself. Each becomes confirmed by the other in his or her true, real, present, authentic self. Indeed, he states, so great is our need for such definition and confirmation that we would rather be falsely confirmed than not confirmed at all—an act of "seeming," rather than "being." True confirmation is mutual and involves making the other fully present in all his or her unity and uniqueness.

Buber on Psychotherapy

In a unique dialogue that took place between Martin Buber and Carl Rogers in 1957 (Friedman, 1965), Buber drew a distinction between acceptance, or affirmation of the other, as emphasized by Rogers ("what one is"), and confirmation, which not only accepts, but actively engages the polarity in the other, including the potential for the worst within, by helping the other against himself or herself ("what one can become"). He further distinguished between the I-Thou relationship and that of therapist-patient, by stating that the helping relationship is necessarily one-sided. The two persons in-volved are not truly equal, in that the patient expects something from the therapist and the latter accepts that responsibility. Buber maintains that the goal of psychotherapy is the healing of the patient and the relation to that goal inevitably differs between therapist and patient. Furthermore, what is explored in therapy is the patient's experience, not that of the therapist. In other words, while the therapist can empathize and extend himself or herself into the world of the patient, the reverse is not usually the case. The patient cannot experience the relationship from the side of the therapist without fundamentally altering or destroying it. (Some thoughts to the con-trary may be found in Miller and Baldwin [this volume] and the work of Virginia Satir.)

Buber describes true dialogue as that occurring "between part-ners who have turned to one another in truth, who express them-selves without reserve and are free of the desire for semblance" (Buber, 1965, p. 86), where neither one is ruled by the thought of his or her effect on the other. He maintains that even the most genuine and authentic of therapeutic relationships cannot permit the awareness of consciousness on the part of the therapist that he or she understands or experiences a greater reality than that of the client. This is not to say that an accepting, positive regard and genuine concern for the full potentialities of the patient on the part of the therapist cannot lead to confirmation and "healing" (whole-ness), but that this, in Buber's mind, is not really a genuine dialogue between equals with equal perceptions of each other's experience and of the situation.

For Buber, genuine dialogue cannot be arranged in advance, and is granted rather than created. The essential quality of therapy is authentic presence—not just being present, although that is neces-sary. Nor is it merely being in the present—that, too, is necessary. What is unique is the quality of presence—of being totally avail-able, in tune with the other, without boundary, without limit. Thus, he goes beyond Rogers' acceptance and "unconditional, positive regard," and Heidegger's solicitude or caring (Sorge) for others, in advocating the offer of one's "total being" to another. Incidentally, it is important to realize that Buber intended his relational concepts to apply to the realities of community living as well (the essential "WE"), a point of relevance for group and family therapy.

Also in 1957, the Washington School of Psychiatry invited Buber to give the William Alanson White Memorial Lectures, along with a series of seminars. In speaking of psychotherapy, Buber stated, "I have the impression [that] more and more therapists are not so confident that this or that theory is right and have [developed] a more 'musical,' floating relationship to their patients. The deciding reality is the therapist, not the methods" (quoted in Friedman, 1965, p. 37). At another point, he states, "There are two kinds of therapists, one who knows more or less consciously the kind of interpretation of dreams he will get; and the other . . . who does not know. I am entirely on the side of the latter, who does not want something precise. He is ready to receive what he will receive. He cannot know what method he will use beforehand. He is, so to speak, in the hands of his patient" (p. 37). In other words, the therapist must be ready to be surprised. "It is much easier to impose oneself on the patient than it is to use the whole force of one's soul to leave the patient to himself and not to touch him. The real master responds to uniqueness" (p. 38).

THE CONCEPT OF THE SELF
IN PSYCHOANALYSIS AND PSYCHIATRY

Arnold Cooper (1974) quotes Otto Kernberg as stating that "psychoanalytic theory has always included the concept of the self, that is, the individual's integrated conception of himself, as an experiencing, thinking, valuing and acting (or interacting) entity—in fact, Freud's starting point in describing the 'I' ('Das ich,' so fatefully translated as 'the ego' in English) was that of the conscious person whose entire intrapsychic life was powerfully influenced by dynamic, unconscious forces" (p. 299). At the same time, it is clear that Freud's focus on building instinctual and structural theories led to difficulties with integrating a broad concept of the self which spoke to its many dimensions. Jung was undoubtedly aware of this problem when he wrote, "as an empirical concept, the self designates the whole range of psychic phenomena in man. It expresses the unity of the personality as a whole" (Jung, 1971, p. 425). He saw the ultimate outcome of the process of individuation as "the realization of the self." This focus on the self, of course, was ultimately based on the assumption of most psychodynamically oriented schools that if you changed the inner self of the patient, behavioral changes would follow, a view held in the reverse by the behaviorists. It is also important to note that until relatively recently, this focus was entirely on the self of the patient and did not expressly involve the use of the therapist's own self in the therapeutic process.

It remained for the neo-Freudians, Sullivan, Horney, and others, to more fully develop and integrate the concept of the self into their theories and practice. Sullivan (1953) refers to the self-system as the central dynamism of human organization, describing dynamism as "the relatively enduring patterns of energy transformation, which recurrently characterize the interpersonal relations . . . which make the distinctively human sort of being" (p. 103). He states that person-ifications of the "good me" and the "bad me," reflected through the appraisals of significant adults, lead to awareness of a sense of "not me," which is overwhelmingly anxiety producing. He believes that the feeling of self-esteem, which is based on the interplay between these, is essential to healthy functioning and to an understanding of mental illness. One of his major contributions was to see therapy as an interpersonal process, requiring active participation by the thera-pist. Since the latter's values, feelings, and attitudes are part of this process, countertransference becomes an important consideration.

Horney (1950) also felt that libido theory and its derived postu-lates did not adequately explain her clinical observations. She de-cided that the nuclear conflict of neurosis was not one of instincts, but of self-attitudes. She views the self as the dynamic core of human personality, "the central inner force, common to all human beings, and yet unique in each, which is the deep source of (healthy) growth" (1950, p. 17). She sees the self as the source of our capaci-ties for experiencing and expressing feelings, for evolving values and making choices, and for taking responsibility for our actions. She, too, believes that self-esteem represents the healthy develop-ment of appropriate self-attitudes, based on real and genuine capac-ities, rather than illusions or self-deceptions. She held a central belief in the inner dignity and freedom of man and the constructive-ness of evolutionary forces inherent in man.

Heinz Kohut (1971, 1985), likewise, eschews drive theory for a more encompassing focus on the concept of the self in his comprehensive theory of the development of the self and the treatment of its disorders. Although his views have evolved over time, he regards narcissism and object love—love of self and love of the other—as two separate but intertwined lines of development, each of which is essential to our ability to function and to love. More relevant to this chapter is his insistence on the gathering of primary data from empathetic observation of the patient's inner experience, and a shift in the role of the therapist toward maintaining an empathetic rather than objective stance. He believes that it is the therapist's task to place himself or herself "in the skin" of the patient and to understand what each situation feels like to that patient. This enables the therapist to create a supportive framework, which serves to replace the missing elements in the primary mother/child relationship, and both provides and models a "corrective emotional experience," which enables the patient to rediscover his or her unique developmental path. He believes that introspection and empathy are essential components of psychoanalytic fact-finding and are key elements in the therapist's relationship to the patient.

The concept of the self likewise holds an important place in the writings of Silvano Arieti (1967) and the Cognitive-Volitional School. Their emphasis, however, is on the symbolic and volitional mechanisms by which the self is defined in its relations with others in the outside world. In addition, they are concerned with the sequence of external influences and the intrapsychic mechanisms by which these influences are integrated into that part of the human psyche that in various terminologies has been called the inner or intrapsychic self. By this very statement, however, Arieti appears to identify the self as some part or substrate of the person, rather than the totality posited by Buber and others. Indeed, Arieti elaborates the existence of a primordial or presymbolic self, a primary self, and a secondary self as stages in development tied to cognitive and volitional capacities. Once again, the shadow of scientific reductionism is implied in this view of the self more as object than as both subject and object.

THE INFLUENCE OF EXISTENTIAL PHILOSOPHY ON PSYCHOTHERAPY

As Frankl, Yalom, and others have pointed out, the nature of neurosis and, thus, of appropriate therapeutic intervention has changed since the days of Freud. A large number of complaints for which patients now seek help derive from a lack of meaning in life, and the search for meaning brings such patients to treatment. Since existential philosophy maintains that the only true absolute is that there are no absolutes, this poses a fundamental question: How does a person who needs meaning find meaning in a universe that has none?

For centuries, of course, this answer has been found in the positing of a God-centered universe in which our purpose was to relate to and, if possible, emulate that God. Since this is patently impossible on an individual basis, most philosophers and theologians have arrived at the point of view, exemplified by the work of Pierre Teilhard de Chardin (1955), that each individual, by recognizing and joining in this cosmic union, is provided with a personal sense of meaning. At the same time, Kant's questioning of the existence of any fixed, objective reality calls such a view into question. Indeed, Camus and Sartre regard the tension between human aspiration and world indifference as the absurdity of "la condition humaine." Satir refers to this as "the cosmic joke," but maintains that the development of a sense of self-worth enables one to tolerate the irony and to find meaning in the principle of the seed and organic growth.

Viktor Frankl

Frankl (1985) clearly acknowledges his existential debt, coining the word logotherapy ("logos," word or meaning) to indicate his central concern with the problem of meaning. He takes issue with Freud's belief in the homeostatic principle, believing it to be basically reductionist and, therefore, limited in explaining many aspects of human life. Frankl (1963) claims that what "man needs is not a tensionless state, but, rather, a striving and struggling for some goal worthy of him" (p. 166).

Frankl ventures a negative response to the idea of self-actualization, stating that it is an effect and not an object of intention. He believes that "la condition humaine"—the insurmountable finitude of being human—is overcome only when we are able to accept our finiteness. "The whole phenomenon of human existence . . . cannot be circumscribed except by the sentence 'I am'" (Frankl, 1985, p. 62). Rather than self-actualization, he would favor self-transcendence as the essence of existence.

He believes that the psychotherapist is not a teacher or preacher, or even a painter. "It is never up to the therapist to convey to the patient a picture of the world as the therapist sees it; but, rather, the therapist should enable the patient to see the world as it is" (Frankl, 1985, p. 66). In this sense, he endorses the therapeutic use of 'maieutic' dialogue in the Socratic sense.

R. D. Laing

Freely acknowledging his roots in existentialism, R. D. Laing (1965, 1969) has written extensively on the role of the self in understanding psychosis. Postulating a "real" self and a "false" self, he believes that the failure to successfully identify each and to distinguish between them is characteristic of patients with schizophrenia. Although these distinctions resemble Buber's "being" and "seeming" and Sartre's "real" and "imaginary" selves, Laing speaks further of the "embodied" and the "unembodied" self. In the latter, "the body is felt—more as one object among other objects than as the core of (one's) own being." This deprives "the unembodied self from direct participation in any aspect of the life of the world" (Laing, 1965, p. 69). Thus, "the individual's actions are not felt as expressions of his self" (p. 74).

Like Buber, Laing is deeply concerned with the act of confirmation, stating, "the sense of identity requires the existence of another by whom one is known; and a conjunction of this other person's recognition of one's self with self-recognition" (Laing, 1965, p. 139). Lack of confirmation, or disconfirmation, from both self and others is seen as leading to the "chaotic non-entity" of the schizophrenic, where there is total loss of relatedness with both self and other.

Laing (1965) believes that the task in therapy is to make contact with the true self of the patient through understanding the existential world of the false self. He quotes Jung as saying that "the schizophrenic ceases to be schizophrenic when he meets someone by whom he feels understood" (p. 165). This does not mean that the self-being of the other is known or experienced directly, but that the self-being of the other is existentially confirmed. Laing (1969) quotes Buber as saying "the wish of every man [is] to be confirmed as what he is, even as what he can become" (p. 98). Such confirmation must come from the "true self" of the therapist if it is to truly confirm the "true self" of the patient. True confirmation, however, does not mean agreeing with the patient's illusions or delusions—a destructive act of collusion on the part of the therapist—but, rather, affirming both the patient's being and becoming, and confirming the validity of his or her unique experience. Quoting Buber again, Laing believes that "an empty claim for confirmation, without devotion for being or becoming, again and again mars the truth of life between man and man" (p. 98). He agrees with Heidegger that the truth of science, which consists of correspondence between what goes on "in intellectu" and what goes on "in re"—between the structure in the mind and that in the world—is not the same truth as described by the pre-Socratics, where truth is "that which is without secrecy, that discloses itself without a veil" (Laing, 1969, p. 129). Indeed, it may well be the experience of this latter truth through the authentic use of the self that brings validity to the former.

Carl Rogers

To underscore his perception of the person seeking help as basically self-responsible and self-directing, in the late 1930s Carl Rogers (1951, 1961a, 1961b, 1987) began to use the word "client" rather than "patient." Characteristics of "client-centered psychotherapy," as it came to be known, included a stress on the self-actualizing quality of the person, a concern with the process rather than the structure of personality change, a view of psychotherapy as but one specialized example of constructive interpersonal relationships, a focus on the inner phenomenological world of the client, and an emphasis on the immediacy of the therapist's presence and attitudes, rather than on skills or techniques as key elements in the process of therapy. Based on his observations, Rogers specified three basic attitudes or conditions he believed are important for the success of therapy: the therapist's authenticity, genuineness, and congruence, complete acceptance and "unconditional positive regard" for the client, and sensitive and empathetic understanding.

Thus, for Rogers, effective therapists should strive to be totally and authentically themselves—without pretense—directly available to clients in a personal sense. In addition, through an attitude of unconditional positive regard, they should endeavor to create a nonthreatening context for therapy, in which it is possible for clients to explore and experience their most deeply hidden feelings. Finally, Rogers believed that therapy is facilitated when therapists are sensitive on a moment-to-moment basis to the clients' universe and are able to sense and understand the latters' unique and personal meanings as if they were the therapists' own. Some of his later ideas on the use of self in therapy are contained in Chapter 2 in this book.

One of Rogers' major contributions, however, was his insistence on research to back up his observations. Believing that the phenomenon of therapy could and should be subjected to rigorous investigation, he pioneered in the use of audio and film recordings of actual therapeutic interviews. Results of these investigations have provided data confirming the hypothesis that the attitudes and behavior of the therapist are important elements in therapeutic movement and change.

SOME THOUGHTS
ON THE USE OF SELF IN PSYCHOTHERAPY

It is not surprising that many philosophers have disavowed identification as existentialists, because as Tillich (1961) has pointed out, "There is not, and cannot be, an existentialist system of philosophy" (p. 9). "Existentialism is an element within a larger frame of essentialism" (p. 10). Like most other philosophical concepts, each view achieves definition largely in terms of its opposite, and neither can be totally accepted without inviting rebuttal from the other. Thus, the apparent triumph of existentialism in the twentieth century must be seen in a historical perspective that considers and balances the opposing views of idealistic or naturalistic essentialism.

Such a philosophical distinction has tremendous implications for psychotherapy. While it is clients' problems that bring them into therapy, it is important to distinguish between those related to their nature and their daily lives and relationships and those arising from their basic existential anxiety. The former are the appropriate concern and within the usual competence of most therapies and therapists, but psychotherapy cannot cure the existential anxiety that arises from the awful awareness of our own finitude—"la condition humaine"— although it can attempt to give meaning to life. It does this in a uniquely human way—through offering to the seeker of help the self of the therapist as a significant symbol of faith and hope in the former's effort to bridge the finite and infinite. Buber's "I-Thou" relationship appears to offer precisely this uniquely human act and experience of confirmation.

The existentially oriented psychotherapist, then, does not manifest a particular technique or theory, nor are the valuable contributions of other psychological theories denied. Rather, a selective approach is used, the central process of therapy being perceived as that of experiencing the full awareness of one's being. Experiential awareness takes precedence over cognitive awareness, the "here and now" is emphasized rather than the past life of the patient, and therapy is regarded as a creative, evolving process of self-discovery. In relating to the patient, the therapist tries to establish a personal bond of trust and meaningful collaboration, based on a genuine belief in the therapist's own potentialities and those of the patient. While remaining observing and objective, the therapist attempts to enter the world of the patient, wrestling with the frustrations and limitations of the therapeutic situation, trying to be fully present and subjectively real. So far as possible, he or she attempts to manifest Martin Buber's "I-Thou" relationship of mutuality, trying to liberate the individual to seek and achieve optimal development. In short, the existential therapist functions as a fully available person in a meaningful encounter with another. As Tillich (1961) holds, "a person becomes a person in the encounter with other persons, and in no other way. . . . This interdependence of man and man in the process of becoming human is a judgment against a psychotherapeutic method in which the patient is a mere object for the analyst as subject" (p. 15).

It appears, then, that for the existentially oriented psychotherapist, the use of self is an essential element in therapy, whether it be with individuals, groups, or families. Support for this position has come from the growing influence of general systems theory in psychiatry, which posits that the therapist must be viewed as an integral part of the therapeutic system and as having a major effect on the system of the patient. What often is overlooked is that this is a two-way street. In general, this aspect is easier to observe and accept in group and family therapy, where the very number and complexity of the transactions involved make cognitive or technical control of the situation difficult at best. In such situations, it may be more effective for the therapist to "go with the flow"—Buber's musical or floating relationship—and to focus on the metamessages of the system and of his or her own internal state of being.

This is not a passive process. An attitude of alert, active attentiveness is required to maintain the essential qualities of contact and receptivity. Nor does this imply having control over the situation or over the patient through authority or technique. Rather, the central core of being within the therapist—the very sense of self—serves to communicate and maintain a centering and stabilizing force or power in the process. While such an approach would appear to abdicate the traditional role of the therapist and encourage chaos to take over, this very act of relinquishment of control is precisely what many patients seem to require in order to rediscover and reassert their own sense of control over their lives. At the same time, this act loses its authenticity if used solely as a technique. It is an intensely real and personal act—that of letting go—putting one's belief in one's self and in the self of the other on the line—exposing one's true and deepest self; in a sense, going naked into the encounter—allowing oneself to become truly vulnerable. This "centered act of the centered self" is truly the source of the creative and life-giving act of self-discovery and transformation (Tillich, 1961, p. 13). Paradoxically, such a use of self implies a deliberate "nonuse" or suspension of self in its usual sense.

Achieving and maintaining such an attitude is never easy, and is impossible for some therapists, whose personal needs or belief systems require them to remain untouched or to be "in charge." Nor is it the province of any one theory or school. Great therapists of all persuasions have always manifested the essential elements of this quality. Nor does it mean that knowledge, skill, and experience are not important. The plethora of self-appointed helpers and gurus, and the unfortunate results of many pseudotherapies and encounter groups led by nonprofessionals attest otherwise.

Can such an attitude be learned or acquired? Despite the existence of "natural" healers and therapists, the answer is strongly in the affirmative. Ideally, the training analysis was intended to accomplish this. Unfortunately, it also modeled the traditional authoritarian, or subject-object, relationship and usually ignored significant dimensions of the self of the analyst in training (as well as of the training analyst!). This resulted in perpetuating, for too long, a focus on technique and theory that often obscured the deeply personal relationship involved. Such lessons need to be learned experientially through intense encounter with others, who are able to share openly in their own continuing search. While the ultimate learning experience is always deeply personal, it almost always occurs in relation with another person. Buber has said that the greatest thing one human being can do for another is to confirm the deepest thing within him or her. It is this act of confirmation which is ultimately implied in the use of self in therapy.

REFERENCES

Arieti, S. (1967). *The Intrapsychic Self.* New York: Basic Books.
Aristotle (1957). *On the Soul* (Trans. by Hett, W.S.). Cambridge, MA: Harvard University Press.
Buber, M. (1923). *Ich und Du.* Leipzig, Germany: Insel-Verlag.
Buber, M. (1955). *Between Man and Man* (Trans. by Smith, R.G.). Boston: Beacon Press.
Buber, M. (1965). *The Knowledge of Man: A Philosophy of the Interhuman.* New York: Harper and Row.
Buber, M. (1970). *I and Thou.* New York: Charles Scribners.
Cooper, A.M. (1981). On Narcissism. Chapter 15, in Arieti, S. and Brodie, H.K.H. (Eds.). *American Handbook of Psychiatry, Volume 7, Advances and New Directions.* New York: Basic Books.
Erikson, E.H. (1950). *Childhood and Society.* New York: Norton.
Erikson, E.H. (1959). *Identity and the Life Cycle.* New York: International Universities Press.
Frankl, V.E. (1963). *Man's Search for Meaning: An Introduction to Logotherapy.* New York: Washington Square Press.
Frankl, V.E. (1985). *Psychotherapy and Existentialism.* New York: Washington Square Press.

Freud, S. (1934). The Unconscious. In *Collected Papers,* Volume 4, London: Hogarth.

Friedman, M. (1965). Introductory Essay. In Buber, M., *The Knowledge of Man.* New York: Harper and Row.

Greenacre, P. (1958). Early Physical Determinants in the Development of the Sense of Identity, *Journal of the American Psychoanalytic Association* 6: 612-627.

Heidegger, M. (1962). *Being and Time.* New York: Harper and Row.

Hollender, M. and Szasz, T.S. (1956). A Contribution to the Philosophy of Medicine, *Archives of Internal Medicine,* 97: 585-592.

Horney, K. (1950). *Neurosis and Human Growth.* New York: Norton.

Husserl, E. (1965). *Phenomenology and the Crisis of Philosophy.* New York: Harper and Row.

Jung, C.G. (1971). *Psychological Types.* Bollingen Series 20. Princeton, NJ: Princeton University Press.

Kierkegaard, S. (1959). *Either/Or.* 2 volumes, New York: Doubleday, Anchor.

Kohut, H. (1971). *The Analysis of the Self.* New York: International Universities Press.

Kohut, H. (1985). *Self Psychology and the Humanities,* Strozier, C.B. (Ed.). New York: W.W. Norton.

Laing, R.D. (1965). *The Divided Self.* Baltimore: Penguin Books.

Laing, R.D. (1969). *Self and Others.* New York: Penguin Books.

Maslow, A. (1962). *Toward a Psychology of Being.* New York: Van Nostrand.

Mead, G.H. (1934). *Mind, Self, and Society.* Chicago: University of Chicago Press.

Roccatagliata, G. (1986). *A History of Ancient Psychiatry.* New York: Greenwood.

Rogers, C. (1951). *Client-Centered Therapy.* Boston: Houghton-Mifflin,

Rogers, C. (1961a). The Process Equation of Psychotherapy. *American Journal of Psychotherapy* 15(1): 27-45.

Rogers, C. (1961b). *On Becoming a Person.* Boston: Houghton-Mifflin.

Rogers, C. (1987). Interview with Carl Rogers on the Use of the Self in Therapy. In Baldwin, M.A. and Satir, V. (Eds.), *The Use of Self in Therapy.* Binghamton, NY: The Haworth Press, Inc., pp. 45-52.

Sartre, J.P. (1950). *Psychology of Imagination.* London: Rider.

Sartre, J.P. (1956). *Being and Nothingness* (Trans. by Barnes, H.). New York: Philosophical Library.

Spiegel, L. (1959). The Self, the Sense of Self and Perception, *Psychoanalytic Study of the Child* 14: 81-109.

Standal, S. and Corsini, R., Eds. (1959). *Critical Incidents in Psychotherapy.* Englewood Cliffs, NJ: Prentice Hall.

Strupp, H.H. (1958). The Psychotherapist's Contribution to the Treatment Process. *Behavioral Science* 3: 34-67.

Strupp, H.H. (1963). The Outcome Problem in Psychotherapy Revisited. *Psychotherapy* 1: 1-13.

Strupp, H.H. (1973). Specific vs. Non-Specific Factors in Psychotherapy and the Problem of Control. In Strupp, H.H. (Ed.), *Psychotherapy: Clinical, Research and Theoretical Issues.* New York: Jason Aronson, pp. 103-121.

Sullivan, H.S. (1953). *The Interpersonal Theory of Psychiatry.* New York: Norton.

Teilhard de Chardin, P. (1955). *The Phenomenon of Man.* New York: Harper.

Tillich, P. (1959). *The Courage to Be.* Paperbound. Clinton, MA: The Colonial Press.

Tillich, P. (1961). Existentialism and Psychotherapy, *Review of Existential Psychology and Psychiatry* 1: 8-16.

Truax, C.B., Wargo, D., Frank, J., Imber, S., Battle, C., Hoehn-Saric, R., Nash, E., and Stone, A. (1966a). The Therapist's Contribution to Accurate Empathy, Non-Possessive Warmth, and Genuineness in Psychotherapy. *Journal of Clinical Psychology* 22(3): 331-334.

Truax, C.B., Wargo, D., Frank, J., Imber, S., Battle, C., Hoehn-Saric, R., Nash, E., and Stone, A. (1966b). Therapist Empathy, Genuineness and Warmth, and Patient Therapeutic Outcome. *Journal of Consulting Psychology* 30(5): 395-401.

Wolpe, J. (1961). The Prognosis in Unpsychoanalyzed Recovery from Neurosis. *American Journal of Psychiatry* 118: 35-39.

Yalom, I. (1980). *Existential Psychotherapy.* New York: Basic Books, Inc.

Chapter 4

Revealing Our Selves

Charles H. Kramer

Finding acceptable solutions for the thorny issue of self-revelation is essential to using our selves. In any meaningful encounter it is impossible *not* to reveal a great deal. How we dress, decorate, questions we ask, information we are or are not interested in all reveal our attitudes, philosophy, and lifestyle. Significant events are hard to disguise: marriage, divorce, pregnancy, parenthood, illness, death. And when we try to be a blank screen, we reveal that we are concealing, which is a message of deception. Furthermore, therapists and patients share a small world. They are likely to hear about us from others, see us in meetings or around town. The longer we practice, the more other therapists come to us, which blows a contrived cover.

Once we accept that we cannot *not* reveal ourselves, questions arise. What is revealed? To whom? How much? In what way? For what purpose? With what timing? In what relation to the dynamics and stage of therapy? With what result? Nothing simple here. Answers to these complex questions hinge on our personalities and styles. We engage in unique interaction with people who have unique personalities and problems. We evolve practices that suit our styles. I present my view of the forces at play so you can compare and make your own decisions.

As a beginner I thought that perfect therapy proceeds using standard techniques and theories without interference from personal

---

This chapter is adapted from Charles H. Kramer, *Therapeutic Mastery: Becoming a More Effective and Creative Psychotherapist*, Redding, CT: Zeig, Tucker and Co., 1999.

life. I soon found that not only is this impossible, but the more closely I approximate a blank screen, the more sterile the therapy. A numbers lover once counted some 250 varieties of psychotherapy. Categories are bewildering. One valuable way of thinking about therapists and the therapy they do is from the perspective of modeling and self-disclosure. What sort of a person should the therapist *be* with patients?

Therapists range from trying to reveal as little as possible to revealing as much as possible. Each extreme is irresponsible and based on ideology, not on what is right for each patient with this therapist at this time. I will spell out principles for disclosure that take into account many variables in both individual and family therapy.

We are *models*, whether we like it or not. We can't help it. Whatever we are, we are. Those who spend time with us will make what they will of what they see and hear. Simply by being in the same space, we present a style of being that may or may not be emulated. We may be a good example, a warning, or both. Post-therapy research confirms that the kind of people we are is most important in a positive outcome. Here is an example of modeling taken from couples group therapy:

> Husband and wife argue bitterly while Jan, my cotherapist and wife, and I try unsuccessfully to help. Next session, the other three couples report how much they learned from watching, fruitful after-conversations, new insights. The first couple propose, "Someone else fight today so *we* can learn. We fought all week and still haven't settled anything."

The fighting couple and our lack of success were a model to learn from. It was not helpful for the couple. It did not demonstrate how to do it right. The couple's pain and discouragement was actually heightened. (We should have cut it short. This happened early in our first group, where we learned as much as the participants.) Yet it was a lively example of their problems. The observers resonated, and were stimulated to explore related issues. The couple was consumed with attacking and defending. There is a seminal difference between participant and observer. The participant is upset and defensive. Energy is spent dealing with conflict. In therapy with two or more people, there are many opportunities to observe, and observing may be more helpful than participating. When we reveal ourselves, patients are the fortunate observers.

What I do *not* mean by modeling: presenting an ideal image, perfection, a "model person" to be imitated. Beginners mistakenly believe they must appear to be paragons of mental health; self-disclosures must show maturity and positive adjustment. Since we don't *feel* all that mature when we embark, it is not surprising we are afraid to open up.

I also do not mean an act put on like an outfit for the occasion. Patients see through pretense. Analysts object to Alexander's "corrective emotional experience," considering it artificial. "Acting is for actors," one purist snorted. No one would disagree. But when the relationship is what it should be, there is no acting. Patients' experience is both different from and corrective of life in childhood. It is corrective because it is compassionate and unambivalent—*different* from experience in the family. We are not contriving, and we do not need to be. Internalization of the new experience modulates the old, becoming a fixture of the inner world, correcting long-standing dysfunctional patterns.

The paradox is that when we make no attempt to be perfect or tell the patient how to be, by the end they have taken in much of our thinking, feeling, and behaving. They pick up both faults and assets from those they admire. This is why we have an obligation, to our patients and to ourselves, to keep growing.

I emphasize the importance of self-disclosure, not because it is a large part of technique but because it is *central*. The best therapists are authentic, fully present, and open to speaking about themselves, without sacrificing power or expertise. I may make only one or two brief personal comments. I am convinced from experience—mine, patients', students'—that these are heard and molded by each person's interpretation. At the same time, I must not distract from patient concerns or be self-centered. I watch to make sure comments are in the patients' best interest, not mine. Their best interest serves mine, but mine rarely serves theirs.

I practiced in my home for forty years. Patients knew our taste in a home—and when it needed painting! They glimpsed my wife, my kids from infancy until college, many details about life outside the office. And when Jan joined me in cotherapy, our relationship was right there to be seen. So I have had plenty of practice handling personal disclosures.

People in distress are searching for inspiration, guidance. They want to be sure they can trust enough to unfold their most precious possession: their story. Small facts about yourself show that you know life, and help them safely reveal themselves. Self-disclosures, like cooking spices, make the difference. Like spices, the pinch must be just right—too little and your dish is flat; too much, and it is spoiled.

I stress disclosure because it is seldom clarified in publications or teaching. Instructors ignore the topic, supervisors do not demonstrate or discuss it, and many students are content not to be troubled about it—just practice stonewalling. Years later, no longer safe within the protective embrace of a training program, they struggle to understand why they cannot keep patients long enough to be effective. It is never too late to look at ourselves with an eye to real change.

WHY SELF-DISCLOSURE?

When we share our life experience, we connect with them and they with us and all of us with life. We offer a personal handle. Therapy is more effective when the therapist is a person, not a scientist, a robotherapist, a walking textbook, or an acolyte for someone's method. Vivid images from everyday life, expressed without pretense, convey powerful messages. The therapist who is not scared by any subject, including self, inspires confidence. We like being with, and more easily trust, someone who is relaxed and having a good time, especially when we are in trouble.

I want patients to know I have wrestled with therapy and with life and will share my journey. I want them to relate to it, to know their journey is also personal. I want them to know my way has been a saga of stress, frustration, humiliation, anger—mellowed by hope, success, joy, romance—without burdening them. It is a big task, but doable and worth doing.

I ask about disclosure in previous therapy, and often hear this story:

I always complained about others—bosses, lovers, friends. I lost them all before I realized I must do something to bring this on. I went into therapy to find out. I asked my therapist how I came across, what his reactions to me were. He always said, "What do *you* think?" When I guessed at his experience of me, he bounced it back. He wormed out of saying anything about what he thought or felt about anything. I felt rejected again, and I wasn't learning what I do to people. I tried to provoke him. Just the usual focus on me as though I were the only one in the room. After a year I was more confused than ever, so I quit. He said I was once again acting out an old pattern, and his reactions were irrelevant.

This story, not as rare as some might think, sets the stage to propose a collaboration, again paraphrased:

If we decide on therapy, I'll let you know how you come across, and you do the same. I may not realize how you take what happens. I may say things you don't want to hear. You might get annoyed and be tempted to quit. That will be the time *not* to quit, but keep our appointments, maybe have an extra, and work on it.

I watch for nonverbal signs of acceptance, puzzlement, rejection. Nearly always the response is positive; this is what they want. Later, however, they may not be so sure. Ambivalence comes out when they ask for examples of the kind of feedback I might give. Typically, I comment on something that has already transpired:

You seem overwhelmed by what you are going through, and I am reminded of times when I felt overwhelmed. (No details.)

I know how sad you are because I feel sad just listening to what's happened between you and your mother.

(Said after evidence of some rapport on both sides.) Several times I asked John a question and he looked frustrated when Mary answered. That must be an important pattern.

The death of your father might be a big turning point in your life. It was for me. (Again, no details.)

These comments, and others like them, are brief and without elaboration. I do not want to detract from the flow. I do not go on about myself. Yet I want to put out an opening statement that if the time is right, I am open to further discussion of my experience.

I comment on something that we all could have observed, without making an interpretation. I pick whatever is moderately significant, neither trivial nor a blockbuster. Trivia have no power for change, unless artfully embedded in a speech. Blockbusters are for one-shot consultations or after much preparation.

I want them to know they will be getting something useful from me, not only relief at pouring out their story. I want them to realize this is a mutual relationship with a human with feelings, opinions, life experiences—one who is not reluctant to talk about them when the time is ripe. Revealing glimpses of my world teaches about life, sometimes using apparently positive examples, sometimes negative. I say "apparently" because events have both positive and negative aspects. What at first looks positive will ultimately reveal a negative. And vice versa.

Principles in teaching patients about life are much like those in teaching students. The teacher's presence is a sustaining model, stronger than words and theories:

> A Jewish tale tells of a man who came back from visiting a famous rabbi. His friend quizzes him as to what great knowledge he acquired from the learned man. The answer was, "I didn't go to the rabbi to learn his theories. I went to watch him tie his shoelaces."

Patients are keenly interested in watching us "tie our shoelaces." Should I tell a story, secretly hoping others will do as I do, I will be disappointed if they don't follow my "advice." And they rightly feel they are being manipulated. I felt frustrated after early attempts to tell about my life. But I learned that patients seldom do things just the way I do—and things turn out OK. Listeners, whether students or patients, hear according to needs at that moment, and in the light of a lifetime. We often agree on the facts. But what the facts mean, and how those facts apply in one's life, are different and individual matters.

GUIDELINES AND SUGGESTIONS

This section includes fourteen guidelines and suggestions, which are numbered for ease of reference. The big self-disclosure questions are: Will what I reveal enhance therapy or interfere, not just in the near future but over the whole therapy and after? Is there a better way? What are the risks of disclosure—and of withholding—and how do they balance advantages? How much is for their benefit, how much for me? What are likely reactions? How can what is disclosed be integrated into therapy and keep it flowing? This is a lot of imponderables for the beginning discloser. But the more extensive our clinical experience, the easier the answers. I still fine-tune.

1. Jan and I plan for likely disturbances, often sharing these with patients. Every therapist is wise to have a plan for illness, interruptions, family crises, or any distraction. We do not know *what* will happen, but we can be prepared for most anything. If something is likely to interrupt a session, I say so. (No phone in my office. I hated it when a therapist used my time to talk on the phone.)

2. Start with small, relatively safe disclosures. When these do not harm, and may even enrich the process, be a little bolder, experiment with greater freedom. It feels appropriate to patients to begin with *comments about how I experience them*—what I see happening, how I feel and think about it, what being with them is like for me, and so on. I am nonconfrontive, neutral, curious, inquiring, not blaming. With more than one in the room, I address all in the early going. If speaking about yourself is new, it takes a while to get comfortable in this heretofore forbidden world. So be patient with yourself and willing to suffer awkward moments early on.

3. I usually start the second session asking each person about reactions to the first, adding I will do the same. I elicit how they felt and what they thought during the session that they did not say. What were their afterthoughts, afterfeelings? Reflections since then? Conversations about how it went? Did anyone have any dreams? We work for a little while on whatever is brought up. A subject not directly related to presenting issues is discussed briefly and tagged to come back to later.

I probe for negatives. When patients are eager for therapy, getting started is such a relief that they do not think of negatives. Wanting to please, they limit comments to the positives they imagine I want to hear. Why jeopardize a good start? If they don't mention negatives, I offer a few: getting the family together, traffic, insurance, budget, painful subjects, and so on. I propose a ground rule: negative thoughts and feelings about therapy—theirs or mine—will be brought out in sessions. When they are not, I say, they accumulate and interfere. People agree, but later need reminding when I suspect they have unexpressed negatives.

After exploring their reactions to the first session, I tell mine: thoughts and feelings I had not mentioned, my ponderings since then, and mild to moderate interpretations. I want to estimate their readiness for change. I say both positive and negative things, on the same principle that my negatives will influence therapy unfavorably when not expressed and resolved.

With psychologically minded people, this exploration may start near the end of the first meeting. But I prefer to wait until the second so we can reflect on the first. First impressions may change, so I usually set up two get-acquainted appointments. I say that our goal is to see whether we have the right "chemistry." I also get clues to the prognosis and some of the difficulties to be expected—a minitrial. The longer I practice, the quicker I know whether we can work together. You will too.

4. With more practice revealing myself, I began to *make small personal comments* even in the first interview. These are brief, not elaborated, and only made if relevant to what is happening:

> I interview a family while the adolescent inpatient staff watch. With gusto, the father rattles off his son's misbehaviors. After listening respectfully, when he pauses for breath I say, "Yeah, my six kids about drove me nuts too when they were teenagers." He smiles, relaxes, sits back, and we hear from the rest of the family. The son angrily recites all that is wrong with the father, sounding just like him. When it feels right I say, "Yeah, I remember when I was a teenager. My parents nearly drove me nuts." He looks understood and relaxes. That consultation succeeded because of my self-disclosures.

Triggering both comments were flashes of specific incidents. To go into these would burden a one-shot consultation. In the beginning, *my responses to the session* are more important than going into personal matters. But with a family in treatment I might bring up later an incident from the past. Emboldened by my openness, someone may say, "You mentioned you and your kids had problems. Were they anything like what we've got? How did you handle them?" I usually oblige.

5. *How do I decide* whether to reveal a thought, memory, feeling, or hunch? Here is how it worked the first few times. In the flow of a session, something personal comes to mind, use of myself, neither theory nor technique. I wonder how useful saying it might be. As an intuitive, thinking introvert, I hesitate, and feel familiar anxiety signals, but say nothing. The interaction moves on, anxiety and thought vanish, and I am mildly incomplete, with self-blame and reassurance. If it comes back, I take it more seriously, go through a similar reaction, and get my nerve up, but again we move on. If it comes back again, I am pretty convinced of its relevance, if not its guaranteed utility. Unless it is clearly out of line, or I want the person to discover it for himself or herself, I tentatively put into words what is on my mind, with anxiety and a flash of dire consequences while I wait for a reaction. The patient notices something different, interesting, personal, perhaps picking up anxiety. Then both parties feel relief, loosening up, a block unblocked. I have taken a leap, an unprecedented risk—and no debacle. Therapy moves forward, enlivened. A pattern has been broken, but not forever; it must be repeated until success prompts more attempts, more success, more confidence on both sides. Not all choice points work well. Mistakes reteach us. I nudge self a little farther, check internally and with others, in a mini-experimental way. Results are immediate, with rare delayed reactions.

Three things are happening, all desirable for success: patient issues are worked on, *how* to work is experienced, and awareness is heightened. Learning about our selves expands throughout therapy, a mutual collaboration. Fears are replaced by fascination. Discovering nuances of one's inner life and motives becomes practical and fulfilling.

By trial and error, I trust intuition and speak sooner with less hesitation. I may say, "I don't know whether it's useful, but I keep having this thought (feeling, image, fantasy, memory). Does it have any value for you?" If it is relevant, we take it from there. If not, I say, "I could be wrong. Maybe it's my own thing. I'll look into it. You might too." I am often on target for something hidden from patients' easy awareness. Or perhaps one sees a connection others do not. We gain insight into a feeling, thought, or memory when it is *pre*conscious, that is, made conscious by focusing attention. An interpretation that goes deep into the unconscious will be rejected as untrue, even if correct. If you do this often, credibility is lost and resistance increases.

With a powerful, positive flow, I keep quiet, especially if I think highly of my brilliant insight. Good therapy is precious and hard to find. Nothing should harm it. *When in doubt* about speaking personally, it is better to wait. I am held back by what I do not yet understand.

6. *The patients' interest* in knowing about your life should be honored. If you do not know whether they are interested, ask them. Some do not want to know, especially if they heard too much from another therapist. What the therapist said that was off-putting often was on target, but they were not ready to hear it. With plenty of preparation, patients eventually may understand their vulnerability. Jan or I may say, "We had a similar incident, but we will tell you only if you want to hear." If they do not want to hear now, maybe later. Some never do. Respect it.

7. *For some therapists, self-disclosure is natural* and comes easily. For others, family reticence and the pseudoprofessional blank screen can be unlearned. Jan claims that when we first knew each other I was spontaneously self-disclosing. Only after years of indoctrination in "judicious silence" did I become a strong silent type.

8. *The more disturbed a patient*, the greater the need for openness. Schizophrenics, borderlines, and psychologically primitive, and the severely abused are exquisitely sensitive to nuances, evasions, and the unconscious of others. They need to test and confirm reality, especially the therapist and therapy. Trying to put anything over on them, despite good intentions, will backfire and destroy the trust they badly need.

9. *Hostile, seductive, or competitive feelings* need disclosure, lest therapy collapse. Strong negative reactions are most difficult to disclose and, paradoxically, most important. We must work on ourselves before sharing. This may mean a consultation with your therapist or a trusted colleague. Disclosure is less likely to be disruptive if done calmly with sincere interest in teaching patients about themselves and shoring up the foundation of treatment.

Patients too must be prepared. Shock is tempered by recalling previous helpful disclosures and by advance warning. "Some of the things I have pointed out about you have not been easy to take. But you have used them well. (Mention one or two.) There is something else I want you to know, but I worry you will take it badly. I've thought about this a lot and decided our relationship is strong enough for strong feelings. Ready?"

10. Over the course of therapy, I am *increasingly self-revealing*. Natural, effortless progression toward greater self-disclosure is a sign of deepening intimacy. I check to see how personal comments are coming across, identifying which are useful and which are not. Impactful stories have parallels in their lives. Areas are opened up to explore that might never have been touched, had I not first told my story. By the end of a long therapy, patients know a lot about me, my wife and marriage, my children and their families, and how we have handled—or mishandled—various crises. People tell me this has been valuable.

11. *Timing* is the essence. Early on, when patients are in pain, they are not in any mood to hear about our lives. "We came here for help with *our* problems, not to help you with *yours*." I hold my tongue while we struggle with the crisis, focusing on what they can do to help themselves. The most I might do is to identify my experience with theirs in brief, perhaps nonverbal ways. When a family is grieving, I might nod and say, "I know how you feel." Or "Yes, I've been through that." Or Jan and I may look knowingly at each other without words, and someone takes note. We do not go into details. It is enough that the message was received.

12. When therapy becomes growth-oriented, the task is: *Do not stagnate. Effective leadership is essential.* Of the many ways to keep therapy moving, none are surefire. We need a range of things to say or do or recommend. Most useful is simply commenting, "I

have been thinking we are in the doldrums," and recall when we were stuck before. Or I may recount a similar stuck time in my life. This stimulates talk about solutions for stalemates. Sometimes what is needed is simply patience and observant waiting to see what comes next. A few key pages from Bridges' *Transitions* (1980) are useful. Commonly, the block is due to unspoken positive or negative feelings toward me or Jan or the whole treatment. Nearly always we have corresponding feelings as well. These need to be talked through and understood. Corrective action may be necessary.

13. *Self-disclosures are related to what I hope they will disclose and work on.* However, keep an open mind about this. Sometimes the mere *fact* that I disclose something is more important than the information. They may be encouraged to disclose also, but the content often is unexpected. My preferred stance—not always achieved—is to be ready for anything at all, and for nothing.

14. *Eventually a self-disclosure backfires*—because it is inappropriate, causes hurt feelings, disrupts the flow. Time to candidly acknowledge the error, apologize (once is enough), make corrections, and learn valuable lessons. Some people tell me immediately when a self-revelation is not useful. This puts the process out front so repairs can be made—the sooner, the better. Others do not own up to being offended or distracted. Watch for clues that the flow has been interfered with: symptom return, irritability, awkward silence, argumentativeness. Gentle probing usually brings out the break in empathy. Until this is done, therapy flounders. Some people harbor a hurt long after being asked. I make it clear early on that it is essential to let me know if my comments are hurtful. Even then, many test out whether I mean it. Unwillingness to reveal when they are hurt provides an opportunity to change a disadvantageous trait.

It is important to recognize subjective signals telling me I have goofed: a sinking feeling in my stomach, uneasiness that something is not right, preoccupation with a session long afterward, or any of the above patient indicators. When I get internal clues and others seem unaware of them, I describe what I am feeling so that we can look for a break in empathy. Putting sensations into words suggests that it is safe for them to do the same.

There is a saying, "We don't know when we've had enough until we've had too much." We may not know when we disclose optimally until we overdo it. This is the value—and the risk—in gently, firmly pushing until we do. But why take an unnecessary risk? Because when you have never upset a patient, never had a break in empathy, therapy has lacked power. It is a cream puff, not transformative, not deep enough. It has been unreal, not true to life. Life is full of mistakes and messes—we bounce from one to another no matter how many years we have been bumbling through. Effective therapy is no exception. The sooner we accept our imperfections and use them to enrich our work, the better.

RISKS OF SELF-DISCLOSURE

Disclosure can go wrong in many ways. Risks decrease and benefits increase when disclosure is done well, and we learn from mistakes. Let's look at two errors: (1) saying too much, at the wrong time, in the wrong way—*bad* disclosure; (2) saying little, putting the onus back on patients, not knowing how this affects them—*avoiding* disclosure.

We are shocked by the first error, lose confidence, and must work hard to save the alliance. Telling personal material looks damaging; cautious supervisors are right, the value of the blank screen is confirmed. I learned plenty in an early group supervision in 1973 at the height of the encounter craze:

> Four supervisees, their spouses, Jan and me. We tell how we got here, what we hope to get. I describe being propelled into medicine by my father's illnesses, and feeling responsible for them. Out of the blue, I sob hard for several minutes. The group is stunned. An ambivalent member is absent, but listens to the tape. She is upset, makes feeble excuses to miss sessions, stops listening to tapes (a ground rule). Not long after we end, she and her husband divorce. Reactions were worked through and the group was stronger in the long run.

Error (2), guardedness, is insidious and cumulative. Some withhold for years, not realizing the effect they have. Cautiousness kills liveliness. Patients quit after achieving little, leaving therapists without a glimpse of why. "Untreatable" is the rationalization. Unfortunately, beginners are taught to say nothing personal "to establish a professional boundary," instead of how to disclose to create an optimal boundary. What starts as a protection for the beginner eventually becomes a hindrance.

Errors of omission are less obvious than errors of commission. Yet guardedness is more common, professionally validated, and damaging. Beginners are careful with patients and supervisors. Commonsensical. There is much to learn; silence is safe. The drawback comes when therapy hits an impasse. The frustrated therapist reverts to what was first taught. Reflexively clamming up, power is lost; we fall back on what we learned as insecure beginners, regress to what seemed to work.

What we first teach should be methods that support students in emergencies. That means training in appropriate self-disclosure. Any short-term gain from blank screening should not be promoted at the cost of becoming open, authentic, and giving. Reticence signals we are not free with thoughts and feelings, yet we expect patients to be free with *theirs*. Being nagged to put everything into words—the "fundamental rule"—by three analysts who did nothing of the kind was frustrating. No example, no forthright expression of what was going on behind my head. Professionalized withholding is a deterrent for a young therapist who aspires to be authentic and responsive.

Whether it is harder to keep your mouth shut or open depends on your personality. Introverts turn thoughts and feelings inward, and do not speak until they know what to say. Extroverts turn outward, and are not sure what they think or feel until they say it. These types have complementary tasks: bringing forth less natural parts of themselves.

Self-aggrandizing turns people off. Name-dropping, religious and political advocacy, competitiveness, and self-inflation may be hard to identify, given the prima donnas in our field and payoffs for speed and quantity. The tidal wave of therapists of every description aggravates dog-eat-dogism. Inflation is the norm, marketing the catchword. Phone books, magazines, flyers, and professional publications trumpet appearance over substance. Solo practitioners with undecipherable "degrees" present themselves "and associates," practicing in one-room "suites." If you want a good, long practice, improve yourself. Word of mouth is the best advertising, effectiveness the best marketing.

Beginners telling personal events may attribute them to others. Freud did. It is easy to get away with this apparently harmless subterfuge, but I do not recommend it. If therapy is to be genuine, it must be based on honesty, however painful. Better to self-reveal in small comfortable doses. The sugar-coated white lies we were raised on need to be seen for what they were and not repeated in therapy. White lies are contagious, spreading until the white liar loses track of them. Sooner or later a cover will be blown that was not necessary in the first place.

You might well ask: "What's the big deal about self-disclosure? If it can interfere with therapy, why bother? Sounds like stirring up unnecessary trouble. I'm very private, and my personal life is not their business." Jourard's (1971) research shows that when an interviewer makes a self-revealing comment, the interviewee soon does. And the number of revelations by the interviewee is greater—which is what therapy is all about—than when the interviewer does no revealing. Follow-up of our cases several years after termination shows no harm. On the contrary, stories about ourselves were often mentioned as the most helpful.

BENEFITS FROM RISKING OPENNESS

The most important benefit of self-disclosure is *diminishing transference*, which arises in every sustained relationship. Transference and self-revelation are reciprocal. The *less* self-disclosure, the greater the transference. *More* self-disclosure, less transference. Control of transference intensity is the responsibility of the therapist, and is guided by self-disclosure.

In four-times-a-week-on-the-couch analysis, the analyst builds transference by minimizing personal information. The patient fills in gaps with fantasy, a transference neurosis, which partially replicates the childhood neurosis. Analysis then may produce a resolution. This has been fine-tuned and standardized for many decades.

But in once-or-twice-a-week-sitting-up therapy, a regressive, dependent transference is not desirable. Should an intense transference be created by the therapist's silence, it results in a transference-countertransference jam unresolvable by the same therapist. Judicious revelation of personal material minimizes this unfortunate denouement. Psychotherapy requires that negative transference be kept from becoming extreme. This is done by letting people know the human being we are, thus minimizing the false image they manufacture when they have few facts. It is done by interpreting transference reactions as they appear. It is done by responding rather than evading, talking rather than stonewalling, giving opinions rather than withholding, being open rather than closed, by having two or more people in the room, by audiotape or videotape feedback. Knowing about the therapist undercuts both idealization and demonization.

Greater openness also teaches us to *take risks and make mistakes.* Taking risks is sine qua non for an authentic therapist. In fact, risks are unavoidable, not only in therapy but in life. "No-risk" therapy is one-dimensional, self-limiting, incomplete. When we do risk self-disclosure, sooner or later we make a mistake that disrupts the flow and jeopardizes the relationship. The irony is that when we gather courage to ever-so-tentatively say or do something pressing for expression, it almost never turns out as bad as expected.

A lifelong benefit from therapy, difficult to acquire any other way, is an ability that few achieve: the skill to analyze thoughts, feelings, and behavior—*to be a therapist to ourselves.* The therapist who shares thoughts and feelings offers a rare gift: an insider's view of what goes on in the heart and mind of someone who compassionately cares about us and who may have insights we have yet to grasp. It does not matter if some perspectives are off the mark. It is the *process* of thinking and feeling that is absorbed. I would be delighted if patients and students only learned how to take a risk, correct their mistakes, and take more risks. After I disclose my inner process, they are more able to help themselves, aided by the internalized memory-image of me—portable, permanent, always available, at no cost. When occasional pretherapy symptom remnants recur—slight headache, mislaying keys, slipping into overwork—they trigger reflection and resolution, not panic.

Benefits for the Therapist

There are many benefits for the therapist. Effective self-disclosure enhances our psyches, thus enhancing our therapy. Especially if we have a background of inhibition.

Babies are free of inhibitions; they gradually learn what is permissible and what is not. But repression of instincts inhibits spontaneity, artistic expression, and emotion. The baby has freedom without responsibility, then has restricted freedom and increasing responsibility. By school age our prohibitions begin a career in benign deception. A child who tells parents everything is a child with problems. Adolescence accentuates secrecy; so does leaving home. By graduate school self-concealment is well honed. This is not a value judgment, but what most of us have done. People of all ages lie, cheat on tests, and otherwise protect themselves.

Parents, too, construct walls to keep *their* lives private. But much withholding is harmful. Both generations build walls of silence that grow more problematic with the passing years. It is similar between spouses. It is routine in marital therapy to find that neither has mentioned a vital subject. Openness between siblings is more common, yet with many limitations. Protection rackets are *projection* rackets. The fact that it is *true* the other may be hurt or angry disguises projection. Assuming the other is fragile is another projection. And failure to appreciate the hurt when concealment is discovered keeps the destructive pattern going.

In graduate school needless secrecy often continues. When personal issues affect learning, individual therapy is advised. We are accused of "doing therapy" when interface issues are pointed out. Training programs turn out incomplete therapists. Still, therapy is so difficult and takes so long, it is probably unfair to complain about graduate schools.

Young adults can mistakenly assume they are emancipated: living away from parents, self-supporting, married, raising children—and being superficial with family. We do not realize that for each family cutoff in the *external* world, there is a comparable *internal* void. Disowned parts cut off from expression carry energy, wisdom, and resources. We are impoverished when these are not available. This can go on for so many years and be so ego-syntonic that we don't know what is missing.

If therapists accept the value of self-knowledge—some do not—then openness in therapy is an excellent way to learn more. Internal parts of us are triggered that might never be touched in other work. We are stirred by events we have not been exposed to: clinical horrors such as incest, child pedophilia and murder, cannibalism, sexual perversions, criminal behavior of every variety. Working with extreme situations, we are challenged to examine our most depraved impulses, impulses that are as strong as the energy it took to repress them. If we are open to our interior, illusions of innocent childhood are hard to maintain.

Self-deception is fostered by individual therapists who have little appreciation that adulthood is a fine time for connecting with parents and sibs. We can be open and self-revealing with each other. When the older generation shares life experience, the younger finds new options. We can repair narcissistic injuries, right wrongs that can be righted, forgive those that cannot. The typical reaction is, "Why talk about those old hurts? Can't change them now. That's the dead past. Why bring them up and feel bad?" Well, the reason is that unresolved feelings are *not* over, hurt is *not* dead and *not* past. The unconscious knows no time limit:

> Middle-aged brothers and sisters angrily disagree on their eighty-five-year-old mother's care. She reacts with anxiety; her health is deteriorating faster than can be explained by her diseases. Through a daughter's private aside, the root of the trouble becomes clear. These sibs, now grandparents, are still upset over childhood sex play, with no lessening of shame, mistrust, hurt, and anger. The subject has never been discussed. Thus they cannot agree on plans for their ill mother.

What does all this have to do with self-disclosure in doing therapy? Openness in the family determines your pattern. When you make changes to greater family openness, it transfers into therapy. And as you are more open in therapy, it is easier to be open in your family. This is the experience of those who have done family-of-origin work.

A frequent criticism of disclosure has to do with boundaries. A slippery-slope mentality is that if you tell a little, where will it end? Separation supposedly maintains professionalism and averts over-involvement, which is ineffective when 5 to 10 percent of physicians have ill-advised sex with patients. I have known thousands of families and couples in conjoint therapy and have never heard of sex between therapist and patient.

Boundaries are established in every therapy, usually without conflict. Try thoughtful experimentation with greater self-disclosure. Borders are not breached by a few honest comments. Trust is built and boundaries are established out of mutual experience, instead of arbitrarily imposed fiat from "authority" presuming to know what is good for everyone.

When you tell people about your life, you offer a bit of yourself for identification. A template. One way, of many, for being in the world. Therapist examples, undistorted by transference, are useful to identify with or reject. They make changes more real, more under conscious control.

Self-disclosure is effective because it demonstrates empathy. People who come to us are deficient in this quality, most noticeably between husband-wife and parent-child. They repeat the same dysfunctional pattern without knowing or changing how they affect others. Training in empathy is one of the world's greatest needs.

Disclosure works because an authentic encounter is corrective. Middle-class therapists are raised by poor self-disclosers, using deceptions from benign little white to malignant big black lies. We become poor managers of anger, inept at resolving conflicts when our most influential teachers do not show healthy disagreement and healing resolution. Kids miss out on learning how to handle emotions, believing niceness is loving and anger is not loving. They do not learn that loving includes being nice at times, angry at others.

Those who come to us are impaired in healthy emotional expression. As parent figures, we are corrective when we do not "protect" patients from the truth about our differences and fumblings. In cotherapy, most helpful are disagreements Jan and I resolve, often while the family or couple watch. If the disagreements are not resolved, we report later. If they do not ask, they wonder, so we tell them. To be corrective, we do not use white lies. At times we may say, "It would be better if we didn't go into that at this point." Or, to problematic questions, "We will tell you, but we must understand what you hope to learn. What do you imagine we will say?"

Occasionally, a patient plunges into a dangerous situation. We may try to head off an impulsive disaster. Or the patient may need to flounder before waking up. Or our judgment is wrong; the person does well despite our well-intentioned reservations. Remember, we are mostly inhibited do-gooders who fear the world's dangers. Willingness to be wrong is an important model for those patients and students whose fear of being wrong keeps them from acting or, contrariwise, act counterphobically. I may give my opinion: "I think you are making a mistake, but I respect your autonomy and will be available no matter what happens."

Sometimes we give patients information they are unlikely to get anywhere else: New ways of thinking about and solving problems, new options for decision making, unexpected consequences of an intended action, and so on. Or we may tell how other patients or friends deal with crises of everyday living. Many patients live narrow lives, with few close friends, and cut off from family. Their families wrapped a shield around themselves so that all the child knew was repetition of familiar dysfunction. "It stays within the family. You can't trust outsiders."

Nothing is more real than telling stories about our clan. Not only do patients have new information about family life, but they see someone actually breaking through his or her own family secrecy, revealing what went on inside—without catastrophe. They may then have courage to expand their horizons. It is an eye-opener to tell isolated parents about kids staying overnight with a friend or at camp where they taste different lifestyles. It disabuses belief that the family's way is the only way. Knowing about differences eases the shock when children grow up and discover how limited their families, and they, are.

There is a vital difference between telling a story about someone else or describing what is "normal," and telling about yourself. When we say something is normal, understanding is cognitive. But when we share our lives, with traces of anxiety, sadness, or catastrophic expectations, people resonate emotionally. The result? Authentic validation, acceptance of self, and expanded awareness of life—those good things we hope will come from successful therapy.

Revealing our lives is what happens in support and self-help groups. People are surprised that they are not the only ones to lose a parent, agonize over children, consider suicide. Normalizing is relieving, for example, in learning about mourning. People frequently worry that depression, preoccupation with the deceased, or hearing the beloved's voice are signs of mental illness. So too with the paranormal, the strange, the uncanny. Most people who have had out-of-body feelings, near-death experiences, distant viewings, or precognitions are unlikely to share these with anyone who remains aloof and "scientific." Self-disclosure is strongly influenced by the reception we expect:

> After a lecture on near-death experiences, a man stands up and announces, "I am a cardiac surgeon. I have resuscitated many patients from clinical death. I've never had one tell me about this kind of stuff. I think it's all poppycock." After a few moments of stunned silence, another man stands up. "Doctor, I was one of those patients you brought back to life, and I'll be forever grateful. But with your attitude I was afraid to tell you about my near-death experience, and I'm not going to tell you now."

Illness and Other Distractions

Therapist illness compels involuntary self-disclosure. Professional and personal lives intersect. Illusions of invulnerability and ever-availability promoted by the reliable, sacred time and space of sessions are demolished—a dose of reality. Patients know we are coping with life's vicissitudes, full participants in whatever comes along.

Therapists are not immune to the agitated chase, the nervous unrest. Most go from morning until night in a flurry of activity. We let ourselves be ensnared by trivial busyness, prisoners of schedules. Preoccupied with making a living, we overdevelop parts that are active, instrumental, quantitative, efficient. Parts that offer nurturing calm, aesthetic pleasure, spiritual reflection, and healing repose are underdeveloped. So it is not surprising that therapists have a high incidence of psychosomatic disease: hypertension, back problems, depression, alcohol and drug misuse, divorce, suicide. Inevitably, these intrude into the therapist-patient arena.

As a young therapist, I uncritically adopted the view of illness from analytic teachers and therapists: "Tell as little as possible. You must protect your patients. Don't burden them with your problems. You life is your private business. Don't make it into *your* therapy." For example:

I have diarrhea, but say nothing to the patient. Concentration is hard as my stomach churns; I stonewall, struggle for control. Finally, I bolt out of the room, muttering, "I'll be right back." When I return, the borderline young woman is distraught, convinced she drove me out by what she said, she is so disgusting I can't stand to be in the same room, I don't really want to treat her, etc. After I explain and apologize, she looks at her reaction and its roots. I ask what I should have done. She says she would have been less upset if I had warned her I might leave. A simple explanation would do, no details.

Her parents were euphemistic and hypocritical; it is corrective to work with someone who learned—from her—to tell it like it is. Upset by stonewalling, calmed by honesty. We overestimate the negative impact of disclosure. Seeing patients as fragile, we discount their adaptive parts. *They always have strong parts. Preoccupation with problems blinds us to them.* We deny dependency, attribute it to patients (they *do* have dependent parts they display to us), and set ourselves up to be perpetual "helpers."

Keeping illness to myself stems from identification with my father. He had grand and petit mal epilepsy from the 1930s to the 1950s. For twenty years he avoided a convulsion at work; colleagues and superiors never knew. So being secretive about illness came naturally to me. He did the right thing, given the stigma against epilepsy and his private, taciturn personality. What worked for him is not necessarily right for me. But secrecy augmented the tense emotional containment that contributed to his hypertension, arteriosclerosis, and early death at fifty-nine.

Professional Attitudes

Although psychoanalysis is in decline in many quarters, its style of practice still subtly pervades the style of most therapists. *Illness in the Analyst* (Schwartz and Silva, 1990) depicts how illness is handled. They conceal as long as possible. Most work as though nothing is wrong, in spite of ominous symptoms. They delay asking for help, with disastrous consequences. They proclaim that the welfare of patients comes before the welfare of analysts, a belief I no longer share. This sacrificial attitude demeans patients as resourceless children. It is repetitive, not corrective, and repeats family alarms: Don't tell children bad news. Protect them from unpleasantness, funerals, divorce. This is a destructive model for both patients and therapists.

Seeing people as in need of protection is disempowering. It insists the patient is too feeble to deal with life; the strong therapist knows best. It feeds young internal characters who feel helpless, and ignores others who do *not*, who have untapped strengths. This stance is based on therapists' avoidance of discomfort with revealing themselves, rationalized as for the patient's benefit. Freud put patients on a couch so they could not see him because he could not stand being watched all day. Therapists who use the blank screen are not skillful with personal questions and inadvertent disclosures.

Giving and Receiving

Therapy can be seen as an exchange of giving and receiving. The conventional view goes something like this.

Some Things Patients Are Expected to Give

- Show up for appointments
- Provide an intimate, probably embarrassing history
- Cooperate with every life detail they are asked about
- Look at and change unhealthy aspects of life
- Take the risk of feeling rejected and misunderstood
- Pay, or get someone to pay, a fee

Some Things Patients Hope to Get

- Guaranteed, exclusive time
- Accurate, compassionate listening
- High-powered expertise
- Healing
- Relief of symptoms
- Love and attention missing in life (unstated, yet most important)

Some Things <u>Therapists</u> Are Expected to <u>Give</u>

- Professional time and expertise
- Attention
- Thoughtful, ethical clinical responsibility
- Techniques based on theory
- Commitment to success

Some Things <u>Therapists</u> Hope to <u>Get</u>

- Expression of altruistic compassion for people in trouble
- Satisfaction of caring for and helping others
- Joy in practicing our chosen profession
- Seeing years of training bear fruit
- Making a living

Patients and therapists get most of what they want. But there are two discrepancies. (1) Patients are expected to reveal their lives, therapists are not—a one-way street. (2) Love, help, *giving* flow only from therapists to patients—another one-way street. It is considered not only unnecessary but harmful to give of the therapist's personal world. And it definitely is not proper to expect caring. Therapists do not *need* love from patients, which should be found elsewhere. Because we are not receiving from patients, we are drained. Receiving is unprofessional. The unvarying theme has been, "Refuse gifts and analyze the patient's motive," assuming pathology. And we are raised to believe receiving is weakness. "Better to give than receive." Receiving obligates, leaves us indebted. Better to give and be one-up. Little effort is made in conventional therapy to make sure learning to give is accorded equal time. I made this error for years:

> He was a very disturbed chronic paranoid schizophrenic. Electric and insulin shock, tranquilizers, and long hospitalization helped, but he still hallucinated and got into trouble. We recently celebrated forty years of therapy, and I believe seeing me kept him out of the hospital and working. After he retired he was bored, hung around taverns, and regressed. Then the

woman he lived with had a ruptured aneurysm, requiring twenty-four-hour care, which he willingly provided. Later, she told me he was mentally healthier and easier to get along with than he had been in twenty years. Giving, a necessity I never thought of, brought healthy balance to many years of receiving from me.

We are increasingly aware of deprivations and violations patients have suffered—good reason for compassion. The assumption is that these traumas are compensated for in therapy. That is fine, but incomplete. We overplay pathology and underplay health. Listen to a case conference. You hear the bad that has happened and the good that has not, the psychic damage and deficiencies, and how therapy must repair and compensate. *The patient is in great need of receiving.* All true. But this half-truth misses the crucial corrective: *The patient is also in great need of giving.* In the yin and yang of life, giving is as vital as receiving. Example: Elderly research subjects enjoy receiving massages, need fewer doctor visits, drink less coffee, and make more social phone calls. But *giving* massages to toddlers is enjoyed even more.

Healthy physiology requires balanced intake of nutrients and output of waste. That patients are given to without giving back violates this body/mind principle. To stay healthy, we cannot receive without giving, and vice versa. Therapists are exhausted, giving our all with little return. And the patient hooked on receiving is blocked from growth.

Twelve-step programs incorporate giving back. The Twelfth Step of Alcoholics Anonymous reads, "having had a spiritual awakening as a result of these steps, we tried to carry this message to alcoholics, and to practice these principles in all our affairs." The Fifth Tradition of AA: "Each group has but one primary purpose—to carry its message to the alcoholic who still suffers." Recovery is incomplete without the Twelfth Step. And groups do not survive without the Fifth Tradition. We have along way to go in accepting that therapy, to be complete, also requires *giving back*. Giving to others need not wait until the end. Some are never "ready." They can start in small ways early on. Unwillingness to give is a good topic for exploration. Giving begins and blossoms with a therapist who gives of self and receives from patients.

The gains to therapists of giving the gift of revealing themselves are as great as to patients. Mutual give and take is life-affirming, mentally unconstipating. Dean Ornish (1998) provides scientific evidence that disclosure of feelings improves physical health and immune function, reduces cardiovascular reactivity, and may even prolong life. The greater the degree of disclosure, the greater the benefits, and the longer lasting they are. Once we overcome apprehension about false vulnerability and become authentic, we are exhilarated, not guarded; freed, not constricted; open, not closed. And this translates into more openness in the family, with colleagues, in life. It leads to fulfillment we never dreamed possible. It counters burnout, makes the career worthwhile. Our addictions and psychosomatic illnesses are due in large part to a stultifying ethic of "patients before therapists."

Patients seldom mention their shame, always taking, never giving. We do not realize how they feel. This often is a motive behind giving a gift to the therapist. When patients do something for us, one-sided obligation and dependency are assuaged. The relationship feels more equal, more mutual, more fair, more balanced, more collaborative:

> Fifteen minutes before a session, I learn that a former student and staff member committed suicide. I am shaken. When I step into the office the couple, both therapists, know something is terribly wrong. My overfunctioning administrative part acts as though nothing happened, babbling a sentence or two. Then I blurt out that I can't go on. I speak of what my colleague means to me and the pain, shock, and tears I feel. These fine therapists listen, and are helpful, supportive, and compassionate. When I calm down—not more than twenty minutes—we set up another appointment.

In later sessions we joke that instead of just not charging them, I should pay them. But they received something more precious than dollars. They explain it is wonderful to give back a bit of what I gave them in three years. It puts us into better balance, makes for more mutual, honest give-and-take. It does not keep me from continuing as therapist. It opens discussions about giving and receiving in therapy and elsewhere. Caring is not a zero-sum game with winner and loser; love increases when given. In therapy it is two-way, even if not recognized. Better to own up to it. Then therapists can savor rejuvenation and appreciate Buddha's recommendation, "If you knew what I do about the power of giving, you wouldn't let a single meal go by without taking the opportunity to give."

Guidelines and Suggestions

In addition to guidelines for disclosure mentioned earlier, I have a few ground rules about illness and other disruptions:

1. When illness or other events might impact patients, I tell them. When this is not possible, if Jan knows them, she tells them. Or our secretary makes sure they are told. She is good at explaining medical matters.
2. I give headlines without details. If asked for more, I provide it, after exploring their need for more. No one has begged. If they did, I would deal with it as with any behavior. Not saying too much is our responsibility. When I decide that is *all* I will say, they get the message. Being clear, calm, and gentle conveys respect, given and received. Full patient disclosure does not require full therapist disclosure. The better the relationship, the easier it goes.
3. Honesty is critical. What they are told is the truth, not necessarily the whole truth. I respond naturally. When I would rather not give specifics, I tell them, "I prefer not to go into details right now." "I can't tell you more without violating a confidence." "This is as much as I'm comfortable telling you." Be candid about the fact that you are holding back. No deception. Nothing artificial. Patients rely on us to stand for reality.
4. If I am likely to be absent for more than a few days, Jan or I keep them informed of important changes, good and bad.
5. I dislike euphemisms. They are evasive and deceptive. They repeat parental dishonesty. I am referring to euphemisms in therapy, not in everyday life. There, they make society's wheels turn more easily; I may not want to reveal myself, and others may not be interested. "Fine" is often the best response

to the ubiquitous "How are you?" Most greeters are just greeting, not starting a clinical interrogation.

6. When I return to work, patients need to know I have recovered and am fully available. I share a brief, matter-of-fact summary, perhaps new insights or ways to hasten healing. Candid acknowledgment that I am both fallible and resilient expresses more respect than evasion. They are encouraged to comment as appropriate—condolences, congratulations, whatever. A normal human exchange reinforces everyone's grip on reality.

THE PULL OF A STYLE

New students who study a smorgasbord of therapists through literature, videotapes, and in person are easily overloaded; diversity is disorienting. Yet, as chaos theory predicts, a disordered mix self-organizes into a new and better order after six months to a year. Knowing different, sometimes conflicting, methods assists students in evolving a style congruent with their personalities. When free to follow what is appealing, they are attracted to teachers and techniques of self-revelation that match their way of being and doing.

Of course, for both teacher and student, a single, party-line method is simpler, quicker, and less demanding. One-dimensional therapies are easier to reimburse, research, publicize, present in workshops, and write about. The field has witnessed a parade of buzzword techniques that rocket into prominence and fade when their incompleteness becomes apparent. Most training goes the univocal way.

But one note doesn't make a concerto. Knowing an array of possibilities, we gain insight into our natural proclivities. After practicing for a few years, most therapists experiment, while looking to heroes for hints. If they are trained in a single method, they find that the practicalities of clinical life demand a broader approach. They become more eclectic, more integrative in their own way. Why not help them evolve that way in the beginning? I have evolved through several phases, oscillating between openness and concealing. I examine my phases in the hope that you are stimulated to do the same. As a patient once said, ruefully reviewing the permutations in his life, "I don't mind if the pendulum swings back and forth, just so the clock moves on."

MEDICAL PRACTICE

Medical student clerkships heightened excitement and anxiety. Excitement because at last I was a real doctor taking care of real patients; anxiety because I did not have the balmiest idea how to be a real doctor. So I acted as though I knew what I was doing, and adopted what I imagined to be a professional, scientific manner. I presented an awkward caricature of probity I did not feel and maturity I did not have, all business, non-self-revelatory. I dealt with people at arm's length—with forceps, not fingers. This was a change, a strain; I was accustomed to being free and silly. I still shudder over asking a sick old man rote questions from a blue card: "Any diarrhea? Borborygmi?"

Graduates were given Osler's *Aequanimitas* (1932). I took too seriously this message: a physician maintains the appearance of confidence no matter how hard his heart pounds, or how critical the patient. I worked with life-or-death crises, but started a harmful, hard-to-change pattern. Later, as a teacher and therapist of medical students, I saw that this is necessary when first dealing with the tragedy of disease. The further tragedy is that many physicians never grow beyond being guarded and stilted.

Internship reinforced my patient-on-the-end-of-forceps mentality. My most abrupt initiation was to arrive on Ward 64 and be told by the senior resident, "These eighty-nine patients are yours. Let me know if you need help. Good luck." And she was gone, leaving me terrified. I had never been solely responsible for even one patient. So I plunged in, counterphobically, and did my best with people facing life-threatening disease—little time for their personal lives, and none at all for mine.

Then for five years I practiced in a Chicago suburb. News, accurate and inaccurate, traveled at light speed. When I was making house calls, the phone often rang—a neighbor had seen the blue Plymouth and wanted me to come over. If anyone needed me in a hurry, the telephone operator knew where I was. My professional and private lives were open to scrutiny. I was surprised the new doc was the target of intense curiosity. Naive!

I compartmentalized as much as possible, something I could do even before medical school. I could focus on one thing, filter out everything else, typical of thinking introverts. (This valuable "skill" was a liability in the family, to my regret.) The final test of objectivity came when Jan and I walked into a party of twelve young, attractive couples. After saying hello to everyone, I realized I had done a complete physical, including pelvic, on every woman. Quite an exercise in compartmentalization, and savoir faire! I became comfortable juggling hats. Patients told me that when I was not obviously self-conscious they could relax and be whatever was appropriate. This small-town practice was groundwork for being at ease in many hats, in family, with students, with patients, with Jan.

PSYCHIATRY AND PSYCHOANALYSIS

Once I entered psychiatry the situation changed again. I was a hospital physician, expected to conform to clear, unbreachable boundaries: doctor in charge, patient expected to be compliant, personal exchanges frowned upon, questions the province of doctor, not patient. Life shifted neatly into work and personal boxes.

At the Chicago Institute for Psychoanalysis there was a rebound of orthodoxy after Franz Alexander left: Patients were to be treated on the couch four or five times a week, expected to vacation only when the analyst did, and corrective emotional experience was a dirty word. In seven years before I graduated in 1967, only Freud and his direct followers were taught. I never heard about Jung, Adler, Rank, Fromm, Horney, or Frankel unless the names were used disparagingly. Quotes from Freud were frequent and reverent.

"The doctor should be opaque to his patients and, like a mirror, show them nothing but what is shown to him. He should not bring his own feelings into play" (Freud, 1966). This was interpreted to mean never tell the patient anything about your feelings or your life.

"The psychoanalyst should deny the patient, who is craving for love, the satisfaction she demands. Treatment must be carried out in abstinence. Ethical motives unite with technical ones to restrain him from giving the patient his love" (Freud, 1966). This meant not only that sex is prohibited—I agree—but also that the student is not even to hint at liking the analysand. If rookies foolishly admitted to having let a patient know we cared, we were chastised for our countertransference.

"Activity on the part of the physician must take energetic opposition to premature substitute satisfactions . . . deny the patient precisely those satisfactions he desires most intensely . . . If everything is made pleasant . . . he is not given the necessary strength for life" (Freud, 1966). While there is clinical half-truth in these statements, they were interpreted in a most extreme and arbitrary way: Never tell the patient anything about your life or your opinions. Talmudlike, answer a question with a question. Put the most negative and pathological twist on all that happens, especially questions, because even the most innocuous-sounding question covers an unconscious, therefore unhealthy, motive.

Lest you think I am exaggerating, look at the context. I was learning psychoanalysis, not psychotherapy. A firm distinction was made between the two. We were striving for analysis: an all-encompassing transference neurosis that could be analyzed. Transference interpretations were to be used rarely and exclusively. "Interpret the negative transference; the positive will take care of itself." The most chilling criticism was, "You are doing therapy, not analysis." Therapy was considered supportive, educational, not producing structural (lasting) change, and done by social workers, psychologists, and clergy who have not been to medical school, are unscientific, and are not qualified to be psychoanalysts.

There have been many changes in thirty-plus years. A few psychologists and social workers have been trained. Self-psychology makes analysts more humane. But in 1991 in Chicago, the birthplace of self-psychology, only 9 percent of the Psychoanalytic Society identified themselves as self-psychologists; the other 91 percent were Freudians. The psychoanalytic influence has been pervasive, and since World War II it has been the dominant psychological paradigm. Its subtle influence shows up in details of practice, even of therapists claiming to be antagonistic to it.

The other major Chicago influence is Carl Rogers' client-centered therapy, which is misinterpreted to mean nonrevelatory responses from therapists who feed back the last thing the client said. This is a distortion of what its founder did and was, but that does not keep therapists from caricaturing the technique when they do not know what to do. A confused version of analytic and client-centered techniques is practiced by many therapists who adopt trappings such as working only with individuals, valuing sessions for many years, and maintaining anonymity. They have usually been in dynamically oriented therapy and have analysts as supervisors and teachers. Analysis is considered the best, most prestigious, high-class form of therapy.

It is easy to see why psychoanalysis was so attractive to me, an introversive, intuitive, thinking, organized personality. Sitting out of sight, speaking infrequently after careful thought, being "scientific," seeming to be in control at all times, having a rationale for not disclosing thoughts, feelings, or personal life—these were appealing and fit my taciturn father's dictum: "If you don't know what to say, don't say anything. People will think you know and are choosing not to say. Open your mouth when you don't know and everyone will know you don't know."

CHILD PSYCHIATRY AND FAMILY THERAPY

Results of child therapy were far from satisfactory. For many reasons, detailed in *Becoming a Family Therapist* (Kramer, 1980), I began to experiment by seeing the whole family when faced with a "problem" child. Gradually I treated couples, families, and groups of couples and families in various combinations. I started out sticking close to the psychoanalysis model: seldom speaking, keeping opinions to myself, focusing on the transference, dealing with resistance by interpretation, and so on. I even went through a brief phase when I sat behind the couple, and pretended I was dealing with two free-associating as one, a pitiful effort to apply what I knew best. (When the only tool you have is a hammer, everything looks like a nail!)

The more couples and families I saw, the more I was impelled to be active and interactive. With lively conflictual families, if I waited to intervene until I thought I understood, I was inundated with *more* data I had no idea what to do with. Much against my training, I was drawn in very early, being responsive, and taking active leadership, especially with disorganized families with no effective leader.

Because I grew as a therapist when video was more available, I had many opportunities to see and hear myself in action, a learning shock all therapists should expose themselves to until it is no longer a shock, merely a dose of reality. For example, seeing over and over a profile of my pot convinced me to lose forty pounds—and keep it off. Video-tapes showed I was more self-revealing than I thought. Besides, it did not seem to do the harm I had been led to expect. In fact, after I told a story about myself, someone often made a personal comment. When I held my body in a certain posture, others followed. When I stood up or moved around, they livened up. Knowing what to look for, it became clear we were in a well-orchestrated, unconscious dance. Watching videotapes of families with them gave us a chance to comment on what was before our eyes. I could no longer limit my remarks to objective analysis of them. They soon commented about me, and not always favorably. The effects were similar when I interviewed families before observers. Colleagues had penetrating comments. This all con-tributed to my steadily becoming more open—with patients, with col-leagues, with students. And with my family and myself. We even videotaped ourselves.

In 1970, when Jan joined me as cotherapist, we saw couples, fami-lies, groups, and did cosupervision, coconsultation, and coteaching. Again my feeble cover of anonymity was blown. Cotherapy by un-related people reveals much about their personalities; all the more so when cotherapists are married to each other. Patients and students not only discovered my partner of many years, but could see and hear a great deal about our personal lives, both overt and implicit.

We took our six kids (ages fourteen to twenty-four) to a week-long family communication workshop in the summer of 1970. We learned more about them—and they about us—in one week than we had before or since. For example, we agonized over the instruction, "Tell your family something important you have never told them before." Powerful. And effective in removing more barriers to openness, especially after I told them with anguish about a brief affair I had had fifteen years before.

Another influence were workshops Jan and I took in 1972 and 1973. The blend of transactional analysis and Gestalt made for direct encounters with leaders and with each other. Participants paired up, taking turns as therapist and patient, dealing with personal issues. We were encouraged to do more nontraumatic and growthful self-expo-sure. This learning translated into therapy, teaching, workshops, and marathons—settings where we revealed more of ourselves than in conventional therapy.

As beginners, we feel more secure learning a single, internally consistent method. There is nothing wrong with that, so long as we do not get stuck in it, making it a handicap to exploring other possibilities. You will do your best work when your method is consonant with your personality. Experiment and find ways that resonate positively. Invent a fit that feels right, at home, natural. You will save yourself from burnout and enjoy a long, productive career. Explore these reflections, alone or in a group:

1. Where are you on a least-to-most spectrum of self-disclosure? Are you the same with each patient? Account for any differences.
2. Trace your journey on the path of self-disclosure. How are you progressing in developing a pattern that fits your personality and therapy style? Are you satisfied where you are now? If not, what will you do about it?
3. Who are the therapists and what are the methods you are drawn to? Compare and contrast them with those that feel alien. Describe the fit or misfit between your person and these techniques.
4. If you were trained in a particular method, how have you adapted it to your practice? Have you been able to use the essence, while finding other ways to compensate for deficiencies? Are there other limitations to the method that need solving? Is your therapy evolving? (I hope so!)
5. How open were/are your parents about their personal matters? How did you feel about it then—and now? How open were/are you with them? With sibs? With your children, other relatives, and friends?
6. Describe your risk-taking style. How did you get to where you are today? Are you satisfied? Are you inhibited? Would you push yourself to take a few more risks? Or are you too burned from bad risks?
7. What were the attitudes toward self-disclosure in training? How did they work for you? Is your view now different from your trainers'?
8. What have you disclosed to patients about your personal life? What effect has it had on them and therapy?

9. What are you willing to tell patients about yourself, if doing so might move therapy beyond an impasse? What are you not willing to tell?

10. How do you know what disclosure is appropriate? When timing is right? What the effects are?

11. Have you ever said anything personal, only to have it backfire? How did you handle it? What did you learn? Did it change your style? Review a self-revelation that worked well. What were the ingredients?

12. How would you handle a patient's request to see your notes? Under what circumstances would you agree? Refuse? Give your reasons.

13. Do patients have a right to see your notes? Why or why not? If you agree, would you edit out comments about yourself?

14. Perhaps you were a lucky one who came into this field without inhibitions about self-disclosure. How has this worked for you? Any advantages? Any drawbacks?

15. Experiment with a little more self-disclosure. If it works, push it farther and see what happens. Try this with a case in deep trouble. What can you lose?!

16. Recall the last time you were ill. What did you tell people? With what results? Are there any changes to make when you get sick again?

17. What are you willing and not willing to tell patients about your illnesses? How do you prefer to handle this?

18. How do you feel about giving and receiving? How do you handle being taken care of when you are sick?

19. How do you handle gifts from patients? Does your answer depend on the patient, stage of therapy, value of the gift, or anything else?

ANNOTATED REFERENCES

Bridges, William (1980). *Transitions: Making Sense of Life's Changes.* Reading, MA: Addison-Wesley. Useful for anyone, no matter how sophisticated.

Freud, Sigmund (1966). *Recommendations to Physicians Practicing Psychoanalysis,* Standard Edition, Volume XII. London: Hogarth Press. (Original work published 1912.) Set a standard to this day for professionalized withholding of self.

Jourard, Sidney M. (1971). *The Transparent Self.* New York: D. Van Nostrand Co. Every therapist who aspires to authenticity should read and reread this book, especially Part 5, "The Disclosing Psychotherapist."

Kramer, Charles H. (1980). *Becoming a Family Therapist: Developing an Integrated Approach to Working with Families.* New York: Human Sciences Press, Part III. If those coming to us are to become more whole, loving, creative, and effective people, we must become so right along with them.

Ornish, Dean (1998). *Love and Survival: The Scientific Basis for the Healing Power of Intimacy.* New York: HarperCollins. Love and intimacy are essential for physical, mental, and spiritual growth. Contrariwise, loneliness, isolation, and withholding self predispose us to dysfunction and disease.

Osler, Sir William (1932). *Aequanimitas: With Other Addresses to Medical Students, Nurses and Practitioners of Medicine.* Philadelphia: Blakiston.

Schwartz, H. and Silva, Ann Louis (Eds.) (1990). *Illness in the Analyst: Implications for the Treatment Relationship.* Madison, CT: International Universities Press. The sad result of Freud's *Recommendations.*

Chapter 5

The Differing Selves

Helen V. Collier

> The failure to see the different reality of women's lives and to hear the difference in their voices stems in part from the assumption that there is a single mode of social experience and interpretation. By positing instead two different modes, we arrive at a more complex rendition of human experience. . . .
>
> Carol Gilligan
> *In a Different Voice*, 1982, p. 173

Accounts of the "what I do in therapy" variety usually come to grief on the twin reefs of egoism and tedium, but as a practitioner my contribution to this collection of writings about the use of *self** in psychotherapy has to be personal rather than scholastic. What follows therefore seeks to avoid those perilous twin reefs by summarizing what I think happens when any of us engage in psychotherapy. My own special aid to navigation is what happens differently when the therapist is a female and must listen to the diversity of voices.

Throughout my professional career, there has always been argument about whether a therapist should reveal self and thereby place personal values in the psychotherapeutic relationship or stay aloof and "objective," relying on scientifically replicable techniques to accomplish the intervention and achieve the clients' goals. I have

---

*Whenever the term *self* is first employed in a chapter as part of the concept of the use of self in therapy, it is italicized to call attention to its special use.

seen all the "schools" of therapy at work, and I have watched colleagues switch from one side of the debate to the other. The need to remain "objective" and the usefulness of replicable techniques have always provided an invaluable sheet anchor in my clinical work. But I have never made them my chief guide, and, for reasons stemming from my educational background, the general debate has caused pause and reflection but not been a major engaging force for me.

Educated young in religion and literature, and later in the philosophy of science, I seem always to have believed—like those disciplines—that absolute objectivity does not exist in human relationships even if the search for it should often be their goal. Once I had completed my academic education, I began the expanding experience of seeking out the major training centers around the country for postdoctoral experience. I knew that the profession had produced many highly sophisticated persons working to weave theory and practice together while always continuing the search for more effective therapeutic approaches. During this energizing period, I met and worked with Miriam and Erving Polster in California and the puzzle pieces dropped into place. The premise they worked from, and which works for me, was that technique and technology are not the center of the therapeutic process but should be present only to enrich the effect of the psychotherapist in the process by which our clients (whether individuals, couples, families, or groups) heal and grow. Today, the Polsters continue to espouse this approach in their work with Gestalt, expanding and changing their theory with the new knowledge and experiences they incorporate.

No matter what "technique" I use in my own work (and I use many), central to everything is my personal presence in the process and my awareness of who I am and how I use that presence. But the reef of egoism immediately looms dead ahead! To dominate clients with my own self is to be a rotten therapist. The therapist's ego is a bore and a distraction. It is the clients' process and ultimate success, not my own, that I must seek. If I become central or dominant, then I guarantee failure in the goal of facilitating their process and experience. Here, then, is the dilemma of the personal approach and the danger of reliance on the use of self.

Far from sinking us, however, that reef makes us navigate better. The awareness of the dilemma of self is the most valuable technique a therapist can have. I find that as long as I am fully conscious of myself as well as my clients during the therapeutic process, I am able to make clear choices as to the role I will play with these individuals in this particular situation. Those roles vary greatly: consultant, catalyst, resource provider, reactor, observer, problem solver, sharing human, sometimes even just a shoulder to cry on. From minute to minute, through awareness and accompanying discomfort, I often receive cues to change roles.

The steady awareness I seek during a psychotherapeutic session is something I can only call "healthy energy." The normal human experience is total presence in the world, constant interaction with a multitude of stimuli in the environment and the physiological self, and steady exchange of energy in a great variety of ways. The therapist, I believe, should always attempt to *enhance that normal human experience in herself or himself during therapy.* How? By staying aware that during therapy the entire composite of her or his experiences (past, present, future) is at work, that all the hopes and failures, all the expertise and ignorance, all the perceptions of self both in the therapeutic process and in the world, all the understanding of the intricacy of being alive is functioning in the here and now between this therapist and this family, couple, or individual client. The difference between therapist and nontherapist, I believe, is the degree of consciousness and responsiveness to the interaction between organism and environment. And are we not, as therapists, to raise and grow that consciousness and responsiveness to the organism and environmental interaction in our clients? Is that not one major element that is missing or dysfunctional in their interaction that initially brings them to the therapeutic setting?

Which leads me to my next point about the presence of self in our therapeutic work. Let me quote from Joseph Campbell (1988) in an interview with Bill Moyers about the human quest in *The Power of Myth.* "People say that what we're all seeking is a meaning for life. I don't think that's what we're really seeking. I think that what we're seeking is an experience of being alive, so that our life experiences on the purely physical plane will have resonances within our own innermost being and reality, so that we actually feel the rapture of being alive" (p. 5). People come to therapy to solve a particular problem—conflict between family members, despair over the addiction of a teenager, a love relationship that has collapsed, helplessness and hopelessness in the face of loss—and we work to impart new understandings, attitudes, skills, and renewed hope for growth and change. This is critical in our work, and I believe we also are present to revitalize "the rapture of being alive" and that we do that by the self being fully present.

The growth and spread of various forms of community, groups, and families in our culture over the past two decades has been a move toward feeling present in like-minded groups so that we feel "alive" and connected. The proliferation of self-help and support groups (AA, ACOA, NA, support groups for CFIDS, cancer, MS, grief, loss of child), religious communities, second-step transition homes, and so on, are all vibrant forms of connection of aliveness between the organism and the environment. We as therapists are part of that vibrant experience by being present with our healthy energy.

Let me look at this presence of self from the viewpoint of a woman, which Carol Gilligan in her groundbreaking work called the "different voice." As have other empirical scholars, Gilligan challenges the theories of Piaget and Kohlberg as based on male standards and models. Studying the psychological and moral development of women over their lifetimes, she finds that "in view of the evidence that women perceive and constitute reality differently from men and that these differences center around experiences of attachment and separation, life transitions that invariably engage these experiences can be expected to involve women in a distinctive way" (1982, p. 171). It is her subsequent conclusion from this basis that makes her work new and exciting. She suggests that the silencing of the female voice through ignoring women's different personality development has resulted not just in harm to women but in an impoverishment of our ability to understand humanity—both women and men. She convincingly proposes that the sex differences in the personality formation of male and female mean that each sex speaks "in a different voice" and that the blending of those voices is the truly human chorus.

The two sexes are trained to experience and express things differently, writes Gilligan. Masculinity is defined through separation, femininity through attachment. Male gender identity is threatened by intimacy, female gender identity by separation. Whereas Vaillant (1977) and Levinson (1978) found separation and attachment to be distinct stages through which people pass, Gilligan finds this to be true only for men, not for women, for whom the two stages are fused, starting in adolescence. The male identity domain holds tight boundaries for the exercise of exclusion; the female identity domain has loose boundaries for the process of interconnection. Males tend to believe that there is one right way to live and their task is to find it. Females tend to believe that there are many right ways to live and their task is to find the right one for now. Inevitably, then, when women and men speak, even of the same thing, they speak in different voices. Other scholars have confirmed and elaborated Gilligan's perception of the different communication styles, including the linguist Deborah Tannen's search for the rituals and barriers in communication between women and men in *That's Not What I Meant* (1986) and *Talking from 9 to 5* (1994). The recently popular books by John Gray, starting with *Men Are from Mars, Women Are from Venus* (1992), describe how these differences play out in intimate relationships as well as the larger world in which we interact.

I recognize, of course, that one cannot say that all behavior characteristics belong to one gender or the other. Apart from being wrongheaded, that would perpetuate the stereotypes which prevent us from seeing qualities as qualities regardless of their gender content. Worse, it would camouflage the differences between individual women and individual men that are the very source of richness they bring to the therapeutic process. It would be as narrowing as making a diagnosis and then seeing all an individual's behavior in terms of that diagnosis only.

On the other hand, empirical research (Maccoby and Jacklin, 1974; Williams, 1982; Gilligan, 1982; Jordan et al., 1991) and studies of the social process (Horney, 1973; Pleck, 1976; Miller, 1987; Collier, 1982; Goldberg, 1983; Milwid, 1990; Thomas, 1992) show that certain values, attitudes, and behavior are related to gender. Much of the groundbreaking work on the gender differences that began with Gilligan's and Miller's work has grown into a major research and training center, The Stone Center at Wellesley College. Now in the 1990s, knowledge and understanding has reached a degree of magnitude and detail that all therapists of both genders need to embrace. In saying this, I do not want to exacerbate the fruitless debate as to whether females or males are "better" in some sense. I advocate an expansion of each sex into the virtues of the other, and a resultant enrichment of our profession's skills and a broadening of that self we bring into the therapeutic process.

And what of that self our clients bring? Can we not only be present for them but also have them fully present for us so that our interaction is fruitful and effective? I am often amazed at the broadness of perceptions brought into the therapeutic setting by a couple or a family. I am currently working with several cross-generational families—children, parents, grandparents all in the same room, each with a self and all with different perceptions. Much of the action is gender as well as role, experience, personality, and age. How can I be present for this chorus of humanity and gather or display each self in order to create a more rewarding home environment for each and all? A couple faced with the trauma of the infidelity of one carries not only the pain each experiences but the entire issue of autonomy and separation, attachment and caring, individuation and interconnection—and communicated "in a different voice." Since I can hear those different voices, how can I help each member of the couple also to hear and even to appreciate them?

Let me summarize what I believe to be the self I bring to the therapeutic process, whether the selves with whom I share this time and space are individuals, couples, families, or groups:

a. My capacity to use the kind of judgment-perspective typical of women strengthens my ability to give equal regard to attachment and autonomy.

b. My perspective that there are many ways to deal with a problem, any of which may be acceptable, enables me to help clients choose a "male" or a "female" way appropriate to all needs, not just to biological gender.

c. When a woman in therapy chooses to act on the basis of the caring in a relationship, I recognize that her choices come not just from dependency needs but from a sense of connectedness to other humans and the need to protect that connectedness. This enables me to help her face choices that involve not only connection but also the option of separation.

d. Aware that every person needs both autonomy and attachment, and with considerable experience at balancing those needs in my own life as daughter, lover, wife, mother, worker, and friend, my flexibility helps clients to decide which quality is appropriate in a particular situation. In therapy this is the real issue more often than is usually admitted.

e. My female training in connecting with others without loss of my self makes both me and my clients comfortable with the different concept that self-identity and fusion with others are not incompatible or mutually exclusive.

f. My identity as a woman brings an awareness of the female reality, the experience that our biology makes us share, our socialization, our sexual development, our work lives, our different sense of the purpose of life.

g. My identity as a woman also enables me to hear and be present for both the female and the male voice, and to respect the different voices.

h. When working with couples and families, I consciously work to hear the voices of the selves, to ask questions if I am unclear in order to assist them in clarifying their existence and nature. Then I can face the crucial matter of whether I reinforce one voice or the other, aim at creating harmony between the two, or (on some pleasurable occasions) encourage a couple or family to transcend them.

i. Wary of the reef of egoism, however, I much prefer to work with a male colleague in couple, family, and group situations. Our joined ability to hear different voices, and our cooperation in tuning in to them, often creates a geometrical increase over either of us working alone or with another therapist of the same sex.

This brief discussion of the different voices and selves brought to the therapeutic process has to end in speculation. Can our profession be enriched by paying more attention to the existence of different voices and selves? Can we balance the presence of the selves in the therapeutic process? What are the lessons we will learn when we hear their symphony? Will they teach that there is a world very different in nature from that bifurcated world we have so far created?

Over my years of private practice, women have come to me mostly with the goal of understanding themselves better and sorting through the complexities which multiple commitments bring to a woman's life. The pattern of men, who have come in steadily increasing numbers, has been different. Those who mostly wanted to understand themselves better used to choose, I believe, male therapists. For many years, men who came to me were mainly those who felt confusion and frustration in regard to women—"What do they really want?" Though often starting with the desire to have me "straighten out" their women, they wanted better to understand themselves mostly in relationship to women. Then a new breed began to come: men wanting to love and to live with women more effectively, men who sensed that they were poor at achieving intimacy. Currently another group is becoming familiar. These are men who embrace the ethic of caring and attachment and want to do more about it, men who are conscious of the limitations of the male life and want to expand, men unsettled by the generally arid life of work and society instead of just by the troubled home. These are the men who, like women since many years ago, want to understand themselves better and develop a life of balance and fullness. These are the men who understand that what we share as humans is much greater than what separates us as women and men.

I attribute this development to a change in male and female choices about how they want to be in the world of the 1990s and into the new century. I think what they seek is the degree and quality of human contact, the feeling of connectedness in a world struggling to find community, the lack of hierarchical directiveness, the flexibility that approves a wide variety of choices, and above all the absence of competitive ego. They feel they can benefit from a deeper experience of the collaborative world in the person of their therapists and expand their own world to a fuller world of being human. If I am right, this is confirming support for saying that the self is crucial to the role of the therapist. The self is not just individual; it is also biological, social, and ethical. It seems transparently clear to me that the most important choice for our clients is not which technique will help them best (though this too is important) but which therapist will offer the widest and most flexible response as an individual to the clients as individuals.

It is just as transparent that the crucial choice for a therapist is to learn to use her or his self with the flexibility and integrity and range that each and every client merits. On the jacket of one of his books, Sidney Jourard wrote, "Shall I permit my fellow humans to know me as I truly am or shall I seek instead to remain an enigma and be seen as someone I am not?" (1971). For a responsible therapist, the question can have only one answer, but the applications of that answer must be as cautious, painstaking, and as selfless as possible.

REFERENCES

Campbell, J. (1988). *The power of myth.* New York: Doubleday.

Collier, H. (1982). *Counseling women: A guide for therapists.* New York: The Free Press.

Gilligan, C. (1982). *In a different voice.* Cambridge, MA: Harvard University Press.

Goldberg, H. (1983). *The new male female relationship.* New York: William Morrow.

Gray, J. (1992). *Men are from Mars, women are from Venus,* New York: Harper-Collins.

Horney, K. (1973). *Feminine psychology.* New York: Norton.

Jordan, J., Kaplan A., Miller, J.B., Stiver, I., and Surrey, J. (1991). *Women's growth in connection.* New York/London: The Guilford Press.

Jourard, S.M. (1971). *The transparent self.* New York: Van Nostrand.

Levinson, D. (1978). *The seasons of a man's life.* New York: Alfred A. Knopf.

Maccoby, E.E. and Jacklin, C.N. (1974). *The psychology of sex differences.* Stanford, CA: Stanford University Press.

Miller, J.B. (1987). *Toward a new psychology of women,* Second edition. Boston: Beacon Press.

Milwid, B. (1990). *Working with men.* Hillsboro, OR: Beyond Words Publishing.

Pleck, J.H. (1981). *The myth of masculinity.* Cambridge, MA: MIT Press.

Tannen, D. (1986). *That's not what I meant!* New York: Ballantine Books.

Tannen, D. (1994). *Talking from 9 to 5.* New York: Avon Books.

Thomas Jr., R.R. (1992). *Differences do make a difference.* Atlanta: The American Institute for Managing Diversity.

Vaillant, G.E. (1977). *Adaptation to life.* Boston: Little Brown.

Williams, J.H. (1982). *Psychology of women.* New York: W.W. Norton.

Chapter 6

Uses of the Self in Integrated Contextual Systems Therapy

Bunny S. Duhl

As a family systems therapist, how do I use my *self** in therapy? To quote Elizabeth Barrett Browning, "Let me count the ways." I draw on everything I have ever experienced, learned or done in this life that connects me to myself and other human beings. I use my awareness and all of these learnings about how we think, image, feel, experience, act, understand, grow, and change. In addition to more formal education, I draw on analogies from my experience as a musician in my awareness of how different instruments can be in rhythm, how they can harmonize or be discordant. As a potter and sculptor for some twenty years, I draw upon a wealth of processes and images, and the knowledge that the same material can take many different forms, and that something that never existed before can evolve and take shape. A delightful series of experiences in theater from an early age through college summer stock definitely provided a way, later, of visualizing family systems, and supported the idea that one could play many roles as both family member and therapist. I constantly draw on that sense of family as theater (Duhl, 1983).

I draw on my experience as a writer, as now, to translate what is holographic into linear language in ways that—hopefully—others can understand. I most certainly draw upon my experience as woman, wife, divorcée, mother of three children, daughter, sister, niece, cousin,

---

*Whenever the term *self* is first employed in a chapter as part of the concept of the use of self in therapy, it is italicized to call attention to its special use.

and orphan. Especially, I draw upon my awareness of being a woman at this particular time in history with my own experiences of changing roles, values, expectations, opportunities, and lifestyles.

So how do I use myself in therapy? In as many ways as I possibly can to tune into what really matters to each client, and which help to transform pain into option, problem into creative solution, and "stuckness" into movement—with the tools for further understanding and movement in the hands of each client.

AN INTEGRATED CONTEXTUAL SYSTEMS MODEL

My model of working with people is an integrated contextual systems model, with a base in family therapy (Duhl and Duhl, 1981). Essentially it derives from general systems (von Bertalanffy, 1968) and learning theory (Piaget, 1952, 1977). The constructs and concepts of social and family systems interactions are intertwined with individual and family developmental models, placing great emphasis on how our minds work at each age and stage, and on how learning to learn takes place in varying contexts (Duhl and Duhl, 1981). Developed at the Boston Family Institute from 1969 through 1986 (Duhl and Duhl, 1974, 1979; Duhl, 1983, 1986), my model focuses on the human capacity for meaning making and the search for coherence. Each of us as human beings makes sense of the world as best we can, given the cognitive stages through which we wend our way and the totality of the contexts in which we are embedded. This model is also cognizant of the miraculous human capacity to believe the products of our own minds—the meanings we ourselves have made—*as if* they constitute the ultimate and only truth about each situation we have encountered and pondered.

Change, in this model, is seen as deriving from internal and external reconfigurations. *Internally*, helping people *to update the way in which they hold beliefs, meanings, and information*, through exploration and reframing, allows them to experience themselves in a new relationship to that information. *Externally*, helping people *to experience and adopt alternative ways of behaving and relating* allows them to experience different relationships to others. Both aspects are necessary for lasting change (Bateson, 1979). Reconfiguring beliefs and behaviors requires offering alternative images and metaphors for those which seem to bind people in fear of the un-known—whether that unknown be the next stage in their lives (Andolfi et al., 1983) or a way of living without fear. Perhaps the most important task a therapist encounters in the change process is tuning people in to their own rich resources which have not yet been tapped, and offering them tools with which to use these resources in daily life and problem solving.

The Roles of the Therapist

Although in family systems therapy the "client" may be a couple, a family, the total important network, or even one person, the role of the therapist, in his or her use of self in totality, is *to safeguard and promote the autonomy of each person's fluid interconnection with others.* The therapist knows that each person influences and is in-fluenced by every other person in the system (von Bertalanffy, 1968), and that each has a personal and idiosyncratic view of issues and events. Each person's view adds a dynamic to the whole. Each is correct, none is complete. Therapists have another view, that of how all members interact in their presence, which allows for a view of how the total family system functions in patterned ways (Duhl, 1983). Since no one view is complete—including their own—con-textual systems therapists must not be bound and bonded to any one individual in a family or extended personal group, but must use themselves in a mobile way so as to be able to "stand behind" each person in the room while seeing the patterns, both flexible and blocked, that interactions among individuals create.

When therapists are with families, they use themselves in multi-ple roles (Satir, 1972a). As empathic listeners, they validate each person's view of events. As artful "dodge 'em car" operators, they carefully maneuver between obstacles, notably the persons in the family who insist their views are the only correct ones. In alerting the family to patterns that are repetitive, they act as a mirror high-lighting that which the family cannot see themselves. They are improvisational theater directors as they ask family members to enact new ways of relating to one another, or place them in motion in a sculptural spatial metaphor of change (Duhl, Kantor, and Duhl, 1973; Duhl, 1983). Much of the time they are weavers, linking images, behaviors, thoughts, and experiences with context, and con-necting all in a textured tapestry of life.

In the instance in which the client is one individual with a contex-tual systems therapist, the therapist acts as historian, anthropologist, and dramatist. In these roles, therapists seek and gather information concerning contexts and other people with whom the client is and has been connected. They need to generate the map of the total system and its interactional nature for both themselves and the client. When they have that map, they are able to encourage those optional behaviors, thoughts, feelings, and beliefs that fit the situa-tion and the particular individuals involved, so that new possibili-ties can take form.

Within a contextual systems model, input from so-called outsiders, such as relatives, agencies, or teachers, is not only accepted but de-sired. Through multiple inputs, the therapist can understand not only the shaping impacts each person has on each other, but can understand the way in which each person holds others in his or her mind—through emotions and a personal glossary of symbolic meanings. Thus the contextual systems therapist knows that to help create fluidity where there are barriers within an individual as well as between people, and to understand the way in which symptoms play a part in the play of life, the therapist must also be a detective and playwright. Listening and imaging with dramatic flair, the therapist then must mentally flesh out the cast of characters with each in specific roles, replete with lines and actions as well as each person's idiosyncratic way of being in and perceiving the world. Grasping how others construct and hold their realities offers the therapist the routes of access for introducing alterna-tive and equally viable constructions (Minuchin, 1974; Watzlawick, Weakland, and Fisch, 1974).

With this model, then, therapists must first know themselves well—to know the meanings they harbor, and where and when they came from. They must also be cartographers and biographers of each person in the room—know each person, understand how each sees the interactive process given the influences of family beliefs, ethnic and contextual background, and developmental time. They must care about the people they see, yet not get caught in that caring.

IMPLICATIONS FOR THE TRAINEE AND TRAINING

How one arrives at being able to do these types of mental schematics is a matter of the type of education—drawing forth, in which all trainees learning to become therapists immerse themselves. Within such a training model as the one developed at the former Boston Family Institute, it is necessary for future therapists to become aware of the systems within the self as well as between persons. In that process, it is equally necessary that they be free (as were the pioneers in the field) to use all of their own life experiences to draw upon. This means, in training, heightening the awareness of one's way of thinking and believing at each stage of life in order to rekindle that which has been dormant. Appreciating the idiosyncratic styles we each have of processing information, and their fit with how we expected ourselves to learn, and our feelings about ourselves, becomes as important as how different learning styles and stages fit together in one family (Duhl and Duhl, 1975; Duhl, 1983, 1986).

To be cognizant of a wide frame within which to work with families means to explore the myths, rules, and bindings that hold families together, one's own as well as others, to examine the stories and core images one has of one's family, to explore and play with the myriad ways family members interact while handling their vulnerabilities and defenses (Duhl, 1976). When we each as trainees investigate the ways in which we hook others into our schemes and get hooked into theirs, we have some sense of approximation of what might also be going on for clients, or for us with clients. Approximation is the closest we will ever get to knowing how another experiences the world. The more we each know about ourselves and the others with whom we learn, the more we can approximate and move with that which is generic in all persons. To be free to use oneself means to recognize many ways that loving, playing, fighting, deciding, and mourning can happen and to know that each person in life is busy trying to maintain a sense of self-esteem (Satir, 1964, 1972b) while going toward imaged goals in a world each never made.

Using oneself fully means to know patterns of clear and muddy communication in one's own systems as well as those one works with and within (Satir, 1964; Watzlawick, Beavin, and Jackson, 1967). Considering the boundaries in one's family, and all the ways those boundaries manifested themselves, takes trainees into looking at family rules, roles, routines, and replications (Duhl and Duhl, 1979). Use of self requires oneself as trainee and as therapist to continually update one's life, while examining oneself as an actor in the systems one is in (Anonymous, 1972).

Using oneself well then means to be involved in an ongoing research project: to be curious about one's own reactions and intentions in varying contexts, and to locate the source of reactivity in one's learned-to-learn patterns. These patterns, developed in earlier contexts, give clues to the current context as well as the context of clients. Such a model implies the continual development of one's capacity to respond creatively in life situations as well as in therapy, to be in touch with one's existential core in relation to one's life in context at each stage in life. It means to play with options for oneself, with a wide range of stances and roles from which to choose. Then one has many creative ways to invent metaphor, humor, and ways of making the familiar strange and the strange familiar (Gordon and Poze, 1973). Most of all, over time, it means to trust oneself—to be able to reach inside and know how to tune into the inner core of oneself en route to other persons, and to know that to be human is to unfold and conserve in varying degrees at different times.

Many ways of specifically describing oneself as a therapist are possible. I will focus here on interventions drawn from life experience, and inventions in clinical practice, hopefully stimulating readers to consider what each brings to his or her practice drawn from life or spontaneously created. After all, one person's invention becomes another's technique.

PROBLEM-SOLVING ANECDOTES: INTERVENTIONS FROM MY LIFE

One's own style as a person obviously is the core of one's style as a therapist. I seem to be one of those people who is both experimental and introspective in life, particularly about actions taken with others. I have always experimented with "what ifs" and recorded in my mind the results of new experimental behaviors. I did that in my creative work with clay, and with my interactions with family and friends. And I found myself naturally doing that in therapy. In addition, long before

I became a family therapist, when I found myself in a pickle, I often found that some unplanned, spontaneous action on my part worked to untangle an interactive knot. Later I would think about the sequences and underlying constructs of such actions, and would analyze *why* they made a difference. This meant I needed to look at the interactive system of which I was a part in a multicentric manner—that is, from the inside out through each one's point of view. I needed to stand in each one's shoes for a moment, to become aware of the probable inner state of each person in the interaction. I needed also to be aware of the dynamics between members arising from those probable internal states.

Naturally then, both playing "what if" and stepping back and analyzing spontaneous happenings became creative forces in my world as a therapist. When I found something worked for me, or was emotionally true for me, I would then consider the possibility that that sequence of thoughts and actions could work for others in similar situations. I found after a while that this was often the case. Over my lifetime, I have built up a large personal repertoire of problem-solving responses that is constantly being expanded. I have learned from the feedback of clients, and added their learnings to my own, and have changed interventions according to that new information. Some of these interventions fit situations that are more generic than others. Some I may have used only once or twice with clients, in very particular contexts. All, however, create a collection of tools coming from the learnings via a full use of self. Thus one person's planned or spontaneous response, when shared and repeated over time by others, becomes a technique. Techniques are interventions which can be described, sequenced, and which have been found to be effective in changing behaviors and thought processes (when used more or less according to directions) in certain generic interactional contexts. These interactional contexts also are replete with recognizable (and therefore predictable) behavioral patterns.

Reading Each Other

Members of families, as well as friends and work groups, derive personal meaning from how others behave with them. We are each an actor in someone else's version of the play (Duhl, 1986). How someone acts with us is usually in some measure feedback about ourselves and the relationship. We read each other's behavior all the time and we cannot *not* make meaning. Often, the meanings we make are negative and not "checked out."

Misreading another person is a very common situation, in which people misinterpret each other's behavior by projecting their own meanings onto each other. The clearer we are about ourselves, the more we can share the meanings we are making and the more we can ask questions of the other person or persons. When misreading is a recurring issue in a couple or family that I am seeing, I often use the following anecdote.

What's My Face Showing?

When my oldest child, a daughter, was about thirteen and a half, we began bumping into each other in a very unpleasant way. For instance, she would ask if she could go to the movies. I would ask all the "proper" mother questions: what movie? with whom? when was it playing? where? and so on. Having received satisfactory answers from this shy child, I would say, "Yes, you can go." She would then mutter something akin to "I thought you would say 'no.'"

I felt annoyed with this response on her part. I felt that my heartfelt intentions to be a good mother, to give her freedom as well as protection, were being misinterpreted. As this type of behavior continued on her part, I found myself thinking, "Keep this up, young lady, and I *will* say 'no'!" I rationalized her behavior with explanations to myself that this was the beginning of teenage rebellion, that although shy, she was beginning to talk back sassy, and that I might as well get used to it and ignore it. After all, since she was the eldest, I had never been there before. However, at the same time, I felt maligned and hurt that she kept attributing negative intent to my best-of-intentions mothering.

Several weeks later, I was busy in the kitchen cooking dinner and thinking about my mother, who was dying of a slow-growing brain tumor. My daughter walked in, looked at me, and asked, out of the blue in a completely atypical manner, "Are you angry?"

"No," I answered, surprised.

"Well, you *look* angry!" she said.

At that point, for whatever reason, I kept my face fixed in its expression and went into the hallway next to the kitchen to look in the mirror there. What I saw shocked me. I saw a heavy frown, brows pushed together with deep furrows between them, eyes squinting and fixed, imparting an intense, penetrating look.

I continued to hold my face in this manner and went back into the kitchen to join my daughter. I said to her, pointing to my face, "I have just looked in the mirror and have seen what you have been seeing, and I can understand how you could see this as angry. Is this what you have been seeing on my face these past few months?"

"Yes," she said.

"And you thought I was angry. Did you think I was angry at you?" Again, "Yes."

"No wonder!" I said. And I let my face relax, as I looked at her.

Of course she kept attributing anger to me! I had looked fierce indeed! Then I told her that I was not angry—or that if I was, it was at God, for as she knew, Nana was dying and I was sad and worried. I did not want Nana to suffer and I also did not want to lose her. I told my daughter that "my eyeballs were turned inward," focusing inside on my feelings and thoughts, and that I was completely unaware of what was on my face. And I reassured her that although it looked to her as if I were angry, I was really worried and sad, and I was not at all angry at her. I then gave her a hug. All the tension between us dropped away.

Most of us are not aware of the expressions on our faces and what we are conveying with them; what meanings others see in our faces that are other than our intent. As result of this incident with my daughter, I devised an exercise for trainees at the family institute, which I also used in workshops as well as with couples and families. I ask people to pair up while I put a list of words on the board. I ask them to enact these words in pantomime with each other, and to mix up the order in which they enact them. I tell them they are to see if each can accurately guess which word the other is enacting. The words are *happy, sad, angry, worried, thoughtful,* and *pensive.*

In my practice I will ask couples and family members to do this exercise right in the office. As per my hunch, time and time again, people will mix up *sad, angry, worried,* and *thoughtful.* Far beyond projection on the part of the viewer, one's face does not always reflect what is experienced internally. The viewer may need to ask questions.

When misreading occurs, and the viewer does not ask questions about the internal world of the expresser, people react and tensions escalate.

I use the anecdote about my daughter and the exercise to throw a monkey wrench into automatic reaction encounters in situations where I sense that the couple or family members are assigning incorrect meanings to each other's facial expressions, and are reacting defensively to what they are interpreting. If I ask them to "check out that meaning" with each other, they often discover how they misread it. When this type of behavior is explored as an exercise, there is no content to be argued about. To read a pantomime of another being "sad" out of any ordinary context means to be able to focus on the face and body expression itself, uncluttered by one's own inner agenda.

I also use this anecdote and set of exercises to encourage an attitude of "benefit-of-the-doubt thinking." I use it to help clients get new information from and about each other which in turn can infiltrate and influence new behaviors toward each other. Many clients are delighted and relieved to get that new information about a partner or other family member. They learn to inquire, to check out what they are seeing, with direct feedback, such as, "You look worried to me. Is that what you are feeling?"

I encourage family members to do as I did—to hold the expression and look in the mirror, so they can indeed see what is being seen by another. In this I often quote a limerick I once heard so that humor can detoxify the situation:

> As a beauty I'm not a great star
> There are others more handsome by far
> But my face, I don't mind it,
> Because I'm behind it—
> 'Tis the folks in the front that I jar!*

Some clients are resentful that they either had been misinterpreting the other or had been misinterpreted by the other. When clients have been misinterpreting others and are resentful, they usually

---

*This limerick is often attributed to Woodrow Wilson, since he quoted it so often. However, according to a Web page on the Internet (http://pwi.netcom.com/~pentatet/myths.htm), it was actually written by Anthony Euwer in a book called *The Limeratomy*, published in 1917.

believe that the others have been trying to trick them, and they are ashamed that they misread an expression, as if they were supposed to know ahead of time its true meaning. Often if one is resentful about being misinterpreted, it carries with it a corollary feeling of shame or blame: "You should have known what I meant." When *either* is the case, it gives me the opportunity to go into the magical thinking and/or rules behind the feeling, which usually take the forms of: "If you really loved me, you would know what is going on inside of me" or the unspoken family rule, "You're supposed to know before you know" where you are held accountable for not knowing what has *not* been clearly expressed. Delving into either myth or rule with couples and/or family members opens up whole new arenas of the substrate structure in which people have been interacting and playing out roles. It creates an opportunity to explore shame and self-esteem and where these rules came from, giving people a chance to update themselves in today's world. Thus a simple anecdote and a simple exercise can lead to a new route of access to very deep material.

I use this anecdote about my daughter to model a right angle turn in behavior on my part with the reception of new information, that is, her question, "Are you angry?" and my subsequent looking in the mirror. I share my own explanation of my daughter's behavior, and my reaction toward her, that is, that she was entering teenagehood and getting mouthy, and that my smoldering retaliatory feelings were moving toward a self-fulfilling prophesy in that I *was* getting angry about being misinterpreted. This sharing normalizes clients' reactions for themselves in a similar situation. I also had not asked my daughter why she was reacting and muttering "I thought you'd say 'no.'" And most probably if I had asked her why she was reacting that way, she would not have told me. One of the suggestions I make to clients is: ask the other person, "What are you seeing or hearing that causes you to think I was going to say 'no'?" In other words, I suggest they inquire for specific concrete behaviors on their part which the other interprets as negative and to which he or she reacts. I am encouraging each client to step back and be curious about what is in his or her face, voice, or body posture that another is reading. When they do, clients become less reactive and more responsive, less fused and more separate and differentiated, as well as more honestly connected with each other.

Ritual Roles with Children

To let clients know that their "stuck places" are places all of us as parents have been in, I occasionally share another anecdote of major importance to me in my life, which has become a generic systemic intervention with myself as well as with my clients.

A number of years ago, when my youngest daughter was about fifteen, I found myself in a peculiar place with her, where we would get into a repeated tangle as I listened to her tales of woe about "what went wrong in school today." I would try to help her sort out what was going on. Each time I would start out open, feeling sympathetic, listening, offering a comment, only to find her objecting and defensive, no matter what I said. I then would get more entangled, enquiring *why* she was defensive. She became even more so, and I felt annoyed and frustrated. Of course I tried to get *her* to change and be "reasonable," which went nowhere. We were into a repetitive loop that I began to dread. And then one day, I realized that I was bored with my own "tape recordings," and I set one new rule for myself: *Whatever I said or did in relation to her in these repetitive situations would be something I had never said or done before.* Now there was an interesting challenge! I would switch my focus to my part of this continuing loop.

The very next day after school she came to talk to me with her latest sad story. I quickly remembered my promise to myself and braced for the unexpected. I did not know what I would come up with. After her opening comment, I looked at her, smiled, and said, "Gee, your eyes are pretty today." She looked startled and went on talking. I then said, "Your hair looks nice too. Did you do something different with it?" At this point she started to complain, almost whining, "Mommmm, you're not listening!" At which point, because I almost started to giggle, I looked out the window and commented on the two squirrels who were chasing each other. She got annoyed. And I kept up my end of the nonhooked dialogue. I was irrelevant, irreverent, silly, absurd. I can't even remember what I said after those first few interchanges. All I know is that I kept myself from saying anything I had ever said before. She slammed out of the room and I smiled, licked my thumb, and gave myself a "medal" on my chest with it. I felt excited. I hadn't gotten into any "tape recorded" dialogue.

The second day a similar event took place, and this time when she went out of the room she not only slammed the door saying "I don't know what's the matter with you!" but she swore at me as well—enough to trigger me to start out of my chair, angry. Halfway up I caught myself and realized *this was only the next level of hooking me into her issues* and into tangling with her in the old angry way. So I sat down again, smiled, and once more felt triumphant and excited.

The third time she came to talk to me about her daily miseries and I said I particularly liked what she was wearing, she stopped to look and to comment nicely that she liked it too. As she again went into her story and I said something absurd, she laughed and countered with something tentatively funny. I knew we were off the dime and into a new dialogue as she began to lighten up and talk about her day in a different way.

Our dialogues have been different ever since, for it takes at least two to make a repetitive interactional pattern. The success of this intervention on my own pattern at that time is strong reinforcement whenever I find myself in such loops with anyone. I use it to get unhooked again.

The Elements for "Success"

As I thought about this long and hard afterward, I realized that there were several elements in what I had done that ensured success, which I had not thought about when I decided to "do something different."

First, when one person changes his or her side of a known script or pattern and holds to that change, the other person *must* change too in order to maintain any kind of connection (Bowen, 1978; Watzlawick, Weakland, and Fisch, 1974).

Second, the opening comments I made to her were positive and about her person. My focus was on *her.* I was paying attention to *her,* not what she was saying. The comments were made with genuine appreciation, for I had chosen things I liked about her each time. It seemed to work as a confusionary set of statements, for she had a hard time getting annoyed with my positive observations about her person.

Third, my voice tone stayed light and interested in whatever I was talking about, which, of course, was everything *but* her "problem." This too was confusionary. The paraverbal message conveyed interest. The content message conveyed disinterest in the problem (Watzlawick, Beavin, and Jackson, 1967). She could not react in her ordinary way to this new noncongruent communication, and therefore had to switch the total communication pattern in a type of second-order change (Watzlawick, Weakland, and Fisch, 1974).

The fourth element here, one of functional autonomy, was my personal agenda not to be bored with myself and therefore not to get hooked, which took primacy over everything else. The sense of delight in my own agenda allowed me to be absurd, and stay free. It certainly beat feeling frustrated!

Yet another element was my refusal to buy into the next level of hooking—that of her swearing. I stayed constant in not reacting to her escalation. That in itself meant that her conversation with me would have to change, if indeed she were to continue to want to talk to me anymore. It was a risk I was willing to take, based on the amount and type of connection we already had.

Lastly, I had already learned that one needs at least three experiences with anything new in one's life to begin to have a sense of pattern and of change (Duhl, 1983). The first time around is experience itself. One has never been there before and one cannot know ahead of time what exactly will happen or what it will feel like. The second time around with any type of experience allows for comparison: This situation is like the first, or is not like the first. The third time around, one has the opportunity for observing a pattern—that events will fall into the first or second category or become yet a third category, in which case one can begin to look for the pattern of categories from the third experience on. And so with this situation, I knew we would need *at least* three go-arounds to begin to get a flavor of what would happen to change our previous ritual hooking pattern.

Uses of This Anecdote

I tell this last story to families and to individuals—to parents without their children present, and sometimes to children without their parents present if they are old enough to comprehend and carry out such behavior. I tell it to wives without husbands present and husbands seen without wives, and to adult children trying to deal with their siblings, friends, and parents. In short, I use it in multiple situations where being hooked is the issue. I call being hooked "the Velcro loop effect" (Duhl, 1976). There are "negative Velcro loops" and "positive Velcro loops." A negative Velcro loop is any repeated pattern or dialogue in which participants end up feeling defeated and incompetent, with concomitant low self-esteem. Positive Velcro loops are mutually enhancing, growth-allowing patterns.

With clients I zero in on and reframe the real issue as one of boredom—being bored with oneself. I suggest that one might as well have a good time and some adventure, since the ongoing repeated dialogue does not seem to be much fun. I stress that the agenda is the personal triumph of novelty over "stuckness," and that it is to be a secret. I suggest focusing positively first on the person of the other, and then, after that, anything is fair game as long as the tone is light, cheerful, as if one were with a wonderful companion on an outing. The imagery I try to evoke is filled with pleasure. I prepare people for the flak of change by assuring them that the more flak you receive, the more you know you are being successful (Bowen, 1978). I warn them that the "opponent" will probably try to escalate the game with the next level of hooking, like my daughter's swearing, and that they must be on guard not to fall into the trap.

A Clinical Example

I was seeing a mother and her twenty-eight-year-old daughter who were caught in their version of negative Velcro loops, each complaining about the other and each wanting something from the other that harked back to much earlier developmental stages for both of them. The daughter had been working sporadically as a waitress for almost a year, though formerly capable of managerial positions, and wanted her mother to "give" to her. Mother in turn wanted the daughter to continue to seek and heed her advice and standards. Each was afraid of the next stage in their lives. They were now living separately. I saw the mother alone, told her this anecdote about my own daughter, and focused on her boredom and frustration. She agreed to try this method out with her daughter.

When I next saw them together, the mother sat smiling as her daughter complained that she "wasn't the old mother that she used to be," and that she "wanted her old mother back." Mother remained unhooked. Shortly after that, the daughter reported that she had begun looking for a new job, more appropriate to her skills, which she subsequently found. This was the first major dislocator in their negative Velcro loop.

In so many interpersonal situations, *doing something different with oneself* is the key to changing self *and* context, yet it often feels like heavy-duty bad medicine. I prefer humor as a vehicle of change, for it feels like an adding on rather than a giving up of behavior, and indeed it is. Moreover, the more one adds on, the less room and time there is for "old" behavior, and the more fun one is having in the process (Duhl and Duhl, 1981).

ONE-PERSON SCULPTURE FLESHED OUT

In another way of using myself, this time physically, I often do a family sculpture with one person (Duhl, 1983) when other family members are not living in the area. The first time I did this years ago, the thirty-three-year-old Southern woman I started seeing reported that she had always been depressed. I wanted to get a picture of the interactional context in which she had grown up.

I had my client enact each family member first, while I momentarily stood in for her. Then I would switch places and become, also momentarily, mother, father, sister, and so on, then put a chair, lamp, or book in the place of each family member. I have done numerous family sculptures in this manner with only one other person, and while chairs and lamps do not give feedback, one can begin to approximate the family system through using oneself first in those positions. Diagramming the system on a large newsprint sketchpad also helps both client and therapist enormously afterward. For many clients, acting out their family systems becomes the first time they have had to move from an egocentric position to a multicentric one, where they too have to *be* each family member in relation to themselves. Such a process suddenly moves them to *see* themselves as part of the whole—as impacting actors, rather than only as receiving victims. Their sense of relationship to themselves and others changes dramatically in this process.

The technique of using myself in doing a family sculpture allows me to feel into each person the client is describing. By assuming their body postures and using their gestures for even a brief moment, I can as an actress approximate what each person might well be feeling and experiencing in that position and role. This in turn feeds my imagery of what was happening for each person and how that manifested itself interactionally as a total system. Feeding my curiosity, this technique offers me new questions, while giving me an immediate and intimate sense of the interactional context. I can then intervene systemically based on my understanding of the client's images of roles and processes in that interactional context.

ROPE AS METAPHOR FOR "BETWEENNESS"

Using myself physically in another manner, particularly when working with one person, I will use a piece of rope to stand for the dynamic tension of a relationship, with me tugging one end of the rope. When I work with a couple or family, I have them pull on the rope in many different setups as physical metaphors for ways of relating, for the "betweenness" quality of their relationships. In addition to being novel and beyond language, the information revealed is simultaneous and directly experienced. Family members cannot hide as they often do in verbal interchange.

When a client is alone, for example, a man who is discussing a relationship that he is considering ending, I will toss a short length of rope to him, and ask him to pull on it. Then all of a sudden, I let go. He reacts, and we investigate that reaction: how it felt, what he thought, and the meaning of being "left holding the rope." I then pick up the end of the rope and ask him to pull again, and tell him that at a moment of his own choosing, he is to let go of the rope. This is often a startling moment for the client. We then talk about the process, where he is the "leaver" and the rope is a metaphor for the relationship between him and his girlfriend. Such active physical concretizations of being the "leaver" or the "leavee" allow meanings and feelings to surface rapidly, and for the client to get in touch with many hidden meanings of power/powerlessness involved in ending a relationship, which have stymied action. The covert is now overt and options and possibilities for new behavior begin to take shape from a different stance.

Relationships have energy and tension in them which I find that words do not convey very well. The idiosyncratic meanings of relationship words—such as "close" or "distant"—have many nuances. They are "empty-vessel" words, which we each fill with our own images, feelings, and meanings (Duhl, 1983). I find that physically concretizing each client's sense of the dynamic tension of a relationship not only fits our earliest way of learning through sensory-motor activity (Piaget, 1952, 1977), but also is a very rapid way to communicate (Duhl, Kantor, and Duhl, 1973; Duhl, 1983). People easily make their meanings clear for themselves as well as for the therapist. The groundwork is now laid for appropriate interventions on the part of the therapist and for new actions accompanied by new attitudes on the part of the client.

In being free to use myself physically as a vehicle for this type of concretization, I participate in creating metaphors and analogues for clients' real-life experience to which we can then refer in quick shorthand. In this process of making meaning overt, I will use myself, my stories, ropes, puppets, wands, toys, drawings, and any other object or process, actual or metaphorical, that will create, explore, and carry the message. When these types of processes are used with couples and families, all are experiencing something new in that moment, rather than relying on memories and inner images and idiosyncratic word usage. Such active usage of self on the part of the therapist gives family members an alive sense that they too can use themselves in new ways. When people *can* use themselves in new ways they grow different edges of themselves, and in that process create new ways of relating to themselves, and in *that* process create new ways of relating to themselves and others. And that, for me, is what the dance of life and the tasks of therapy are all about.

REFERENCES

Andolfi, M., Angelo, C., Menghi, P., and Nicolo-Corigliano, A.M. (1983). *Behind the Family Mask*. New York: Brunner/Mazel.

Anonymous. (1972). "Towards the Differentiation of a Self in One's Own Family," in J.L. Framo (Ed.), *Family Interaction: A Dialogue Between Family*

Researchers and Family Therapists. New York: Springer Publishing Co., pp. 111-173.

Bateson, G. (1979). *Mind and Nature*. New York: E.P. Dutton.

Bowen, M. (1978). *Family Therapy in Clinical Practice*. New York: Jason Aronson.

Duhl, B.S. (1976). "The Vulnerability Contract: A Tool for Turning Alienation into Connection in Individuals, Couples and Families." Paper presented at the First International Family Encounter, Mexico City, November.

Duhl, B.S. (1983). *From the Inside Out and Other Metaphors: Creative and Integrative Approaches to Training in Systems Thinking*. New York: Brunner/ Mazel. Republished by the author, 1996.

Duhl, B.S. (1986). "Toward Cognitive-Behavioral Integration in Training Systems Therapists: An Interactive Approach to Training in Generic Systems Thinking." *Journal of Psychotherapy and the Family*, 1(4): 91-108. Winter 1985/86.

Duhl, B.S. and Duhl, F.J. (1974). "Another Way of Training Therapists." Paper presented at Nathan Ackerman Memorial Conference of Family Process, Cumana, Venezuela, February.

Duhl, B.S. and Duhl, F.J. (1975). "Cognitive Style and Marital Process." Paper presented at the Annual Meeting of the American Psychiatric Association, Anaheim, CA, May.

Duhl, B.S. and Duhl, F.J. (1981). "Integrative Family Therapy." In A. Gurman and D. Kniskern (Eds.), *The Handbook of Family Therapy*. New York: Brunner/ Mazel, pp. 483-513.

Duhl, F.J. and Duhl, B.S. (1979). "Structured Spontaneity: The Thoughtful Art of Integrative Family Therapy at BFI." *Journal of Marriage and Family Therapy*, 5(3): 59-75.

Duhl, F.J., Kantor, D., and Duhl, B.S. (1973). "Learning, Space and Action in Family Therapy: A Primer of Sculpture." In D. Bloch (Ed.), *Techniques of Family Psychotherapy*. New York: Grune and Stratton, pp. 47-63.

Gordon, W.J.J. and Poze, T. (1973). *The Metaphorical Way of Learning and Knowing*. Second Edition. Cambridge, MA: Porpoise Books.

Minuchin, S. (1974). *Families and Family Therapy*. Cambridge, MA: Harvard University Press.

Piaget, J. (1952). *The Origins of Intelligence in Children*. New York: International Universities Press.

Piaget, J. (1977). *The Essential Piaget*. H.E. Gruber and J.J. Voneche (Eds.). New York: Basic Books.

Satir, V. (1964). *Conjoint Family Therapy*. Palo Alto, CA: Science and Behavior Books.

Satir, V. (1972a). Speech given at Uses of the Self Conference, New York Family Institute, Southbridge, MA, March.

Satir, V. (1972b). *Peoplemaking*. Palo Alto, CA: Science and Behavior Books.

von Bertalanffy, L. (1968). *General Systems Theory*. New York: George Braziller.

Watzlawick, P., Beavin, J.H., and Jackson, D.D. (1967). *Pragmatics of Human Communication*. New York: W.W. Norton and Co.
Watzlawick, P., Weakland, J., and Fisch, R. (1974). *Change*. New York: W.W. Norton and Co.

Chapter 7

The Person and Practice of the Therapist: Treatment and Training

Harry J. Aponte
Joan E. Winter

Clinical training is an intensive learning process undertaken to develop the professional skills and competence of a practitioner. The training process is the bridge that enables and enhances the application of academic and theoretical treatment concepts to the specific clinician within the context of actual therapy. Within the field of psychotherapy, a plethora of models and beliefs about human behavior and change exist. Likewise, an abundance of training interventions and strategies have been developed. In any case, one element is common to every training model: therapy is conducted by people. The vehicle for therapeutic change is a social relationship. Thus, at bottom, the single instrument each training model actually possesses is the "person" of the therapist in a relationship with a client. Despite one-way mirrors, personal psychoanalysis, videotapes, supervision, and so forth, it is a human person who is alone in a room with a client or a family. In the psychotherapy session, individual therapists utilize their own expertise and knowledge, as well as their personal life experiences and value system, to engage with clients in ways that will improve the quality of their lives.

As a result, an intriguing question emerges and challenges the psychotherapy profession: how to develop the competency of the "person of the therapist"? This puzzle is amplified by the trainer's challenge to simultaneously help the therapist enhance clinical skills in tandem with personal skills.

FUNDAMENTAL THERAPEUTIC SKILLS

The "Person and Practice of the Therapist" training model emphasizes four essential skills a clinician needs to attain in order to effect a positive therapeutic outcome (Winter, 1982). The areas of expertise include the following:

1. *External skills*, or the actual, technical behavior utilized by the therapist in the conduct of therapy
2. *Internal skills*, or the personal integration of the therapist's clinical training and life experience in order to become a maximally useful therapeutic instrument
3. *Theoretical skills*, or the acquisition of theoretical models and conceptual frameworks necessary to identify and guide the therapeutic process
4. *Collaborative skills*, or the ability to coordinate one's therapeutic efforts with other professionals and agencies, including schools, lawyers, therapists, ministers, physicians, or any other relevant service provider on behalf of clients.

Given the differences in treatment methodologies, practically every school of therapy accepts the importance of theoretical skills. In most psychotherapy training programs, prior to delivering services, it is essential for a practitioner to master at least one cognitive framework. Academia has consistently contributed to theory, which undergirds practice. Professional training programs, representing "schools" of therapy, also offer a sound foundation regarding their particular theoretical framework. With today's push to certify and license practitioners, there are many sources of pressure to understand and master theory.

In addition, some training programs note the value of collaborative skills, a time-honored professional ethic. Despite the fact that, in reality, few models devote training time to the nuts and bolts of developing a practitioner's collaborative abilities, general agreement prevails regarding their value. Essentially there are two main areas of collaborative skills: (1) with agencies and professionals who provide services other than therapy, and (2) with other psychotherapists.

Due to changes in family structure, as well as the complexity of issues facing families today, it is crucial that a therapist understand his or her own limits. Knowing how to appropriately refer and work effectively with other professionals can no longer be viewed as ancillary to the conduct of theory. Rather, it is a necessary but not sufficient condition in our litigious, malpractice-oriented environment. Additionally, the shift in medical economics today has therapists collaborating, willingly or not, with managed care insurers of mental health treatment. The opportunity to offer, much less extend, treatment to families often depends upon persuasive written and oral communication with managed care case reviewers (frequently, people who have little, if any, experience in providing psychotherapy).

The necessity of collaborative skill development is further heightened by both the increased mobility and technology of today's world, and the effect divorce is having on family life. Cases requiring collaboration include those with legal issues such as divorce and child custody, school problems, chemical addiction, medical problems, psychopharmacology, and so forth. The possibility of being the only service provider in today's world is lessening for psychotherapists. Successful clinicians learn how to deal with a variety of contexts and service providers in the client's world. In a major family therapy outcome study, Virginia Satir kept 96 percent of high-risk dropout families engaged in treatment (fifty-seven out of fifty-nine families). This result occurred, in large measure, due to the collaborative approach she utilized with agencies and the court system (Winter, 1993).

The second type of collaborative relationship skill is called for in instances in which parallel treatment is provided by more than one therapist to a family unit. Although outcome research evaluating the effectiveness of two or more therapists concurrently providing service to one family does not indicate an improved outcome by adding clinicians (Gurman and Kniskern, 1981), frequently therapists have little choice but to work collaboratively. This is particularly true in divorced and blended family systems, especially if the natural parents do not live in the same locality. Consequently, an increasingly complex society and medical care delivery system call upon practitioners to master the skills of collaborative professional relationships.

Although both theoretical and collaborative skills are generally viewed as requisite expertise for the practitioner, a major division exists regarding emphasis in teaching technical and personal skills to clinicians. This is especially the case among family therapy training models. Historically, in the field of family, marital, or systems therapy, there have been essentially two schools of thought with regard to training. One method focuses on the external skills or the technical and behavioral actions of the therapist, and the other emphasizes the internal skills or the personal integration of the clinician.

Proponents stressing external, technical skills, such as Haley, Minuchin, and Falloon, have written that the trainer/supervisor should focus on the actual therapy behaviors displayed by practitioners and help them acquire the necessary direction and effective therapeutic responses. For advocates of a technical skills method, the practitioner's personal life is not the object of change or discussion in training. Haley advocated that training for family therapists should be confined to evaluating the metaphor and function of the family's symptom (Minuchin, 1984), and then developing or helping the therapist devise an intervention strategy. Haley asserted that therapists' problems and personal lives were not an appropriate topic to include in a family therapy training curriculum (Winter, 1986). Specifically, he reported that:

> A bill of rights being drafted by clinical students is now in the planning stage. The list included an item that says no teacher may inquire into the personal life of a therapy student, no matter how benevolently, unless (1) he can justify how this information is relevant to the immediate therapy task in a case, and (2) he can state specifically how his inquiry will change the therapist's behavior in the way desired. (Haley, 1976, p. 176)

In an externally focused training model, students are given client families and a supervisor. It becomes the job of the supervisor to interpret the meaning and theoretical implications of the client's symptoms and then to develop, through the trainee's conduct of therapy, an effective technical intervention to alleviate the client's problems.

On the other hand, proponents who emphasized the vital role of internal, personal skills, such as Bowen and Satir, advanced that a fundamental task of a systems training program should be to help therapists resolve personal conflicts and address their own problems and blind spots to enhance therapeutic outcome. Teachers in these models assert that by assisting the therapist to become more personally integrated, the clinician will be able to intervene with a greater range of choice, insight, and creativity in the lives of clients.

Satir and Baldwin enunciated this perspective:

> The therapist's ability to check on his own internal manifestations is one of the most important therapeutic tools he has. If his internal experience of an interview is different from all other data he is observing and he is fairly sure his reaction is not related to something going on in his personal life, then the most effective way to proceed is on the basis of that internal data. It takes time for the therapist to become aware and be able to trust his internal manifestations, but when he does, he will always have another way to proceed in a therapy situation when he feels stuck. (1983, p. 233)

Bowen took an unequivocal position about training therapists. He stated, "I am not training people to utilize techniques or telling them how to say hello" (Winter, 1986, p. 302). Bowen asserted that training the person of the therapist should be oriented toward developing an intact, complete person.

It is postulated within internally oriented skills training programs that when therapists have resolved their salient problems, they can alleviate or be cured of some of their selective psychological blindness. This improvement in therapists' levels of functioning allows them to better understand their own psyches and those of their clients. Such practitioners, it is asserted, have increased access to their own wisdom, which enables them to be more effective with a variety of clients.

Because educational models differ in their focus on skill development and curriculum, trainees are often faced with making an "either-or" choice: to develop expertise in technical or in personal skills. Few clinical programs offer the opportunity to have both supervised treatment with client families and an in-depth focus on the practitioner's personal functioning, and how it relates to the conduct of therapy.

Fewer still adopt a flexible training approach that simultaneously integrates the therapist's technical and personal skills. It is uncommon to find a training model that consistently maintains a focus on both the conduct of therapy, with specific case interventions, and the practitioner's personal issues and the *interaction* between the two. Systemic links and the interdependence between the therapist and client are frequently overlooked. Specifically, *assisting a therapist to incorporate his or her own personal qualities into technical interventions with clients is the core process in the use of self in therapy.*

In essence, a person needs both a biological father and mother in order to be born. One needs both a right and left brain to make sense out of the world. A therapist needs a training process that can effectively focus on both sides—technical and personal competence—and helps integrate the two. Clearly, a practitioner can manage with less, but the loss of one or the other dimension, and a lack of amalgamation of the two competencies, will inhibit the range of skills and, ultimately, the clinician's effectiveness.

The training approach presented here, the Person and Practice of the Therapist (Person-Practice) model, is the result of the work of two clinicians and teachers, with distinct treatment, training, and research experience in both external and internal training methods, developing a system which encompassed both trainers' theoretical models. One trainer's background was primarily Structural Family Therapy and psychoanalysis. The other trainer had worked extensively with Erickson, Satir, and Bowen. Out of this theoretical diversity a different training process emerged. The Person-Practice model is an atheoretical model for training. Very different treatment approaches can be utilized in this training method. As Gurman and Kniskern's landmark outcome research literature review revealed, selective choice of treatment methodology with specific therapists is a critical variable for change:

> The well-worn, but still salient reminder that the ultimate empirical *and* clinical question is, "What treatment for what problem? (with what therapists, etc., etc.) . . ." (1981, p. 748)

The original developers of the Person-Practice model utilize a variety of treatment strategies in both case discussions and live family interventions, including Structural Family Therapy, Bowen Theory, Satir Process Model, Ericksonian hypnosis, and organizational development. Even so, this training approach does not depend on any particular clinical or theoretical framework. It utilizes a generic teaching method that can accommodate a variety of technical interventions.

Figure 7.1 is a paradigm of the four fundamental therapeutic skills underlying the Person-Practice training model. In this model it is advanced that each clinician needs expertise, ease, and integration in all four dimensions.

FIGURE 7.1. Four Fundamental Therapeutic Skills: A Systemic Paradigm

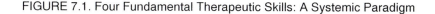

External   Internal

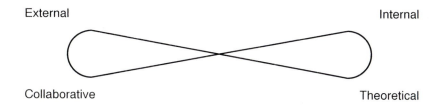

Collaborative   Theoretical

The figure eight symbol represents the dynamic movement inherent in a therapist's emphasis and choice regarding clinical skill development.

THEORETICAL FRAMEWORK

Although a variety of treatment approaches are utilized by the participants training in the Person-Practice model, a primary value system and theoretical framework underpins both the treatment and consequent training process. This cognitive map does not prescribe a specific treatment intervention strategy for every case or participant. Rather, the theoretical framework is designed to elicit each participant's development of his or her own convictions and beliefs regarding theory, as well as technical and collaborative skills, and how to use self to attain positive outcomes for clients.

The internal or personal skill of the therapist, and its impact on practice, has been an area of inquiry since the inception of psychotherapy. The interaction between the process of therapy and the participation of the therapist provides definition for training the person of the therapist.

The Person of the Therapist: A Historical Perspective

Not surprisingly, psychoanalysis was the first of the therapies to formally include in its training method a process of understanding and changing the person of the therapist. It was also the first treatment model to emphasize and utilize the relationship between the patient and the therapist as the primary vehicle for ameliorating psychological problems. Psychoanalysis formally instituted the "training analysis" for the therapist. Freud was concerned with issues inherent in the therapeutic relationship and developed the term transference (for the patient) and countertransference (for the analyst) to describe their interaction. Freud initially wrote:

> We have become aware of the "counter-transference" which arises in him (the analyst) as a result of the patient's influence on his unconscious feelings, and we are almost inclined to insist that he shall recognize this counter-transference in himself and overcome it. . . . We have noticed that no psycho-analyst goes further than his own complexes and internal resistance permit; and we consequently require that he shall begin his activity with a self-analysis and continually carry it deeper while he is making his observations with his patients. (1957, pp. 144-145)

Freud believed that the personal reactions of the analyst were critical to the patient's process of change. Countertransference was viewed by Freud as "unconscious feelings" that were related to the analyst's unresolved, neurotic "complexes." Originally, his solution for counter-transference was self-analysis (which Freud applied only to himself). For his students Freud eventually established the training analysis, the precursor of present-day models of change for the person of the therapist.[1]

Freud (1964) worried about "the effect of a constant preoccupation with all the repressed material which struggles for freedom in the human mind . . . stirring up in the analyst . . . all the instinctual demands which he is otherwise able to keep under suppression" (p. 249). He saw the demands of continually facing others' psychological struggles causing problems for analysts in their own personal, internal lives. Freud's concern went so far that he modified his earlier requirement for self-analysis to the expectation that the therapist "submit himself to analysis" not once, but "periodically—at intervals of five years or so." In other words, his "own analysis would change from a terminable into an interminable task." Freud was prescribing a continual process of work on self for the analyst (Freud, 1964, p. 249).

Although in the Person-Practice model the importance of a therapist focusing on and mastering personal issues in order to function effectively with clients is advocated, there are a number of salient differences from a psychoanalytical approach. First, as indicated, Freud's countertransference model refers only to the analyst's unconscious "complexes." The Person-Practice model draws primarily from the field of general systems thinking and family therapy. The total, existential life experience of both family and therapist, conscious and unconscious, real and fantasized is incorporated in the Person-Practice theoretical framework. Within a systemic framework it is advanced that "every part is related to the other part in a way that a change in one brings about a change in all the others. Indeed, everyone and everything impacts and is impacted by every other person, event and thing" (Satir and Baldwin, 1983, p. 191).

The psychoanalytic process, on the other hand, is technically structured to maximize fantasy and projection on the part of the client. The analyst is directed to maintain a passive, almost anonymous position vis-à-vis the patient. In Freud's treatment room, the patient was lying down on a couch, facing a window, with no eye contact, never sitting up or turning his or her head to see the analyst. Likewise, Freud's chair was at a 90 degree angle to the patient. His literal gaze was at an ornate collection of anthropological artifacts.

Contrary to this method, in family therapy the clinician not only sits within the family circle, but plays an active role in creating family change. Outcome studies of family therapy reveal that: (1) a therapist's relationship skills (even in behavioral models), (2) elevated activity level, and (3) ability to structure early interviews were all related to successful outcome (Gurman and Kniskern, 1981). Whittaker and Keith succinctly concluded, "We are very active as therapists" (1981, p. 207).

Active therapist involvement integral to successful family therapy does not encourage the projective process of a Freudian induced transference. In contrast, in a psychoanalytic transference it is vital that the analyst provide a blank screen or tabula rasa for patients to write their own fantasies and thoughts upon. Conversely,

> Family therapy requires a use of self. A family therapist cannot observe and probe from without. He must be a part of a system of interdependent people. (Minuchin and Fishman, 1982, p. 2)

Such involvement anchors and increases the *reality* of transactions between the patient and the therapist (as opposed to the *fantasy* in psychoanalytic treatment). Nonetheless, even in family treatment, it is inevitable that both patient and therapist will bring into the therapeutic relationship each person's real and psychological linkages with their respective lives. Herein, all participants bear the scars of their past along with the wounds inflicted in their current lives. In the Person-Practice model it is acknowledged that in such active interaction both client and therapist are emotionally vulnerable. They must form alliances and develop trust with one another. They get close. They will also inevitably clash as tension builds from their differences. The therapist draws out the client family to change even as the family protects itself against the perceived peril of change. The client-therapist connection enters the risky waters of human contact even in the strictest professional environment. The therapist had better know those waters and be skillful in navigating them.

Moreover, because the family therapist plays an active role in the therapeutic relationship, one is less protected than was the analyst from imposing one's own personal values, culture, and spirituality on the patient, especially if the patient's life struggles resonate with those of the therapist (Aponte, 1994a, 1996). It is inevitable that therapists will evaluate and judge problems through the lens of their own worldviews, that they will naturally conjure up goals that fit with their ideals, and be inclined to propose solutions that fit with their own views of life. Few psychotherapists will argue today that practitioners can actually be "value-neutral" in therapy.

In the Person-Practice model we contend that even as therapists make room for clients' values, they will use insight derived from their own values to understand and work with clients' values. Clinicians need to be explicitly trained to use their potential influence over a client's values judiciously. The role of the family therapist demands enormous personal self-knowledge and discipline from the practitioner; thus the special necessity of personal work for the family therapist.

From this perspective, the therapist has a dual clinical task: first, to seek to define self and resolve personal issues that affect one's work; and second, to learn to recognize and contend with one's flaws, since there is no possibility (as Freud implicitly admitted) that a person can ever achieve full resolution of current or past afflictions. Acknowledging to self the lasting presence of one's human flaws is crucial in the Person-Practice model.

Beyond the historical exploration of the person of the therapist, other salient aspects of the therapeutic relationship further clarify the connection between the clinician and treatment.

Mutuality and Metamorphosis: Implications for the Therapeutic Relationship

In therapy, clients and therapists join together to create a new, actively evolving entity. All participants bring into the treatment room their own distinctive life experiences, worldviews, and personal relationships. In turn, the therapeutic relationship generates yet another set of life experiences, which is shared by therapist and client. In the Person-Practice model the therapist is accessible to being influenced and changed by the family. Indeed, therapeutic affiliations can and do affect the lives of therapists. Although treatment is for the benefit of the client family members, all participants in the process, including the therapist, take back to their personal lives, to a greater or lesser degree, effects from the therapeutic association. Even when family members and friends are not actual participants in the treatment process, the clinical relationship impacts upon their lives as well.

Therapy is a personal relationship operating within the parameters of a professional structure. Essentially, that professional structure prescribes that the therapist and clients be engaged in their efforts for the beneficial outcome of the family. However, due to the interrelatedness of the participants, a treatment relationship cannot deny the therapist's individual needs. While effective therapy subordinates the therapist's needs to the family's, ideally, the family and therapist should be able to work together in a way that serves and enhances the therapist through the same efforts that are directed toward the family's advancement.

From this perspective, clinicians can and should actively conduct treatment in a manner that utilizes all that the therapist is as a person. Learning how to effectively employ the therapeutic alliance in such a comprehensive manner is training the person of the therapist. Within the Person-Practice framework, the practitioner must:

1. Have a working understanding of one's own emotional make-up and family relationships, both past and present, as well as one's values, culture, and spirituality. Such awareness encompasses the dynamic evolution and current role these aspects of self play in the therapist's life.
2. Be conscious of what themes one brings into the relationship from one's own history and life experiences—what is bestirred in self by the current interaction with the client? (Winter and Aponte, 1987)
3. Learn to manage self within one's theoretical framework, therapeutic model, and clinical strategy during the session to maximize therapeutic effectiveness.

Moreover, a clinician needs to be aware of how the therapy one conducts affects self. How one is in the therapeutic relationship should be congruent with the meaning of one's own life and values so that it supports and, perhaps, even contributes to the effort being made to enhance the practitioner's own level of functioning. Learning to make the therapy conducted with families work for self is also part of training the person of the therapist.

Thus, a positive treatment outcome depends on the therapist's ability to harness self within the social relationship of therapy. Successful clinicians learn to be aware of what material they currently bring into the therapeutic process, both strengths and problems, and how to employ these resources for the client's growth and change. Generally, clinicians wish to grow and resolve their personal issues. They seek to unchain and emancipate self, not only for their own benefit, but also for their clients' well-being. Even with their admitted flaws, therapists aim to bring what is healthiest in self to the clinical relationship. However, therapists, like everyone else, are a work in progress and need to develop the ability to learn from their own struggles, converting the pain of their flaws into life wisdom to better help clients.

Nevertheless, even though there is an intrinsic interdependence in the treatment process, a practitioner may or may not want to change his or her personal life in order to better serve families in treatment. Regardless of the therapist's choice in this matter, when clinicians' issues become an impediment to their clients' development, and they become aware of the situation, a sense of discomfort develops. Getting consultation in problem resolution and management of self is also training the person of the therapist. In the Person-Practice model, as practitioners strive to foster change and growth in clients, they also work to better self in order to be more effective therapists.

One important side effect resulting from a training focus on the use of self with clients is that through this process of personal development the practitioner tends to maintain a greater degree of involvement and empathy with clients. Certainly, this endeavor reduces the prospect of burnout and also increases the therapist's commitment to clients and to attaining a successful therapeutic outcome.

Therapy As a Catalyst for Practitioner Change

Engaging in clinical work with family systems is a social context which jostles a therapist's own personal issues in ways that few other encounters do. As Freud foretold, the continuous reflection on people's personal struggles leaves little of the therapist's own internal life untouched. Repeatedly, such a process moves clinicians to seek resolution of their own life issues, especially as their personal dilemmas and limitations are inevitably brought to the foreground when attempting to help others change.

From the vantage point of the Person-Practice model, training for the person of the therapist becomes an occasion for a clinician to obtain an intervention for self within the context of one's work. Accordingly, as therapists seek to improve their clinical effectiveness, they can also improve themselves.

There are aspects of the person of the therapist that are specifically, and often only, revealed to the clinician through the unique experience of conducting treatment. Practitioners observe some of their personal struggles in the lives of their clients. In the treatment room therapists encounter some of their own private torments and limitations when attempting to respond empathetically and helpfully to clients. Because therapists are not locked into the same person-specific struggles in their work that they have in their own families, they are not so defended against looking honestly at self. For this reason, clinicians are often more able to pursue change in a work context, rather than at home or even in personal therapy or analysis. As a consequence, providing treatment acts as a potent stimulus to personal growth and fosters a variety of possibilities for change in practitioners. This catalyst is rooted in several components of the therapeutic process.

Role Structure

Due to the nature of therapeutic roles, the clinician acts as a guide and mentor who can challenge a client. In the course of providing such leadership, one is called upon to relate in ways that may not normally surface in daily life. The professional role can give a therapist emotional protection and support to risk dealing with aspects of clients' lives that touch on the therapist's life, without having to expose or directly examine one's personal vulnerabilities.

Motivation

Repeatedly, therapists have demonstrated a willingness to master personal life struggles because their own dysfunctional patterns are limiting the full use of self, thereby handicapping their effectiveness with clients. Outside the defensiveness of therapists' personal relationships, and their own emotional family systems, they may find reason to change. The desire to attain excellence in one's work is a powerful motivator. If therapists can improve their own lives in the process of assisting a client's functioning, the forceful drives toward both professional achievement and self-actualization are served.

Courage

Clients often call forth a sense of determination in the therapist which one is unable to generate just for self. Within the therapeutic context, a clinician may be willing to face difficult issues for the benefit of a client that would not be confronted just for self or for one's own family. Being outside the repeatedly reinforced fences of habitual or conflictual personal family relationships is once again a plus. For the sake of commitment to a client, a therapist will travel to unknown territories.

Awareness

In the midst of guiding a client through certain events or life stages, a therapist's awareness may be heightened about issues in his or her own life which, until that point in time, may have been avoided, suppressed, hidden, or buried. One may dare to look honestly at self in a context where the old, familiar personal foes are not operating.

Identification

An essential element of successful therapy is empathy (Margulies, 1989). As a therapist joins with a family, he or she often develops, in some way, an identification with the client (Freud, 1957). When practitioners move into the pain in a family's life, within the hopeful treatment environment created for and with the client, therapists gain access to similar pain in their own lives. Due to the indirectness of the transactions (outside the context of a practitioner's own life), and in the necessarily accepting treatment environment, a therapist may be better able to endure and face personal failures.

Vantage Point

Since the foundation of providing treatment is not for the purpose of changing the therapist, the clinician may be less defensive and more able to observe in this environment. From such a unique vantage point, a powerful paradox emerges: while a therapist is one step removed from the phenomena, at the same time, through the bond with the client, a therapist is also intimately close to it. This contradictory and inconsistent situation creates a potent indirect passageway to the therapist's psyche. The practitioner's own protective shield is down because he or she is not the target of change.

Vicarious Change

Therapists may be changing self without their own knowledge by actively instructing and participating in the client's developmental process. Without awareness, a clinician may have hypnotically effected a complex, difficult problem within self. The same directions and suggestions therapists give clients are simultaneously given to their own unconscious minds, wittingly or unwittingly.

Special Relationships

As in the therapist's personal life, certain clinical relationships can be so challenging or congenial, or in other ways reinforcing or provocative, that they provide a clinician with an unusual learning opportunity. Such therapeutic alliances may support steps toward a practitioner's own desired growth.

Due to these compelling catalytic forces, the conduct of therapy can create unique, almost unprecedented opportunities for personal change of the therapist. Curiously, practitioners previously may have been defeated in achieving the very same aim in their own personal or family treatment. The process of therapy can generate dynamic movement for both the client and the practitioner. In most instances, the key that unlocks a therapist's successful use of self, for the beneficial outcome of clients, is effective clinical training and supervision.

TRAINING MODELS FOR THE PERSON OF THE THERAPIST

A variety of methods for training the person of the therapist exist. An overview of predominant training models, a summary of the Person-Practice method, and a training transcript explore this dimension.

Overview of Predominant Training Methods

Psychoanalysis approaches the development of the person of the therapist through the training analysis. This type of personal search is independent of the therapist's practice except to the extent that an analyst's conduct of treatment should overflow into one's own analysis (Freud, 1958). If the insight gained into the analyst's own psyche aids his or her clinical perceptions, this may also be a by-product of the training analysis.

With the advent of a systems approach, family therapy models developed a variety of methods for training the person of the therapist. Most of these models have evolved from the internal or personal skills schools of therapy training (Bowen, Satir, Whittaker). The external or technical skills schools of training (Haley, Minuchin) have emphasized the therapist's technical interventions and, to a lesser degree, theory.

Gurman and Kniskern (1981), in their comprehensive review of family therapy outcome, assert that therapist relationship skills have increasingly revealed a relationship to treatment outcome. They stated:

> A reasonable mastery of technical skills may be sufficient to prevent worsening or maintain pretreatment functioning in very difficult cases, but more refined relationship skills are necessary to yield truly positive outcomes in marital-family therapy. (p. 751)

Except for Aponte (1992), the external skills models of treatment and training have not focused on the person of the therapist as a point of inquiry and change. Accordingly, an examination of internal models follows.

Although Bowen would perhaps have bristled to be grouped with the internal or "personal" skills school of training (since he repeatedly emphasized the fundamental need for and development of theory), his training approach, nonetheless, had a clear focus on the development of the person of the therapist. In 1960, Bowen was the first family therapist to present his method of training the person of the therapist to other clinicians, using his own family-of-origin work as an example. He subsequently circulated an "anonymous" paper on his efforts. This seminal paper became a landmark in the family therapy training field—or, to use Bowen's language, a "nodal event" (Bowen, 1972).

Bowen diverged from his psychoanalytic background when he proposed that "'training' psychotherapy as we have known in the past (for therapists in training) may one day be considered superfluous" (1972,

p. 164). Parallel to the analysts though, he believed that the therapist's own life was a major factor which affected treatment outcome. Differing from the projective training process common for an analyst, Bowen advanced that therapists gain much greater ground by working directly with their own specific emotional family systems. He conceived of a therapist's continual process of "differentiation" (distinguishing self) in one's own family as the essential ingredient in the development of a mature, effective therapist. Otherwise, Bowen believed that therapists were doomed to displace their own unmet needs on the families they treated (Winter, 1986).

Toward this end, Bowen developed a training approach that "coached" the therapist trainee in working with his or her own family of origin, in a type of self-excavation and development process within the family system. In this effort a supervisor, trainer, or therapist acted as a "coach," providing greater objectivity for a trainee. Bowen's method prescribed the usefulness of a therapist researching his or her own family of origin, visiting family places of residence including the ancestral home, and, most importantly, learning how these forces directly related to his or her parents and family members. He postulated, "If you can accomplish half of what you want with your family, you are doing great. . ." (Winter, 1989). According to Bowen, no family will ever scare or intimidate a therapist as much as the therapist's own family. As therapists contend with their own anxiety in their respective family systems, then client families will be "easy" by comparison (Bowen, 1972).

Satir may be the figure in family therapy who made the development of the person of the therapist most central to her training. As she unequivocally stated, "Our approach assumes that the therapist in his person is the chief tool for initiating change" (Bandler, Grinder, and Satir, 1976, p. 2). Her training efforts through the Avanta Network provided month-long, residential programs for groups of therapists. In this context, Satir employed an in-depth method of "Family Reconstruction" for trainees. This process involves an intensive enactment of a therapist's own family history and dynamics. An individual reconstruction usually takes at least five hours (Nerin, 1986). Satir's training method utilizes workshop participants to play roles in the therapist's own family and recreates life events and significant interactions that affect the practitioner.

Satir had three primary goals for the family reconstruction intervention, including: (1) to reveal to clinicians the source of their "old learnings" or worldview; (2) to develop in therapists an awareness of their parents as people (beyond their role as parents); and (3) to assist therapists in developing their own individual views and definition of self (Satir and Baldwin, 1983). Therapists not only participate in their own family reconstruction, they also learn to conduct reconstructions for other therapists, as well as for clients. The reconstruction teaching method enables family therapy trainees to gain further knowledge of how systems operate, beyond their own unique family circumstances.

In addition to the reconstruction technique, Satir and her designated leaders also utilized other methods for therapist change including "Parts Parties," which employ a Gestalt therapy approach to personal integration (Winter and Parker, 1991, 1992). By utilizing a residential group training context, away from the therapists' ordinary life contexts, the therapists were continuously immersed in systems processing. There they were more able to focus on their personal development and access to self. Additionally, in the Satir Process Model, therapist family-of-origin meetings are viewed as an invaluable catalyst for enhancing a practitioner's level of clinical effectiveness.

A basic tenet of Satir's systemic training model is committed to the development of the therapist.[2] She stated:

> Using oneself as a therapist is an awesome task. To be equal to that task one needs to continue to develop one's humanness and maturity. We are dealing with people's lives. In my mind, learning to be a therapist is not like learning to be a plumber. Plumbers can usually settle for techniques. Therapists need to do more. You don't have to love a pipe to fix it. Whatever techniques, philosophy or school of family therapy we belong to, whatever we actually do with others has to be funnelled through ourselves as people. (Satir and Baldwin, 1983, p. 227)

The Person-Practice model differs from all of the previous training approaches in one major respect: it focuses primarily on the *bridge* between the therapist's personal life and the actual conduct of treatment. The model emerges from an ecological framework with the therapist's clinical practice as the central context or setting for training the person of the therapist.

The Person-Practice Model: Change in Context

Systems thinking suggests that efforts to bring about change for a person should not be limited or circumscribed by any particular context of one's life. (Context is defined as the interrelated conditions in which something exists or occurs, the setting or environment where a phenomenon manifests itself.) Efforts to bring about change in a person's life most often require work in a variety of interrelated contexts. Change in one context may or may not contribute to change in another context. Successful therapeutic strategies require a considered evaluation regarding which contexts or systems in which to intervene to maximize the client's change. Likewise, an effective clinical training program must utilize a variety of contexts to impact the therapist, including clinical practice, supervisory relationships, marital relationships, nuclear and family of origin, practice setting, collegial relationships, and personal therapy.

In essence, the Person-Practice model calls for a skillful selection of the context for intervention. The support and development of links between various contexts enhances the trainee, both as a therapist and as a person. The training model corresponds to a therapeutic approach that delineates the power of continuity among interrelated systems:

> Underlying this therapeutic perspective is the assumption that there is a structural continuity between the structural patterns linking the individual, the family and the community, and that an intervention in one of these systems may have a corresponding impact on the others, depending on the strength of the linkages between the organization(s) . . . (Aponte, 1980, p. 332)

GOALS IN TRAINING
THE PERSON OF THE THERAPIST

Given an ecological and contextual model for change, the aim of the Person-Practice training model is twofold. First, the *primary* or core purpose of the training is to improve and enhance the quality and success of the therapist's clinical work. Second, a *complementary* goal is to assist the therapist's efforts for improved individual functioning and personal development.

Toward the *primary* goal of improving a clinician's therapeutic results: the fundamental treatment objective is to enhance the client's functioning and quality of life. By gaining more understanding and mastery of self, the therapist does, indeed, gain greater ability to penetrate the meaning of a client's struggles. By developing greater mastery over personal issues, a practitioner is better able to manage and therapeutically direct the use of one's person in clinical interactions. Thus, the practitioner can more effectively utilize personal assets, as well as deficits, along with life experiences, good or bad, in the implementation of technical interventions. When a therapist is not absorbed in his or her own emotional needs and pain, there is a substantially greater ability to devote observation skills and energy to the client. The practitioner's resolution of personal issues not only decreases the projective process, it also allows more effective use of self with the client and, therefore, increases avenues for change in the therapeutic process.

In the Person-Practice model the goal is also to enable therapists to develop an increased capacity to live with and learn from their own struggles. This effort allows for some distance to be taken from personal vulnerabilities and these particular frailties can be better utilized on behalf of the client and the treatment process. In the Person-Process training approach flaws are viewed as part and parcel of the human condition. How many personal issues can anyone resolve to finality?

Toward the *complementary* goal of developing the therapist's own integration: by employing a work-related context, which has influential and catalytic forces, training becomes a powerful supplement to the clinician's efforts to move his or her own life toward greater fulfillment. Training that utilizes and explores with the practitioner the personal context of therapy and one's use of self becomes an opportunity to invest more in the work and in the people who are being treated. The alterations therapists make in their own lives, especially those occasioned by their work, enhance their ability to be instrumental in the client's change.

This model implies that a clinician's effectiveness is not limited so much by what has been resolved in life, but by what one has learned to recognize and work with in self. Being able to handle certain issues may require in some instances that one achieve a degree of resolution in one's personal life, but in *all* circumstances it will mean knowing how to manage within the therapy one's own reactions to unresolved personal issues in ways that will benefit the client. As therapists learn to be more fully aware of self, having greater access to their own emotions and memories, they are better able to determine how to use self in the here-and-now of the treatment process. The point of focus is the human interaction between therapist and client within the context of the therapeutic relationship and clinical goals.

Training and supervision are designed to help not only a specific case, but also to create an autonomous and effective therapist with all cases. By resolving individual issues, or by learning to work with unchangeable or unresolved issues, a clinician attains greater freedom and ability in the use of self with clients. Moreover, by learning how to relate and mange self, the clinician increases technical expertise. These goals illustrate the need for an interactive and flexible approach toward therapist development.

PERSON-PRACTICE TRAINING FORMAT

The Person and Practice of the Therapist model of training has been formalized at the Family Institute of Virginia in Richmond into a year-long program. The number of trainees in a group is no more than fourteen, and the participants meet monthly for two intensive, consecutive days. To acquire sufficient clinical skills, most people participate for at least two years. On a rotating basis, each trainee has an individual presentation time, designed to examine a clinical or personal dilemma. In both instances trainees have previously prepared a written examination of their own personal issues or clinical cases.

The clinical presentation can consist of: (1) a verbal examination of a case, (2) a videotaped session presented for review and discussion, (3) supervision of a live family interview, or (4) a simulation of a difficult case or a dilemma a clinician experiences during therapy sessions. The personal presentation can also be: (1) a discussion of a therapist's own issue, (2) a meeting with members of a trainee's own family, or (3) a meeting with people in a trainee's work system with whom he or she may be entangled.

In recent years, along with clinicians, the training program has been including organizational consultants (in organizational development, OD) and other business types who bring in management or organizational situations for discussion. Frequently the OD trainees bring in, or simulate, a work group to which they provide consultations (similar to the clinical presentations), or they may ask colleagues in their work setting to join them for a consultation regarding their working relationships (similar to a personal presentation).

Prior to making a presentation, trainees prepare a written description for class distribution that examines their selected issues. The written assessment is intended to help develop the therapist's or consultant's theoretical and conceptual skills. Additionally, it intensifies a trainee's personal involvement and understanding of the selected issue.

A trainee presents to two leaders, male and female, and to their colleagues in the group. The training group serves as a significant source of support, feedback, and challenge to the members. The program gives each participant a variety of contexts in which individual issues may be addressed as they relate to one's personal life and clinical performance. The group itself is an extremely powerful and vital learning context in which participants can address their issues, both during the formal meetings and between sessions.

For anything but a live clinical session or simulation, trainees are given an hour for the presentation, fifty minutes in discussion with the trainers, and approximately ten minutes with the group. The live presentations are allowed an hour and a half, including time before and after the live session to discuss the presentation with both trainers and the group.

All training sessions are videotaped so that trainees can review the experience afterward without the stress and anxiety of being on the "hot seat." The videotapes allow trainees an unprecedented opportunity to observe self, rather than to participate. The opportunity to learn via both direct participation and later observation enhances the quality of a trainee's learning. Participants are urged to view the tapes with other group members or with family. Sometimes viewing a tape alone is also helpful.

Presentation formats each have a different merit, and therapists are encouraged to make use of all methods, including:

1. *Discussion of personal or clinical issues.* In this medium, the person presents a clinical case or personal issue to the leaders. The therapist utilizes the transactions between self, the leaders, and group members to better understand the case, oneself, and the relationship between the two. Also, a trainee can explore consequent clinical strategies.

2. *Videotape or audiotape of a clinical session or training presentation.* Such recordings provide a possibility to observe the therapist in action. This method affords an opportunity to examine a treatment segment of usually no more than fifteen minutes. It allows the clinician and the trainers the opportunity to see the therapist in action. In this context a trainee can observe what could not have been seen before about self. Here, practitioners can develop a new perspective and improve, refine, or, as necessary, formulate their clinical hypotheses. They can literally see how they are using self on behalf of the client. In this method, a trainee can later view both the clinical and training tape alone, or with a colleague, when the group is over.

3. *Role play of a clinical issue.* The leaders have a chance, with the direct involvement of group members, to make observations and intervene with a therapist in vivo. A simulation provides safety and the freedom for a therapist to experiment with change, which cannot be offered in a live or videotaped therapy session. Therapist and role-playing "clients" are asked to spontaneously create a treatment situation or problem. Such enactments draw from the participants fresh reactions to one another, and allow for the possibility of a "take two," corrected intervention.

4. *Live session with a patient's family, a therapist's own family, or work colleagues.* The live session provides the most direct opportunity for the leaders to intervene with a therapist concerning his or her clinical work or personal or professional life. In interviews with a clinician's own family, the therapist and group leaders pursue identified issues with the leaders

conducting the session, while the group views through an observation mirror. In patient family interviews, the leaders can observe from outside the interview room, telephone input to the therapist, or join the therapist and clients. Therapists can also bring in supervisees or other colleagues to develop aspects of their professional or collegial relationships.

An important element of the Person-Practice training method is the utilization of videotape. All therapist presentations are taped to permit review on their own time. Consequently, the therapist has an opportunity to hear and see what was not known or observed before. When a live clinical interview is taped, the therapist can review it with the clients. One can share the tape viewing with a member of the training group, and others who are not part of the training group, including one's own personal therapist, and experience the presentation in yet another context. Some participants choose to return a year or two later and observe where they were at an earlier stage of their professional development. These tapes become an invaluable learning tool for years to come.

In the course of a year, a therapist's decision to focus on personal life or therapy skills varies. In the Person-Practice method, each participant generally elects a concentration for professional growth and change. Regardless of whether the principal concern at a point in time may be clinical work or personal development, a trainee is expected to examine both arenas during the course of the training program. At various times therapists will be motivated to acquire skills in different dimensions and look at particular aspects of their lives. The clinical training program remains adaptable in order to accommodate the participants' individual differences. The unique pattern of a person's life is inextricably woven into the therapist's choice of skill concentration. The variability each trainee exercises, coupled with the format's flexibility, provides a variety of experiential opportunities.

Occasionally, a trainee only feels comfortable presenting in one dimension. For example, some therapists may feel safer presenting a case from a strictly clinical viewpoint. On the other hand, some therapists are afraid to reveal their practice skills and enjoy talking about themselves. Since the model holds that *internal* and *external* skills, as well as *theoretical* and *collaborative* expertise, are instrumental in creating competent practitioners, a trainee may need to be encouraged to look at and risk self in another dimension. There may be strategic reasons for encouraging a therapist to work on one area at a particular moment in time. Once safety and trust have been established with the leaders and the group, however, shifts in skills emphasis usually occur naturally without prodding from the trainers. As therapists develop personal and clinical mastery, their choice of emphasis tends to be more congruent with their needs and current dilemmas in life.

The following transcript illustrates the range and variability of both external and internal skill development in one participant in the Person and Practice of the Therapist clinical training program. Included is a transcript of a training session and the participant's written reaction to that intervention. Following this is a transcript of a live therapy interview the trainee conducted, with the leaders' supervision, at the training seminar one month later. Several contexts, including clinical practice, case evaluation, marital relationship, family of origin dynamics, personal therapy, collegial relationships, and practice setting are exemplified.

TRANSCRIPTS FROM A TRAINEE'S PRESENTATION

A trainee, Devan, presented a clinical problem for discussion. She wanted a case consultation because she knew she was having an unusual amount of difficulty in helping a couple she was treating. She presented the case to the two leaders, Winter (W) and Aponte (A), in the group's presence. The entire intervention took approximately one hour. The excerpted transcript begins when Devan is revealing how the wife had recently stopped an affair:

> **D:** . . . the event that got her to stop the affair . . . I mean the therapy event that four weeks ago she came in and told me . . . [was] that she had talked to this daughter about the affair, and I just went crazy. And I told her that that was awful. . .
>
> **A:** She was trying to get her daughter to collude with her?

D: Yeah, and I just really told her that that was just unacceptable and that I was no longer willing to have that information and have her daughter know, and we know, and her know, and her husband not know, and that she either had to cut it off completely and stop it, as in *now*, or I was going to make her deal with her husband about it. I was really upset with her and uncomfortable about the three women having the secret and her continuing to be duplicitous and then dumping that on the daughter. But, it was clear that it took her daughter for me to get that clear about it, you know it took her . . . [inaudible] . . . daughter for me to decide.

A: That's what I was going to ask you . . . it has been quite a while . . . to have this kind of secret . . .

D: Right, and I have been saying all along, "stop it, stop it," but I have never just actually thrown a fit and said "I am not going to collude with you anymore" until she used her daughter.

Devan started by describing that she had strong personal convictions that it was wrong for the woman client to maintain this deception with her husband, and to attempt to involve the therapist in keeping the secret. However, Devan was unable to take a decisive position with the woman until the information surfaced that the client's daughter had subsequently become involved in the affair secret. Aponte underlined her struggle by his questioning. A short time later in the presentation, Devan identified a personal reason why this case was difficult for her:

A: . . . sort of brought allusions to your marriage, a hint that there is some connection between your marriage and this marriage.

D: [My husband] and I had this discussion about a week ago . . . the reason why I decided to present this is because we are having this discussion about a week ago. I wasn't understanding what he was saying, and he said, "If you had a client that was like this and was saying this to you, what would you do?" I said, "Actually, I do have a client. And I don't know what to do with them." I am stuck with them.

A: I see.

D: So, the connection is real clear to me. In this particular couple that connection is clear to me. I have two other couples that I also really don't feel like I am doing dynamite therapy with, and their specific issues are not as clear to me. With them [all three cases] the generic issue is that the men are not very expressive, kind of withdrawn, deny that there are problems, say that it is their wives' problems [not the husbands'], . . . that there is a depression [the wives'], and that they want me to fix their wives. . . . One of them drinks too much and doesn't think he has a drinking problem. . . . Also, I feel as if when I meet with the men individually I can connect with them and I can say . . . you know, I can be real direct with them and it feels okay. When I get there with a couple, I feel like I am absolutely not doing anything, and at the end of the couple's session, my impulse is to take the wife and say, "Get a good lawyer."

A: Right. You identify with women and distance yourself from the men.

W: And it says here [in Devan's case presentation commentary written before the seminar] "Maybe she should go get her happiness where she can." Does that say anything to you?

D: Yeah, as a matter of fact, I thought about whiting out that sentence, but then . . . I thought . . . no, I would go ahead and do it. That is why I am here. Well, I am real clear that I can identify in here, not only her and me, but I can also identify her and my mother . . . about wanting this man to give her something. She wants him to say . . . I mean, she just wanted some . . . Anne [the client] is saying . . . she said to him, "I just need you to tell me that you love me." Well, she told him that when they got separated in June. Since June, he hasn't told her that he loves her. He refuses to tell her that he loves her; he tells her that he likes her okay, he tells her that he needs her, but he refuses to say the words to her, "I love you," because she asked him to. . . . So, there is a part of me, when he starts pulling that chill on her that really feels like "you don't need this crap." You know, because I don't think that the things she is asking him for are that far out of . . . are that far out.

Winter then further explores Devan's emotional entanglement with the woman. The question of the client's level of honesty with the therapist is examined:

W: The "other man" moved away from the time she stopped the affair?

D: When she told him that she was absolutely not going to see him anymore. But see, all summer she has been going to him and saying, you know . . . he knew she was in therapy and she has been going to him, saying, "We've got to cut this off." He threatened to kill himself if she cut him off. It has just been one of those . . .

W: I don't understand why you see yourself as really identified with . . . her, and involved with her . . . when she lies to you like this. I don't understand where you are, you know . . . you are so involved and on her side.

D: Well, because I guess I feel sorry for her. I feel like she is, she is much more clear with her pain. Well, I guess the mental machination that I do in this head is that I see her as not being in control of this. I see her as being helpless and confused, and just not . . . [pause]

W: Do you mean that she is entitled to anything that she wants to do because her husband doesn't say that she is attractive? She is entitled to mistreat you, mistreat her daughter . . . because he doesn't "mow mow" and "wow wow" over her? Is this it? . . . I am trying to find out where *your* vulnerability is.

D: I mean one of the first things that comes to mind—but I am sure this isn't all of it—one of the first things that comes to my mind is that she acts much more kind of helpless and depressed, and you know all of her symptoms are like my mother. And so, I am much more able to respond to that and take care of her in spite of what she is doing. The other part that comes to me is that there is like a . . . it is really a shitty thing to be doing to him [the husband] and the second part that comes to me is that I wonder if I am not . . . if there wasn't some kind of underlying motivation for me about the power that I got from being that shitty to him.

A: The picture I get of you is both contexts: as the wife, as the woman who gets what she can; and as the woman who will seduce the guy but not really give herself to him, as the somebody who doesn't trust anyone, who is basically alone and says, "I have got to have all the strength myself. I can't depend on anyone." But, if you follow this scenario, as I pointed it out, and if you and your husband were in therapy, and he is having the affair, and the male therapist that you were seeing really got you to let down your guard with him, so you cry to him and you came to depend upon seeing him and then found that he has a secret and that he was saying to [your husband], "Why don't you ditch this broad anyway? She's not going to deliver."

D: Whew! I am sitting here feeling real scared and vulnerable because . . . that is really shitty therapy. I am really feeling real vulnerable about that part of me, besides the other part, because it is just like real bad. . . . I am wondering how I get myself out of it . . . dig myself out of the hole.

A: My question is, can you get that scared about what you do to you in your personal life as you get about what you do in your therapy? Are you as guarded in your personal life?

D: I don't feel like I have people who I trust except maybe . . . sometimes alternately, I trust [my husband] and sometimes I don't . . . and I trust my mother, you know . . . that's about it. You see, I don't know if people would even . . . it is like, what is wrong with me is that I don't really know how to be honest with people. I lie a lot. Some of them are just little lies; some of them are bigger. I lie a lot. In order to be close to me, people are going to have to take the time. I am going to have to not lie, you know. I am going to have to stop playing those games.

A: Are you in therapy?

D: Yeah, but I don't trust my therapist.

A: Then you're not in therapy. That is the function of your therapist. And, see, the thing is, that you are not taking that risk with your therapist.

W: But have you really decided that you are tired of suffering, you are tired of this lonely [life] . . .

D: Oh, yeah. I have had it with . . . I have been tired of it for six weeks. Ever since I had a severe case of the flu. I have been tired of it. I am not going to do . . . I am not going to live like this. I have been trying to do what I know to do, you know. . .

The therapist revealed that she identified with the woman client's deception with people because she, like her client, did not trust that people would care for her if they knew her as she knew herself. The presentation also dealt with how much Devan wanted her husband's love and commitment, but how fearful she was of openly testing her marriage, lest her husband fail her. Later, she expressed her desire to raise those issues directly with her husband. Also, Devan voiced her determination to deal with her own therapist, whose approval she also wanted and feared losing. Since co-workers were in the group, Devan talked directly with them about her long-standing anxiety that they would not want to work with her, nor would they want her friendship. Devan left the presentation indicating a determination to be straightforward with the people in her life. She committed to helping Anne, the client, develop the courage to take the personal risks required to reach out for the love she, too, wanted from her husband. Rather than maintaining a fraud in the marital relationship, the therapist left determined to change her unspoken collusion with the wife's secret.

Subsequent to this intervention, Devan reviewed an audiotape of her previous training group presentation and reported how listening to the tape affected her. First she addressed the personal effect of the tape on her:

One morning, I was here early and had a few hours set aside for administration. The transcript was on top of the pile of papers, so I picked it up and decided to listen to a few pages of the tape. As it turned out, I spent two and a half hours without moving from my chair and finished the tape. It felt like I was in some kind of trance or altered state. . . . I was totally focused on the process of how the presentation was unfolding.

I was also aware that I was processing the tape on at least two levels. The therapist in me was saying, "What an interesting case study," and was focused on the interview skills of Aponte and Winter, and how they fit together as a co-therapy team. I was struck by how involved they were with "the client" [me] and how direct they were about their sense of what was going on. I could literally see Winter's eyes tearing up while she asked me if I believed she would kick me out of the practice; and I felt kind of sad and ashamed that Aponte was *so* right when he accused me of not reaching out to people and then blaming them for my loneliness.

I had the sense of humanness of the whole thing, and a feeling of universality. I don't know, just that me, the person, and me, the therapist, are always growing and changing, and so is everyone in that group experience, and so are my clients. And it just felt like a type of circular "watering process." The flowers grow because they are watered, and they produce moisture that goes into the air and forms clouds that water the flowers, etc. Anyway, that was the trance.

Then Devan described the effect listening to the tape had on her clinical work:

I finished the tape on a Wednesday and that afternoon, I had a few families to see, but no noticeable effect from the morning's experience. The next day, though, I did three separate hours of therapy with three women clients that were absolutely different from any therapy I have ever done. It was like watching myself do therapy, almost like I was really in there with these women and I was taking risks with them, and touching them (literally, at one point, I was physically holding one of my clients), and another voice was saying, "Good God," and I was not afraid of myself. I knew (really knew) that my confrontation wouldn't destroy them (or me) and that we were in it together. It's really hard to put into words, but I just felt "on" and exhilarated and gleeful in a way I haven't ever felt as an individual therapist. I have sometimes in the past gotten some of that same feeling with a really difficult family, when I know I'm right at the core of the issue and that the family absolutely will leave the room changed. But never with an individual client. It's always been too risky to get there with them and possibly lose (myself?), or lose control or whatever. This time I didn't, though, and it was *so* real. During the past week, I have felt moments like those. They aren't as steady as they were that day, but they are more often and it's somewhat like following a map or playing hide and seek with myself. I have a hint now when I took the right fork in the road or when I'm getting hot or cold. I'm not always choosing to move toward hotter (sometimes I run for the ease and safety of cold), but I know it's there and it's possible.

One month later, in Devan's next presentation in the training group, she conducted a session in which she was supervised live by the leaders. The client Devan interviewed was a different one than in the earlier presentation made to the training seminar, but the themes of trust and honesty were the same. This client (C) was a young woman (twenty-two) who had also been having an affair with a married man:

D: How do you feel about the way things are between us in therapy?

C: I guess right now they're sort of like at a standstill. I mean, it could go either way. You know, it was like improvement and then, stop, it's just right there.

D: What do you think that's about?

C: I don't know, I guess it's just, I don't know. I mean, I've been honest as far as . . .

D: You've been honest?

C: Yeah, with you, as far as what's going on here and at home and at work, you know . . .

D: But there are a lot of situations that you and I haven't [*sic*] gotten into where you were not being honest with me.

C: Um, no, I feel like I've been honest with, well . . .

D: I feel like you weren't being honest with me on a couple occasions.

C: Like, specifically?

D: Well, content-wise, there have been a couple of situations where you told me a half truth. Like, specifically, the time I tried to schedule the doctor's appointment for you and you said you couldn't make it because you were meeting friends, and you weren't meeting friends; you were meeting Ron. So I felt like it was not complete; my information was not complete and I was being led to believe you were in one situation when you were in another. I think I've never told you before that I thought you were lying to me . . .

At this point, Devan was able to face with her client the deficits in their therapeutic relationship. The therapist was aware, unlike her presentation a month before, of the dishonesty in the client and how that trait spilled over into other aspects of the client's life, including the therapy:

D: I'm saying that's what needs to change. I need to go out on a limb, and you need to go out on a limb for us to develop some trust.

C: Well, uh huh.

D: How do you feel about what I'm saying? I feel like I'm saying some pretty difficult things and you have your pretend person here.

C: I'm just listening, I mean, I don't know what to say . . . I mean, of course, I don't like when I say those things because I know I don't mean them. But I guess when I'm hurting I want someone else to hurt. I just make up lies or scare them. It's the only way I know.

D: What do you think would happen if you called me and said, "Devan, I'm really hurting and feeling lonely, and I need to talk for a few minutes so I can calm down . . ."

C: Well, that sounds better than what I do now.

D: Do you think I would say "no" and hang up on you unless you're threatening to kill yourself, or run away, or something?

C: No, but I just remember one day when I made four phone calls to four people in my family to let them know how I was feeling and, yet, they were too busy and didn't have time to talk. All in the same week—to my brother, my sister, my father and mother. And each one said, "I don't have the time," click, "I don't have the time," click.

D: Did you tell them what you needed?

C: No.

D: Well, see, I think that's the key here, because I see that happening with your family, and it probably happens with other relationships. It probably happens between you and me, too. Because if you come in and pretend it's all nice and hunky dory, and never say what you really need, then they let you down and they don't know how badly they hurt you.

Devan was able to risk engaging with her client in a confrontation over the client's trust of her. She was able to see the client's loneliness and how she protected herself from intimacy, as Devan herself does, for fear of rejection. Also, the therapist was able to effectively address the client's affair without becoming personally entangled or threatened by the therapeutic material.

CONCLUSION

Much is expected of therapy. Much is expected of clinicians today when therapy has become more active and interactive than during classical psychoanalytic days. Therapy is the vehicle by which people attempt to change their losses into fulfillment. Therapy has become a modern-day tool to address the interaction and complexities between people and their environment. The instrument common to every therapeutic model is the person of the therapist in a relationship with the client. Considering the clinician's task, it is no wonder that the person of therapist and one's use of self become a central focus of professional development.

The Person and Practice of the Therapist training model is an atheoretical, generic training approach, not bound to any specific school of therapy. It concentrates primarily on the *bridge* between the actual conduct of treatment and the therapist's personal life. The model strives to enhance psychotherapists' ability to utilize their life experiences and personal assets and struggles on behalf of improving professional performance. The training is aimed toward generating effective therapeutic outcomes and supplementing clinicians' efforts to advance their own lives. The learning context is focused on the practitioner's actual conduct of therapy, utilizing live supervision, videotapes, and cases or personal presentations within a collegial training group.

From the perspective of the Person-Practice model, a process that fully explores with a therapist the personal context of one's work and how to master self within that framework is the bedrock element of clinical training. In this approach it is postulated that when a person's work becomes an opportunity to improve self, a clinician more easily makes a greater commitment to the people in treatment and discovers new avenues to improve the quality of clients' lives. In essence, helping therapists to utilize their own unique personal qualities in clinical or technical interventions is the core process in the use of self in therapy.

NOTES

1. Murray Bowen initially set out to discover the "scientific link" between Darwin's and Freud's theories. At the end of his life Bowen unequivocally stated that there was "nothing scientific about Freudian Theory" except for the clinically observable process of "transference and counter-transference." Otherwise, Bowen believed that Freudian theory did not evince the rigor of a scientific, systematized method of research. That is, where: (1) a hypothesis is formulated after systemat-

ic, objective collection of data; (2) the hypothesis is tested empirically; and (3) results of the experiment can be retested or verified again (Winter, 1993).

2. Satir (1975) also emphasized the importance of technical skills. She emphatically stated that how a therapist looked, spoke, and touched clients was crucial to treatment outcome. She also asserted that collaborative skills were vital to a therapist's effectiveness (Winter, 1993).

BIBLIOGRAPHY

Aponte, H. J. (1980). Family therapy and the community. In M. S. Gibbs, J. R. Lachenmeyer, and J. Sigal (Eds.), *Community psychology, theoretical and empirical approaches* (pp. 311-333). New York: Gardner.

Aponte, H. J. (1982). The person of the therapist, the cornerstone of therapy. *The Family Therapy Networker*, March-April, 19-21, 46.

Aponte, H. J. (1985). The negotiation of values in therapy. *Family Process, 24*(3), September, 323-338.

Aponte, H. J. (1992). Training the person of the therapist in structural family therapy. *Journal of Marital and Family Therapy, 18*(3), 269-281.

Aponte, H. J. (1994a). *Bread and spirit.* New York: Norton.

Aponte, H. J. (1994b). How personal can training get? *Journal of Marital and Family Therapy, 20*(1), 3-15.

Aponte, H. J. (1996). Political bias, moral values, and spirituality in the training of psychotherapists. *Bulletin of the Menninger Clinic, 60*(4), 488-502.

Aponte, H. J. and Winter, J. E. (1987). The person and practice of the therapist: Treatment and training. *Journal of Psychotherapy and the Family, 3*(1), 85-111.

Bandler, R., Grinder, J., and Satir, V. (1976). *Changing with families.* Palo Alto, CA: Science and Behavior.

Bowen, M. (1971-1974). *Murray Bowen family therapy seminars.* Seminar presentations at the Medical College of Virginia, Richmond, VA.

Bowen, M. (1972). Toward a differentiation of a self in one's family. In James L. Framo (Ed.), *Family interaction* (pp. 111-173). New York: Springer.

Duhl, B. S. and Duhl, F. J. (1981). Integrative family therapy. In A. S. Gurman and D. P. Kniskern (Eds.), *Handbook of family therapy* (pp. 483-513). New York: Brunner/Mazel.

Durkin, J. E. (Ed.). (1981). *Living groups: Group psychotherapy and general systems thinking.* New York: Brunner/Mazel.

Falloon, I. R. H. (1991). Behavioral family therapy. In A. S. Gurman and D. P. Kniskern (Eds.), *Handbook of family therapy,* Volume II (pp. 65-95). New York: Brunner/Mazel.

Freud, S. (1957). The future prospects of psycho-analytic therapy. In J. Strachey (Ed. and Trans.), *The standard edition of the complete psychological works of Sigmund Freud,* Volume XI (pp. 144-145). London: Hogarth Press. (Original work published 1910.)

Freud, S. (1958). Papers on technique: Editor's introduction. In J. Strachey (Ed. and Trans.), *The standard edition of the complete psychological works of Sigmund Freud,* Volume XII (p. 87). London: Hogarth Press.

Freud, S. (1964). Analysis terminable and interminable. In J. Strachey (Ed. and Trans.), *The standard edition of the complete psychological works of Sigmund Freud,* Volume XXIII (p. 249). London: Hogarth Press. (Original work published 1937.)

Gomori, M. and Winter, J. E. (1995). Le modèle évolutif de Virginia Satir: Les implications pratiques. *Panorama des therapies familiales* (pp. 417-429). Paris, France: Éditions du Seuil.

Gurman, A. S. and Kniskern, D. P. (1981). Family therapy outcome research: Knowns and unknowns. In A. S. Gurman and D. P. Kniskern (Eds.), *Handbook of family therapy* (pp. 742-775). New York: Brunner/Mazel.

Haley, J. (1976). *Problem solving therapy* (pp. 176-177). San Francisco: Jossey-Bass.

Margulies, A. (1989). *The empathic imagination.* New York: Norton.

Minuchin, S. (1984). (Interviewed by Richard Simon, Ed.) Stranger in a strange land. *Family Therapy Newsletter,* November-December, 20-31, 66-68.

Minuchin, S. and Fishman, C. H. (1982). *Family therapy techniques.* Cambridge, MA: Harvard University Press.

Napier, A. and Whitaker, C. (1978). *The family crucible.* New York: Harper and Row.

Nerin, W. F. (1986). *Family reconstruction: Long day's journey into light.* New York: W. W. Norton.

Satir, V. (1975). When I meet a person. In R. Spitzer (Ed.), *Tidings of comfort and joy* (pp. 111-127). Palo Alto, CA: Science and Behavior Books.

Satir, V. (1988). *New peoplemaking.* Palo Alto, CA: Science and Behavior.

Satir, V. and Baldwin, M. (1983). *Satir step by step.* Palo Alto, CA: Science and Behavior.

Whitaker, C. A. and Keith, D. V. (1981). Symbolic-experimental family therapy. In A. S. Gurman and D. P. Kniskern (Eds.), *Handbook of family therapy* (pp. 187-225). New York: Brunner/Mazel.

Winter, J. E. (1979a, July). *Interview with Murray Bowen and Bowen Theory therapists.* Washington, DC: Georgetown Family Center. Unpublished Manuscript.

Winter, J. E. (1979b, November). *Interview with Jay Haley and Strategic Family Therapy therapists.* Washington, DC: Family Therapy Institute of Washington, DC. Unpublished manuscript.

Winter, J. E. (1980, November). *Interview with Virginia Satir and Process Model Avanta therapists.* Richmond, Virginia. Unpublished manuscript.

Winter, J. E. (1982). *Philosophy of supervision.* (No. 2511004). Richmond, VA: Commonwealth of Virginia, Board of Behavioral Sciences.

Winter, J. E. (1986). *Family research project: Family therapy outcome study of Bowen, Haley, Satir.* Unpublished 1978-1980 interview transcripts.

Winter, J. E. (1988). *Family therapy outcomes with Bowen, Haley, and Satir: Engagement, dropout, completion, and recidivism.* Williamsburg, VA: College of William and Mary. Manuscript.

Winter, J. E. (1989, August). *Meeting with Murray Bowen.* Washington, DC: Georgetown Family Center. Unpublished manuscript.

Winter, J. E. (1993). *Selected family therapy outcomes with Bowen, Haley, and Satir,* Volumes I and II. Williamsburg, VA: College of William and Mary. Dissertation.

Winter, J. E. (1995). Le modèle évolutif de Virginia Satir: Les fondements théoriques. *Panorama des therapies familiales* (pp. 387-416). Paris: Éditions du Seuil.

Winter, J. E. and Aponte, H. J. (1987). The family life of psychotherapists: Treatment and training implications. *Journal of Psychotherapy and the Family, 2,* 97-133. Reprinted in F. Kaslow (Ed.) (1987), *The family life of therapists* (pp. 97-133). Binghamton, NY: The Haworth Press, Inc.

Winter, J. E. and Bjornsen, C. (1991). Selected outcomes of Bowen Therapy with families of juvenile offenders. *American Family Therapy Association Newsletter, 44,* 33-34.

Winter, J. E. and Parker, L. R. E. (1991). Enhancing the relationship: Virginia Satir's parts party. *Journal of Couples Therapy, 2,* 59-82. Reprinted in B. J. Brothers (Ed.) (1991). *Virginia Satir: Foundational ideas.* (pp. 59-82). Binghamton, NY: The Haworth Press, Inc.

Winter, J. E. and Parker, L. R. E. (1992). Enhancing the marital relationship. In G. F. Muller (Ed.), *Virginia Satir Wage zum Wachstrum* (pp. 209-231). Munich, Germany: Pederborn/Junfermann.

Chapter 8

Use of the Multicultural Self
for Effective Practice

Judith F. Bula

INTRODUCTION

Multiculturalism has been called the "fourth force" in counseling, following the forces of the psychodynamic, behavioral, and humanistic movements (Pedersen, 1991). Many authors have noted the rapid growth of multicultural awareness for counseling and therapeutic practice in recent years (e.g., Hollis and Wantz, 1990, 1994; Hills and Strozier, 1992; Ivey, 1995; Quintana and Bernal, 1995). Professional associations such as the National Association of Social Workers, the American Counseling Association, the American Association for Counseling and Development, and the American Psychological Association have cultural counseling competencies in their ethical guidelines (Pope-Davis and Coleman, 1996). With this long-overdue emergence of multicultural awareness in the helping professions (the first known publications on the subject were in the mid-1950s), it is incumbent upon the individual practitioner to be knowledgeable about her or his own multicultural reality in order to use that information effectively in work with clients of various ethnicities, genders, ages, socioeconomic classes, religions, sexual orientations, differing abilities, and with those who use different languages.

The assessment of multicultural competencies and the acquiring of those competencies are essential steps in enhancing the effectiveness of practice in working with a wide variety of clients. The trend

---

The author wishes to thank her colleagues Dr. Maria Yellow Horse Brave Heart and Dr. Antonio Ledesma for their helpful consultation.

of the current literature is most often in one of these two directions (e.g., Cushner and Brislin, 1997; Dana, 1997; Kiselica, 1995; Paniagua, 1994; Pedersen, 1997; Pedersen et al., 1996; Pope-Davis and Coleman, 1996). Less frequently seen is the emphasis of this volume, the focus on use of *self*,* and in this instance, the use of the multicultural self. One exception is Dr. Lee Knefelkamp, who, in association with the Institute for Intercultural Communication, teaches a seminar on the "Development of the Multicultural Self." Dr. Knefelkamp emphasizes the importance of "attending to the development of one's self in the context of gender, race, ethnicity, culture, generation, sexual orientation, socioeconomic class, and disability; and exploring the major theoretical models, research, and assessment in each of those areas" (in Bennett, Bennett, and Pusch, 1998). The counselor's awareness of her or his own assumptions, values, and biases is an important first step before understanding the worldview of a culturally different client and before developing intervention strategies and techniques.

To use one's multicultural self effectively in the helping context, there must be the sense of perceiving that self as multicultural. In Chapter 1, Virginia Satir indicates the damage that can be done by someone in the helping role who is not aware of all aspects of self and how that self is being used. To perceive one's self as multicultural, in turn, implies that there is knowledge about what is meant by "multicultural" to begin with, and then there is an active identification with that meaning in one's day-to-day existence. A multicultural self, by very nature of its designation, implies a self-with-context.

This time-honored concept from social work history, the self within the context, dates back to the mid-1800s and has gone through several transformations: person-or-environment (an either-or view of the source of problems); person-and-environment (with emphasis on environment); person-and-environment (with emphasis on person); person-IN-environment (still widely used today); and person-WITH-environment (the form preferred and advocated by this author because of its implication of active participation

---

*Whenever the term *self* is first employed in a chapter as part of the concept of the use of self in therapy, it is italicized to call attention to its special use.

"with" one's context rather than the more passive residing "in" that context). In recent years, an interesting similarity has emerged from cultural identity theory:

> Drawing on many authorities in cultural identity theory (e.g., Cross, 1971; Helms, 1985, 1990; Jackson, 1975; Jackson and Hardiman, 1983; Sue and Sue, 1990), liberations psychotherapy focuses on helping clients learn to see themselves in relation not only to themselves but also to cultural/contextual influences, with special attention to the family. *Self-in-relation* replaces our traditional conception of the individual self (Miller, 1991). (Ivey, 1995, p. 53)

This chapter provides an opportunity for readers to know self as it relates to eight multicultural factors, or perhaps more realistically, according to David Keith's suggestion in Chapter 12, to gain or further strengthen one's "familiarity" with a multicultural self. Second, this chapter also offers guidelines for readers to assess their own cross-cultural counseling competencies. With this twofold focus (knowing self and assessing one's competencies) one potential outcome is the integration of the personal with the technical; of one's core beliefs and values with learned skills, techniques, and professional behaviors. With this goal in mind, the following discussions focus on becoming familiar with one's multicultural self, seeing ourselves for the multicultural persons we are and, finally, looking at the multicultural self as professional and, in particular, offering the opportunity to assess our own use of the multicultural self for effective practice by considering cross-cultural competencies.

DEFINING THE MULTICULTURAL SELF

Other discussions in this volume provide guidance in the importance of knowing self as well as the dangers that can lurk in the therapeutic setting when there is a lack of self-knowledge. What is meant, though, by knowing oneself as a *multicultural* self? The term "multicultural" has been defined as implying "a sense of simultaneous loyalty to and embracing of more than one culture (i.e., not simply the presence of two or more races or cultures)" (Williams,

1992, p. 281). Multicultural factors have been identified as including ethnicity, gender, age, religion, socioeconomic status, sexual orientation, differing abilities, and language (Schniedewind and Davidson, 1997). Therefore, to define the self as a multicultural self would imply the regular and conscious experiencing of self as "loyal to and embracing" these multicultural factors. To the degree one is able to do this with one's self, one is also able to embrace these multicultural qualities and characteristics in others.

The eight multicultural factors identified previously do not compose an exhaustive list of possible factors, but they do reflect those multicultural factors which consistently appear in current literature. Several other factors that also appear, but less consistently, are race, developmental stage, and family form. Arguments against the inclusion of race on a list of multicultural factors include "the confusion and misunderstanding it creates among people," "its ambiguous meaning as a measure of difference referring to culture," and that "racism is often equated with prejudice and . . . raises to the level of social structure the tendency to use superiority as a solution to discomfort about difference" (Pinderhughes, 1989, p. 89).

Those who argue for the inclusion of developmental stage as a multicultural factor recognize the frequent discrepancy between age and developmental stage (Bula, 1998a). This can refer to the difference between chronological age and the corresponding developmental stage or it may refer to a person's emotional age as compared with his or her developmental stage. It can also include those with developmental delays as well as those who are developmentally advanced. "Middle age," for example, contains certain "values, norms, beliefs, attitudes, folkways, behavior styles, and traditions that are linked together to form an integrated whole that functions to preserve the society" (Leighton, 1982, in Pinderhughes, 1989, p. 6), which is the earlier definition given to the term "culture."

The same is true for family form (Bula, 1998a). Blended family, single-parent family, nuclear family, dual-career family, and others can all have their own traditions, beliefs, behavioral styles, and attitudes which form a whole to preserve society. Awareness of these two factors, both family form and developmental stage, in our own lives and in the lives of those we serve can add a great deal to our understanding of the completeness of those persons as well as having an impact on practice decisions. These terms point to the evolving and emerging nature of the definition of the term "multicultural."

Definitions for each of the eight factors are common throughout the literature. The ones identified here are merely meant to inform readers of the commonality of perspective that is currently found in the literature, but these particular definitions are not meant to limit individual views or applications of those terms to one's own life. To do so would defeat a very important purpose of this chapter, the knowing of one's self as a multicultural self. With that said, the following are common definitions of these areas of multicultural social identity (Schniedewind and Cathers, 1996):

- Ethnicity—"connectedness based on commonalities (such as religion, nationality, region, etc.) where specific aspects of cultural patterns are shared and where transmission over time creates a common history" (Pinderhughes, 1989, p. 6);
- Gender—a social, not a psychological, concept denoted by the terms "femininity" and "masculinity," which "refer to a complex set of characteristics and behaviors prescribed for a particular sex by society and learned through the socialization experience" (Ruth, 1990, p. 14);
- Age—number of years since one's birth or conception, noting that some cultures begin counting at the time of conception rather than from the time of birth;
- Socioeconomic class—"class is more than just the amount of money you have; it's also the presence of economic security" (Langston, 1995, p. 101);
- Religion—"In most societies it is the basis for morality and for all human relationships, especially where it is believed that there is a divine law controlling all things, and it gives meaning to life" (Allen et al., 1993, p. 626);
- Sexual orientation—one's feelings of sexual attraction to people of the same sex, to people of the opposite sex, or to people of both sexes (Marcus, 1993, p. 6);
- Differing ability—having abilities that differ from the established societal norm, some of which may include living with impaired sight or hearing, needing to use a wheelchair, having intellectual capacity which exceeds that of one's peers, or utilizing different patterns of learning;

- Language—includes one's first and primary language as well as later learned languages, with emphasis on bilingual and multilingual skills as a definite strength.

To take these eight factors then and to "become familiar with one's multicultural self," the first important step is to give each of these factors an individualized meaning according to one's own experience and perspective. Ask: What is the meaning *I* give to ethnicity? to gender? to age? to socioeconomic status? to sexual orientation? to differing ability? and to language? How does my own meaning agree with or differ from those definitions given above? Answers to these questions can help one get closer to the intended purpose here, that of the use of self, based on an in-depth knowing of self, toward the end of maximizing the effectiveness of the helping process and the use of ourselves in that process. Each client, client couple, client family, client agency, or organization seeking services will also come to us with individual ideas about the meaning of each multicultural factor, and it becomes one of our practice tasks to listen carefully and discover these ideas rather than to assume that the ways we each define such complex terms might possibly carry similar meaning for the other.

MULTICULTURAL SELF AS PERSON

Once there is some sense of what is meant by each of the factors, the next step is to determine one's own declarative statement about each:

I am _____(ethnicity)_____.
I am _____(gender)_____.
I am _____(age)_____.

Even such simple self-identifications can sometimes raise a sense of a person's history. For example, these comments came from several people who were participating in a recent workshop: "I came from a poor background and still often identify with those experiences, but now would call myself middle class" and "I was born into a Protestant family but converted to Catholicism when I got married." Emotional responses are common as well: "I was barely out of the coma when I knew nothing was moving below my waist and that the accident had changed everything about my life." These self-statements of "I am" can also reveal feelings of ambivalence or certainty, acceptance or rejection, and positions of power or of oppression. Both the content and the affect of these statements provide valuable information regarding the individual's perception of "who I am as a multicultural being."

After determining personal meanings given to each term and then using these meanings in one's own self-statements, the next step in becoming familiar with one's multicultural self is to learn more about one's beliefs, attitudes, and knowledge related to each statement. Sue, Arrendondo, and McDavis (1995) list the following four statements of beliefs and attitudes for "Counselor Awareness of Own Assumptions, Values, and Biases":

1. Culturally skilled counselors have moved from being culturally unaware to being aware and sensitive to their own cultural heritage and to valuing and respecting differences.
2. Culturally skilled counselors are aware of how their own cultural background and experiences, attitudes, and values and biases influence psychological processes.
3. Culturally skilled counselors are able to recognize the limits of their competencies and expertise.
4. Culturally skilled counselors are comfortable with differences that exist between themselves and clients in terms of race, ethnicity, culture, and beliefs. (p. 633)

Awarenesses related to knowledge are identified by these same authors as follows:

1. Culturally skilled counselors have specific knowledge about their own racial and cultural heritage and how it personally and professionally affects their definitions and biases of normality-abnormality and the process of counseling.
2. Culturally skilled counselors possess knowledge and understanding about how oppression, racism, discrimination, and stereotyping affect them personally and in their work. This allows them to acknowledge their own racist attitudes, beliefs, and feelings. Al-

though this standard applies to all groups, for White counselors it may mean that they understand how they may have directly or indirectly benefitted from individual, institutional, and cultural racism (White identity development models).
3. Culturally skilled counselors possess knowledge about their social impact upon others. They are knowledgeable about communication style differences, how their style may clash or facilitate the counseling process with minority clients, and how to anticipate the impact it may have on others. (p. 634)

To know the multicultural self as person, using the eight factors and the previous statements of skill, we must be willing to ask ourselves such questions as: What are my deepest values, beliefs, and attitudes about being Latino/a, African American, Anglo/Euro-American, Asian, Native American, about being a woman or a man; about being poor, middle class, or wealthy; about being young, middle aged, or elderly; about being gay, straight, lesbian, bisexual, transsexual; about being Protestant, Catholic, Jewish, Buddhist, Muslim; about living with blindness, deafness, in a wheelchair, with a long-term illness; about being unilingual, bilingual, multilingual? Am I really loyal to these parts of myself or are there some for which I have also fallen into stereotypical or prejudicial thinking? Can I experience a true sense of empathy for this self of mine which struggles to make sense of the privilege I experience on the one hand and the oppressions on the other? How have I worked to resolve inner conflicts when different parts of my multicultural self are at odds with each other? How do I make sense, for example, when the teachings of my ethnic and religious backgrounds violate the rights of my gender? What kind of discipline do I exercise in learning other languages when the shortcoming of knowing only one language becomes painfully apparent? This list of questions could be endless, but what is most important, especially given the work of how to use my multicultural self in the setting of therapeutic practice, is that the questions shape themselves for each individual person from her or his stance in relation to each of the multicultural factors. Some helpful tools are available to assist with this endeavor: two versions of a multicultural matrix (Ledesma, 1997; Bula, 1998a; Schmitz, 1998) will be presented (see Tables 8.1 and 8.2), and readers are also referred to a self-evaluation form (Leigh,

1998) that evaluates skill level in ethnographic interviewing, and a Person in Culture Interview (Berg-Cross and Chinen, 1995).

One useful tool for self-assessment using these awarenesses, one which helps identify gaps as well as knowledge that is in place is a multicultural matrix (see Table 8.1). Dr. Antonio Ledesma (1997) has also encouraged the use of a "Values" column in such a matrix, coming even closer to those areas which are so central to a person's core identity that they would be unlikely, or very difficult, to change.

TABLE 8.1. Multicultural Matrix—A

	Beliefs	**Attitudes**	**Knowledge**
Ethnicity			
Gender			
Age			
SES			
Religion			
Sexual Orientation			
Differing Abilities			
Language			

In the process of making one's beliefs and attitudes more overt, the culturally aware may also recognize that they find themselves considering positions of both privilege and oppression. Dr. Cathryn Schmitz (1998) presents another version of a multicultural matrix (see Table 8.2).

Both matrices presented here, plus others responsive to the needs or expectations of various learning environment, can serve as helpful exercises for knowing one's multicultural self. This work in self-awareness is considered as crucial to the helping professional engaged in cross-cultural counseling as family-of-origin work is to family

TABLE 8.2. Multicultural Matrix—B

	Privilege	Oppression
Ethnicity		
Gender		
Age		
SES		
Religion		
Sexual Orientation		
Differing Abilities		
Language		

counselors and therapists. One point which emerges as the "multi-" in "multicultural" comes into clear view is that of the relative impossibility of experiencing a same-cultural or "unicultural" interaction with any other person. Even if all of the eight factors coincide for two people, once they begin a conversation about their beliefs, attitudes, and knowledge of each factor, the likelihood of similarity in all twenty-four areas of the matrix becomes rare.

MULTICULTURAL SELF AS PROFESSIONAL

What are some of the ways we in the helping professions can become more highly aware of our multicultural nature in order to use that information to better understand and assist those with whom we work? Values clarification, in which one participates in an experience with people of a culture or religious setting different from one's own, an age or single-gender group different from one's own, for example, can be first steps in increasing multicultural awareness with others. However, Dr. James Cole (1997) cautions that such experiences can never bring about the fundamental changes required to be able to truly embrace differences beyond prejudice and stereotypes. It is only with an experience of empathy, of "walking in that person's shoes," that the transformation to multicultural acceptance can occur.

After becoming more familiar with one's multicultural self, the next step toward an effective use of that multicultural self in the therapeutic practice of helping is to have a way of assessing one's cross-cultural counseling competencies. Before considering that assessment process, however, there is one contextual statement which will help to create the background for that discussion.

The term "therapy," used in its traditional connotation, is absent in this chapter. This is intentional. "Traditional forms of treatment should be modified because they are geared primarily for mainstream Americans" (Sue and Zane, 1987, p. 38). Jose Sisneros (personal communication, 1998) points out that people of minority cultures do not typically seek what is known as "traditional therapy" because it is not seen as a resource that will be helpful nor as one which will meet their needs. James Leigh (1998) mirrors this statement by saying, "Techniques of helping are constantly changing, and social workers must avoid the trap of using techniques and methods that do not fulfill the service needs of ethnic minority persons" (p. 6):

> In effect, traditional . . . therapy theories are White, male, Eurocentric, and middle-class in origin and practice. Therapy can be described as centrally concerned with maintaining the status quo.
>
> In this frame of reference, traditional . . . therapy, to paraphrase Eldridge Cleaver, is more problem than solution. Today even the most cursory review of the influential journals and texts still reveals a naive Eurocentric approach. The increasing influence of the multiculturalists is recognized, but they are still clearly a minority voice. (Ivey, 1995, pp. 55-56)

If not traditional therapy, then what? What is it that the multiculturalists recommend? The answer to these questions is what Ivey refers to as "development of critical consciousness" or the process of *conscientizacao*. It draws on the work of Paulo Friere (1972) and the literature on cultural identity theory (Cross, 1971, 1991; Hardiman, 1982; Helms, 1990; Jackson, 1975; Jackson and Hardiman, 1983; Ponterotto, 1988; Sue and Sue, 1990). Five stages of consciousness development have been identified as central: naivete; acceptance, passive or active; naming and resistance, passive or active; redefinition and reflection; and multiperspective integration (Ivey and Payton, 1994). Major concepts one will find are *client colleagues, cointentional education, self-in-relation, coconstruction of reality,* and *reference group orientation*. Further elaboration of the process of *conscientizacao* is outside the parameters of this chapter; however, readers are encouraged to pursue the works of the multicultural authors listed above and, in particular, the work of Paulo Friere.

Now that the stage has been set with this contextual qualifier about the absence of the term "therapy," it is time to turn to the focus of this section, the multicultural self as professional. Whether in the helping profession for two months or twenty years, how is it that one becomes aware of one's level of competence when it comes to working multiculturally? The belief that such an awareness is imperative has been voiced by many (e.g., Korman, 1974; Pedersen and Marsella, 1982; Sue, Arredondo, and McDavis, 1995) including the American Association for Counseling and Development (AACD) and the American Psychological Association (APA). Both of these organizations published ethical guidelines in 1981 making it imperative for counselors and therapists to have formal training on cultural differences. Sue, Arredondo, and McDavis (1995) even go as far as saying that "professionals without training or competence in working with clients from diverse cultural backgrounds are unethical and potentially harmful, which borders on a violation of human rights" (p. 630).

Once again Sue, Arredondo, and McDavis (1995) offer specific guidelines for a counselor self-assessment of cross-cultural counseling competencies. Their framework for presenting these competencies is divided into three major sections: counselor awareness of own assumptions, values, and biases; understanding the worldview of the culturally different client; and developing appropriate intervention strategies and techniques. Within each of the major sections are subsections on attitudes and beliefs, knowledge, and skills. This final skills section is quoted at length for purposes of the present discussion but it is important for readers to know that this occurs as only one part of the broader framework. (The complete document can be found in Ponterotto et al., 1995, pp. 624-644.)

The skills Sue, Arredondo, and McDavis (1995) have identified for developing appropriate intervention strategies and techniques include the following:

1. Culturally skilled counselors are able to engage in a variety of verbal and nonverbal helping responses. They are able to *send* and *receive* both *verbal* and *nonverbal* messages *accurately* and *appropriately.* They are not tied down to only one method or approach to helping but recognize that helping styles and approaches may be culture bound. When they sense that their helping style is limited and potentially inappropriate, they can anticipate and ameliorate its negative impact.

2. Culturally skilled counselors are able to exercise institutional intervention skills on behalf of their clients. They can help clients determine whether a "problem" stems from racism or bias in others (the concept of healthy paranoia) so that clients do not inappropriately blame themselves.

3. Culturally skilled counselors are not averse to seeking consultation with traditional healers or religious and spiritual

leaders and practitioners in the treatment of culturally different clients when appropriate.

4. Culturally skilled counselors take responsibility for interacting in the language requested by the client; this may mean appropriate referral to outside resources. A serious problem arises when the linguistic skills of the counselor do not match the language of the client. This being the case, counselors should (a) seek a translator with cultural knowledge and appropriate professional background or (b) refer to a knowledgeable and competent bilingual counselor.

5. Culturally skilled counselors have training and expertise in the use of traditional assessment and testing instruments. They not only understand the technical aspects of the instruments but are also aware of the cultural limitations. This allows them to use test instruments for the welfare of the diverse clients.

6. Culturally skilled counselors should attend to as well as work to eliminate biases, prejudices, and discriminatory practices. They should be cognizant of sociopolitical contexts in conducting evaluations and providing interventions, and should develop sensitivity to issues of oppression, sexism, and racism.

7. Culturally skilled counselors take responsibility in educating their clients to the processes of psychological intervention, such as goals, expectations, legal rights, and the counselor's orientation (p. 636).

Multiple levels of the client system are addressed in this list of skills: the individual level (5); the one-on-one dyad (3, 7); the institutional level (2); the societal/political level (6); and the communication process which links them together (1, 4). This breadth implies the importance of counselors being able to view the systemic totality of their clients' experiences, from the individual to the societal. It also implies the necessity of defining interventions that are systemic and of providing a "good fit" for the various needs of each client. From this list, counselors and other helping professionals can identify strengths and gaps in their own competencies.

The step of knowing self as a multicultural professionally skilled self is the precursor to knowing how to use one's self in a cross-cultural or multicultural helping situation. After this, the verbal and nonverbal communication skills of the counselor can promote or block the further development of connection and rapport with each client.

James Leigh (1998) offers some extremely helpful guidelines for refining one's communication skills for cultural competence. "Crucial to this cultural mix is the need to discover something in common between the two perspectives. Effective helping requires that the cultural gap be bridged" (p. 4). Leigh is writing specifically to social workers about working with people of different ethnic minorities, yet his words can apply to other helping professionals and other groups of the multiculturally diverse as well:

> A social worker should develop communication skills that elicit the ethnic minority person's narrative. It is in the narrative that the helper will find the client's hopes, aspirations, values, and views of the world. It is through the narrative that the client is understood, is helped, and feels better rather than through the theories about how people in distress improve, are helped, and are made to feel better. (p. 4)

Eliciting a person's story, his or her narrative, can be enhanced through the use of the procedures for ethnographic interviewing, according to Leigh, and he presents these procedures in his book, *Communicating for Cultural Competence*. He has also, with two colleagues, James Anderson and Gloria Richardson, identified "Seven Principles for the Culturally Competent Social Worker" which agree with those of Sue and colleagues previously, yet they are even more specific to the professional practice interactions with clients:

1. I accept the fact that I have much to learn about others.
2. I have an appreciation of the regional and geographical factors related to people of color and contrasting cultures, how the individual may vary from the generalizations about their regional and geographic group, and how regional groups vary from the total cultural group.
3. I follow the standard that knowledge is obtained from the person in the situation and add to my learning about the situation from that person before generalizing about the group-specific person.

4. I have the capacity to form relationships with people from contrasting cultures in social, work, and professional relationships.
5. I can engage in a process characterized by mutual respect and conscious effort to reduce power disparities between myself and persons of minority status.
6. I have the ability to obtain culturally relevant information in the professional encounter.
7. I have the ability to enter into a process of mutual exploration, assessment, and treatment with people of contrasting cultures and minority status in society. (Leigh, 1998, pp. 173-174)

Putting all of this together, the definitions of a "multicultural self" and thinking about the person of the multicultural self as well as the professional use of the multicultural self, no discussion about the use of a multicultural self for effective practice would be complete without an example of what this looks like in the actual work with a client. An abbreviated description of Joseph Glenmullen's (1993) work with a Korean-American couple provides an excellent example of the counselor's use of self in the therapeutic setting and of the use of culturally sensitive communication skills. It also provides an interesting interweaving of multicultural factors of ethnicity, religion, age, gender, and family-of-origin dynamics. In the sensitivity of Dr. Glenmullen's work with them about the culturally taboo subject of a sexual problem, one can also see aspects of *conscientizacao*. Two, in particular, that stand out are encouraging the exploration of the clients' worldview and belief systems and, second, the invitation to tell their story, the narrative.

Case Example*

Carl and Lee were a soft-spoken, appealing couple in their mid-twenties. They came from the same tightly knit Korean-American community, which they described as politically and socially very conservative. Carl was born in this country. Lee and her parents moved to the United States when she was ten, so her family was

---

*Adapted from *The Pornographer's Grief* by Joseph Glenmullen, MD. Published by HarperCollins Publishers. Copyright © 1993 by Joseph Glenmullen. This usage granted by permission of the author.

"even more steeped in the Old World culture, even more conservative."

They began seeing each other in high school. The tradition that adolescence is a time when young people concentrate almost exclusively on studies in preparation for their careers and future has its roots in Korea. There is a lot of pressure for academic achievement, and what dating goes on is largely platonic.

When they came to see me, the couple had been married six months. Carl was a lawyer and Lee a systems analyst. They were well educated and articulate, but their demeanor changed when they began discussing the specific problem for which they came to see me.

"We have a sexual problem," Carl began hesitantly.

"I see," I said, nodding.

Carl and Lee glanced uncomfortably at each other and me for some moments. They seemed uncertain about how to proceed. Eventually, Lee said awkwardly, "We haven't been able to . . . to consummate our marriage." Looking at Carl, she asked, "Do you want to tell the next part?"

Carl explained that sex was never discussed in their cultural milieu, even among close friends, making it extremely difficult for them to talk about their concern. He then blurted out the words *impotent* for himself and *frigid* for Lee. Having gotten that far in describing the problem, he asked anxiously, "What is the cure?"

"Well," I said gently, "I would need to know more about you—your history and what you mean by the words *impotent* and *frigid*—before I could suggest a treatment."

Crestfallen to think they would have to explain in any more detail, they asked, "What do you want to know?"

"How you got to this point sexually. What your relationship was like before marriage. And what the six months since your wedding have been like."

Slowly, they explained that their protracted courtship and engagement had produced considerable sexual tension between them. Unable to resist, they developed a fairly involved sexual relationship, "without having intercourse."

"We wanted to be monogamous and contain our sexuality within the relationship. Our religion is just as negative about masturbation as it is about premarital sex. So if we were going to have a sexual outlet, if we were going to break the rules, we figured we may as well do it with one another."

Could they tell me more about their religious background, I asked. They explained that the Korean church has a pervasive influence on the national culture. It is a Protestant sect, quite narrow and rigid. Sex before marriage is "out of the question" for both men and women. Virginity at marriage is "totally assumed."

"The position is not just moralistic," said Lee. "For example, my mother told me in no uncertain terms I should be a virgin when I was married unless I was not married by the age of thirty, and then I should go ahead and have sex."

"Why did she say that?" I asked.

"She was trying to say it was something not to be missed in life but you should try to do it a certain way."

"I see. That's not something a Western European, Catholic parent would say."

"That's what I mean by it's not just moralistic. There's also this pragmatic element that ties in with what we were saying earlier about education. There is a prescribed order in which you are supposed to do things in life. Of course, it's very strongly held, and you feel ashamed to deviate from it."

"You keep using the word *shame* when I would use the word *guilt*," I commented.

"Yes," they said, smiling.

Carl explained, "Asians feel shame when Westerners would feel guilt. It's not so much one's struggle with an internalized moral code. Rather, it's more one's sense of duty and obligation to the family and community, and one's shame in letting them down."

Lee countered, "It's easier for Carl to be less ashamed. He would be held less accountable."

"There's a double standard?" I asked.

"Not officially. But men are more easily forgiven for sexual transgressions," Lee answered.

I commented that whatever shame the couple did feel could be holding them back: feeling ashamed for partaking of forbidden pleasures before marriage, they might now feel undeserving of the ultimate pleasure, intercourse, within marriage. We would keep this possibility in mind while investigating other potential causes. I reassured them that in all likelihood their problem, whatever its cause, would be treatable.

Having visibly put Carl and Lee at some ease, I said I needed to know more about their sexual histories. In their premarital sex, both Carl and Lee had no difficulty being fully aroused and reaching orgasm. Indeed, that was "the norm."

"Did you try intercourse?" I inquired.

"Just a few times," Carl answered, "but we never managed it."

On their wedding night, the couple attempted intercourse and failed. Having looked forward to it, they made a more concerted effort than in the past. For a while the two continued to be fully aroused sexually. The more focused they became on effecting intercourse, the more miserably they failed. By about four months into the marriage, neither of them could achieve sexual arousal. In the past two months they had become aversive, almost phobic, about sex. The couple reiterated their diagnoses: Carl's "impotence" and Lee's "frigidity."

"I'm still not sure what you mean by that. You say you 'failed' at intercourse, but that could have happened in a number of ways."

"He never entered," Lee replied. "I was in too much pain."

"Too much pain?"

"Yes. It hurt when he tried to enter."

"Eventually," said Carl, "we thought maybe I wasn't using enough force. So a few times I tried quite forcefully, with Lee's consent."

"What happened?"

"It hurt too much," said Lee. "It didn't work. We had to stop."

"That's when our sexual relationship completely fell apart," Carl sighed. "Here I was not succeeding and hurting Lee in the process. I couldn't bear it. I stopped being able to get erections."

I was moved but also relieved. The problem was now clear to me. "Let me tell you where I think things stand. As I now see it, your 'impotence' and 'frigidity' are both secondary to a problem with penetration."

"What's the significance of that?" asked Lee.

I explained that a problem with penetration raised very different concerns than a primary problem of impotence or frigidity. Pain and difficulty with penetration can result from a number of possible causes. By far the two most common are vaginismus and an intact hymen. To my surprise, Lee said she had never had a gynecological exam.

"Why not?" I asked.

"I've never had anything much wrong with me and in my family we only go to doctors when something is really wrong. That's an idiosyncrasy originating with my mother." In none of her sexual activity had she ever been penetrated vaginally. This information led me to conclude an intact hymen was the most likely reason why the couple had not been able to consummate their marriage.

I explained to Lee that she would need to see a gynecologist for a pelvic exam. I referred her to a particularly sensitive, relaxed gynecologist. I suggested Carl go with her and be present at the exam so that they both could see what the problem was.

When they returned, Carl and Lee were beaming. Their problem had in fact been an unusually strong, intact hymen. Lee had already had the minor surgical procedure to remove it. Their sex life was immediately facilitated.

One final point regarding Carl and Lee: In my experience, the position of many Asian immigrant groups in the United States today is highly reminiscent of some Western European immigrants a few generations ago. One sees the clash of the old versus the new culture, particularly the wide gap between the first and second generations in this country. In the children, one sees the confusion and conflicts on issues such as premarital sex, sexual identity, or deviation in any way from the parental norms. These are difficult transitions for both children and parents and often take several generations to resolve (Glenmullen, 1993, pp. 155-167).

*　　*　　*

It is possible to see in this example how Dr. Glenmullen inquired about the couples' belief system and worldview before attempting any diagnostic conclusion. He invited the narrative and learned the interaction of ethnic, religious, gender, age, and family-of-origin dynamics. Within a traditionally secretive area, that of a sexual problem, he helped create a place of safety and mutual problem solving.

Viewing a brief moment of effective practice in this way does not necessarily allow others, including clients, to know the depth of the counselor's work with self that is a prerequisite to such work. And yet, the evidence is abundant that such effectiveness is highly unlikely to occur without such an awareness of the multicultural self.

REFERENCES

Allen, D.A., Kaur, R., Jackson, E.M., and McLeish, K. (1993). Religion. In K. McLeish (Ed.), *Key ideas in human thought* (pp. 626-627). New York: Facts on File.

Bennett, J., Bennett, M., and Pusch, M. (1998). *The Summer Institute for Intercultural Communication.* Portland, OR: Intercultural Communication Institute.

Berg-Cross, L. and Chinen, R.T. (1995). Multicultural training models and the person-in-culture interview. In J.G. Ponterotto, J.M. Casas, L.A. Suzuki, and C.M. Alexander (Eds.), *Handbook of multicultural counseling* (pp. 333-356). Thousand Oaks, CA: Sage.

Bula, J.F. (1998a). The multicultural matrix. Lecture presentation. University of Denver Graduate School of Social Work, Denver, CO.

Bula, J.F. (1998b). What is family? Lecture presentation. University of Denver Graduate School of Social Work, Denver, CO.

Cole, J. (1997). The triad model: A powerful, safe process for reducing subtle, prejudicial behavior. Presentation at the Seventh Annual Conference of the National Association for Multicultural Education, October 28. Albuquerque, NM.

Cross, W. (1971). The Negro to Black conversion experience. *Black World, 20*(1), 13-25.

Cross, W. (1991). *Shades of Black.* Philadelphia: Temple University Press.

Cushner, K. and Brislin, R.W. (Eds.) (1997). *Improving intercultural interactions: Modules for cross-cultural training programs, Volume 2.* Thousand Oaks, CA: Sage.

Dana, R.H. (1997). *Understanding cultural identity in intervention and assessment.* Thousand Oaks, CA: Sage.

Freire, P. (1972). *Pedagogy of the oppressed.* New York: Herder and Herder.

Glenmullen, J. (1993). *The pornographer's grief and other tales of human sexuality.* New York: HarperCollins.

Hardiman, R. (1982). *White identity development: A process oriented model for describing the racial consciousness of White Americans.* Unpublished doctoral dissertation, University of Massachusetts, Amherst, MA.

Helms, J. (1985). Toward a theoretical explanation of the effects of race on counseling: A Black and White model. *The Counseling Psychologist, 12*(2), 153-165.

Helms, J. (1990). *Black and White racial identity.* Westport, CT: Greenwood Press.

Hills, H.I. and Strozier, A.L. (1992). Multicultural training in APA-approved counseling psychology programs: A survey. *Professional Psychology: Research and Theory, 23*(1), 43-51.

Hollis, J.W. and Wantz, R.A. (1990). *Counselor preparation 1990-1992: Programs, personnel, trends* (Seventh edition). Muncie, IN: Accelerated Development Inc.

Hollis, J.W. and Wantz, R.A. (1994). *Counselor preparation 1993-1995: Vol. 2, Status, trends, and implications* (Eighth edition). Muncie, IN: Accelerated Development Inc.

Ivey, A.E. (1995). Psychotherapy as liberation: Toward specific skills and strategies in multicultural counseling and therapy. In J. Ponterotto, J. Casas, L. Suzuki, and C. Alexander (Eds.), *Handbook of multicultural counseling* (pp. 53-72). Thousand Oaks, CA: Sage.

Ivey, A. and Payton, P. (1994). Towards a Cornish identity theory. *Cornish Studies, 2*(2), 151-163.

Jackson, B. (1975). Black identity development. *Journal of Educational Diversity and Innovation, 2*(1), 19-25.

Jackson, B. and Hardiman, R. (1983). Racial identity development: Implications for managing the multiracial work force. In R. Vitvo and A. Sargent (Eds.), *The NTL managers' handbook* (pp. 107-119). Arlington, VA: NTL Institute.

Kiselica, M.S. (1995). *Multicultural counseling with teenage fathers.* Thousand Oaks, CA: Sage.

Korman, M. (1974). National conference on levels and patterns of professional training in psychology: Major themes. *American Psychologist, 29,* 301-313.

Langston, D. (1995). Tired of playing monopoly? In M.L. Andersen and P.H. Collins (Eds.), *Race, class, and gender: An anthology* (pp. 100-110). San Francisco: Wadsworth.

Ledesma, A. (1997). Presentation to the Diversity Project Committee. University of Denver Graduate School of Social Work, Denver, CO.

Leigh, J.W. (1998). *Communicating for cultural competence.* Boston: Allyn and Bacon.

Leighton, A. (1982). Relevant generic issues. In A. Gaw (Ed.), *Cross-cultural psychiatry.* Littleton, MA: Wright-PSG.

Marcus, E. (1993). *Is it a choice? Answers to 300 of the most frequently asked questions about gays and lesbians.* San Francisco: Harper.

Miller, J. (1991). The development of women's sense of self. In J. Jordan, A. Kaplan, J. Miller, I. Stiver, and J. Surrey (Eds.), *Women's growth in connection* (pp. 11-26). New York: Guilford.

Paniagua, F.A. (1994). *Assessing and treating culturally diverse clients: A practical guide.* Thousand Oaks, CA: Sage.

Pedersen, P.B. (Ed.) (1991). Multiculturalism as a fourth force in counseling [Special issue]. *Journal of Counseling and Development, 70*(1).

Pedersen, P.B. (1997). *Culture-centered counseling interventions: Striving for accuracy.* Thousand Oaks, CA: Sage.

Pedersen, P.B., Draguns, J.G., Lonne, W.J., and Trimble, J.E. (1996). *Counseling across cultures.* Thousand Oaks, CA: Sage.

Pedersen, P.B. and Marsella, A. (1982). The ethical crisis for cross-cultural counseling and therapy. *Professional Psychology, 13*(3), 492-500.

Pinderhughes, E. (1989). *Understanding race, ethnicity, and power: The key to efficacy in clinical practice.* New York: Free Press.

Ponterotto, J. (1988). Racial consciousness development among White counselor trainees. *Journal of Multicultural Counseling and Development, 16*(2), 146-156.

Ponterotto, J., Casas, J.M., Suzuki, L., and Alexander, C. (1995). *Handbook of multicultural counseling.* Thousand Oaks, CA: Sage.

Pope-Davis, D.B. and Coleman, H.L.K. (Eds.) (1996). *Multicultural counseling competencies: Assessment, education and training, and supervision.* Thousand Oaks, CA: Sage.

Quintana, S.M. and Bernal, M.E. (1995). Ethnic minority training in counseling psychology: Comparisons with clinical psychology and proposed standards. *The Counseling Psychologist, 23*(1), 102-121.

Ruth, S. (1990). *Issues in feminism: An introduction to women's studies.* Mountain View, CA: Mayfield.

Schmitz, C. (1998). Presentation to the Diversity Project Committee. University of Denver Graduate School of Social Work, Denver, CO.

Schniedewind, N. and Cathers, K. (1996). Open minds to equality: A sequenced approach for teaching about diversity. Presentation at the Sixth Annual Conference of the National Association for Multicultural Education, November 9, St. Paul, MN.

Schniedewind, N. and Davidson, E. (1997). *Open minds to equality: A sourcebook of learning activities to promote race, sex, class, age, language, ability, sexual orientation and religious equity.* Des Moines, IA: Allyn and Bacon.

Sue, D.W., Arredondo, P., and McDavis, R.J. (1995). Multicultural counseling competencies and standards: A call to the profession. In J.G. Ponterotto, J.M. Casas, L.A. Suzuki, and C.M. Alexander (Eds.), *Handbook of multicultural counseling* (pp. 624-640). Thousand Oaks, CA: Sage.

Sue, D. and Sue, D. (1990). *Counseling the culturally different* (Second edition). New York: John Wiley.

Sue, S. and Zane, N. (1987). The role of culture and cultural techniques in psychotherapy: A critique and reformation. *American Psychologist, 42*(1), 37-45.

Williams, T.K. (1992). Prism lives: Identity of binational Amerasians. In M.P.P. Root (Ed.), *Racially mixed people in America* (pp. 280-303). Newbury Park, CA: Sage.

Chapter 9

Are All Therapists Alike? Revisiting Research About the Use of Self in Therapy

Meri L. Shadley

Searching for the Atman among the Samanas, he [Siddhartha] tried to escape the Self, only to learn that it is the Self that he must discover and come to know. Now in the midst of seeking a teacher, he "has discovered that comforting secret that a teacher is unnecessary."

S. Kopp
If You Meet the Buddha on the Road,
Kill Him, 1972, p. 41

In Herman Hesse's (1951) story of Siddhartha, ultimately "one must find the source within one's own self" (p. 8). A major conclusion of a multidimensional study of family therapists conducted in the mid-1980s was that this is the case with therapists, too. They frequently experience intense emotional reactions to their clinical work. How therapists respond to this intensity and use themselves therapeutically is unique and individualized. One's own personal and professional experiences become the ultimate guide to effective use of *self.**

When this research was originally completed, the author anticipated much would be written in the next few years about the use of self in therapy. As the field of family therapy had evolved, the focus

---

*Whenever the term *self* is first employed in a chapter as part of the concept of the use of self in therapy, it is italicized to call attention to its special use.

had become very "model-oriented." It seemed only natural for the pendulum to move to therapeutic relationship issues. This did not prove to be the case. Although articles about models and theories have decreased in number, Naden et al. (1997) found that 61 percent of all writings in the field between 1980 and 1995 centered on clinical issues. Sprenkle and Bailey (1996) reported that clinical manuscript submissions to the *Journal of Marital and Family Therapy* between 1993 and 1996 had increased by approximately 50 percent, but submissions about training had decreased by 60 percent.

Obviously the advent of managed care demands that the family therapy field focus on assessment and intervention. Being less theory driven but even more expedient in clinical work has become the calling of the times. The field's attendance to problem- and solution-based models also keeps our training focused primarily on client change. How therapists develop and the methods they utilize to most effectively use "themselves" have apparently become less applicable to education in our time-sensitive therapy era. Fewer than 10 percent of the training and professional issues articles encountered by Naden et al. (1997) were about the self of the therapist.

With so little written about this topic over the past ten years, what are we to surmise? Do the original results of this study remain? Does the self of the therapist matter in the practice of family therapy as we understand it today? The answer depends on whether we are seeking another pendulum swing or whether we are searching for integrative information about what supports efficient and successful outcomes with clients.

The foremost result of the original study (Shadley, 1987) was that the manner in which therapists made use of themselves in therapy had less to do with their theoretical stance than with personal realities such as gender, developmental stage, and personal attributes. This made psychological sense then and continues to do so today. Lynn Hoffman (1998) most recently suggested that "setting aside the model" to look at "common practices" allows a tapestry to emerge. The tapestry of common practices detailed in this use-of-self study remains as vivid today as it was when first described.

Although this study has not been replicated, the results have been discussed with student practitioners and experienced clinicians alike. Other writers have also detailed their own thoughts and studies on the potency of personal life experiences (Catherall and Pinsoff, 1987; Guerin and Hubbard, 1987; Wilcoxon, Walker, and Hovestadt, 1989). Consistently, therapists continue to find and detail how their personal styles and life experiences frame the manner in which they use themselves in therapy. As the feminist perspective has looked at family therapy models and practices (Goldner, 1985; Hare-Mustin, 1987; Knudson-Martin, 1994), gender is also indicated to influence therapist practices. And finally, developmental stage is frequently determined to be a relevant variable in how one "is" in therapy with client families (Dreyfus and Dreyfus, 1986; Falicov, 1998).

The picture that emerged from this study's thematic analysis of use-of-self patterns is similar to an old newsreel. Initially viewed in black and white, the information was not startling, but it did highlight important information of the day. As we review these news briefs, we can more clearly see how history is significant in today's world and perhaps anticipate some of tomorrow's possibilities.

Hoffman stated (1998, p. 154) that Virginia Satir was "a voice so ahead of its time that only now can it be heard." Perhaps, then, it is time to "rehear" research that supports her contention that "the person of the therapist is the center point around which successful therapy revolves" (Satir, 1987, p. 24). As we revisit this "old news," it is important to remember that some therapists never saw the original broadcast. What might seem obvious to the seasoned clinician may bring clarity to a "grainy" image for our newer colleagues.

Developing a congruent use-of-self style can be difficult and initially uncomfortable. Attempting to understand how family therapists discover, change, and effectively use themselves clinically, the researcher inquired into issues concerning the therapeutic relationship. Subjects overwhelmingly reported that their own personal history—cultural and familial realities and events—as well as their professional experiences during and after training influenced their therapeutic style. For some therapists, their style of using self incorporated accepting self as a fellow human who offers more than professional expertise. Others reported keeping the personal self more insulated while sharing their professional skill. Still others indicated that acknowledging their personal vulnerabilities and capabilities provided clarity about which parts of themselves to withhold and which to use in order to retain strength, health, and integrity.

This multidimensional investigation into family therapists' use of self was part of broad-based research on the professional development process. The thematic analysis and quotes detailed in this chapter were derived from semistructured interviews of thirty therapists across three regions of the United States (Reno/San Francisco Bay Area, Chicago, and New England/New York). From this section of the research, themes about therapists' use of self broke down into four general areas: (1) therapists' definition and awareness of self, (2) qualities considered critical to therapeutic relationships, (3) personal characteristics related to therapeutic use of self, and (4) use-of-self dimensions and styles. Differences across developmental stage, gender, or theoretical orientation that remain important to today's family therapist will be detailed. Otherwise, the case examples will be descriptive and attempt to show the tapestry of how therapists use themselves effectively in therapy.

THERAPISTS' DEFINITION
AND AWARENESS OF SELF

Consistently, the question, "What is the self of the family therapist?" provided the most difficulty for subjects. Typically, the answers were filled with complex thoughts, incomplete sentences, pauses, and a quiet, almost reverential, sound quality. Many started their answers with a statement such as, "That's really hard to describe. I've not tried to put this into words before because it seems like something beyond words. Hmm. Hmm. Hmm. Let's see. Well, it's . . . it's all levels of self. Includes all kinds of awarenesses—spiritual, emotional, psychic, physical, mental—expressed in different ways."

Within each personalized definition, interviewees frequently included a variation of one of the following phrases: "All systems interacting," "everything within a dynamic interplay," "all life's experiences transformed," "patterns formed by past, present, and future," "natural responsiveness to each context," "integrity of all self parts," and "the essence of who or what I am as a person."

Even with slight variations, this researcher's premise that the professional self is a constantly evolving system which is changed by the conscious and unconscious interplay of the numerous systems impacting the clinician held true. Emphasizing the belief that the personal and professional selves cannot be separated into distinct entities, Tony states: "This is who I am and there is a certain need I have for the client to be able to organize around that. I mean I can change it. I can access different parts, but still only within a limit." Statements such as this suggest that while the professional self might need to be a controlled version or modification of the personal self, the two selves are intricately interwoven.

CRITICAL ASPECTS OF THERAPEUTIC RELATIONSHIPS

Based upon Carl Whitaker's belief that the self "gains in definition and potential" when it is in "communion with others in relationship" (Neill and Kniskern, 1982, p. 20), another relevant issue is: "What personal qualities are critical to one's use of self within therapeutic relationships?" Although this question was not asked directly, it emerged from the interview questions about how therapists use themselves in therapeutic relationships. Since many subjects referred to their own qualities of being with clients and qualities that came out of the therapeutic situation itself, both of these are interwoven within the described results.

The information given by the subjects sorted into nine categories. The first four—empathy, warmth, humor, and genuineness—are well-known qualities that have been found to be highly related to positive clinical outcomes in family therapy as well as individual therapy (Alexander et al., 1976; Gurman and Kniskern, 1978). Descriptors used by the interviewees include the following:

Empathy—understanding, sensitivity, caring, patience, compassion, willingness to listen because of similarity to personal issues, feeling an affinity with another person's situation

Warmth—nurturing, sharing, accepting, able to be touched

Humor—playful, clowning, making fun of situation or self

Genuineness—humanness, openness, naturalness, congruence, responsiveness, using whole person rather than just expert

The additional aspects—respect, trust, connection, encouragement, and objectivity—sorted from the following word examples:

> *Connection*—attachment, resonate, open one's self to pain, be part of a whole with the family, invest oneself
>
> *Encouragement*—challenge, confront, enable, want success, push for goals, desire movement
>
> *Trust*—create safe environment, go with the flow, use one's intuitiveness, sense the spiritual relationship
>
> *Respect*—being awed or inspired by the client family's resilience, politeness, not provoke intensity unnecessarily
>
> *Objectivity*—setting limits, maintaining distance, being selective, reserved, wanting another's picture or view

The interview dialogues frequently indicated the same category several times, yet most of the therapists found two or three categories particularly valuable to their use of self. Examples include:

> I try to be me—open, human, nonjudgmental, confrontive, up front, humorous—and use my high energy.
>
> I believe that it is important to show respect for clients. Outrageous behavior such as yelling, etc. is disrespectful. . . . I like to share my understanding, humor, and warmer feelings . . . . People who succeed in this field have a lifelong history of connecting with people.
>
> I've been told that I'm able to create a sense of trust very quickly. I know I'm comfortable moving back and forth between confronting and understanding people. Maybe people feel they're safe with me in therapy because I make them come to me. I see myself as a tool and it's up to them to decide how they are going to use me.

Probably the most important research result in this section of the study was that therapists from all orientations found genuineness to be one of the most important qualities for effective use of self. It was also interesting to note that very few of the subjects mentioned objectivity without making a comment about one of the other qualities. For example, one subject stated that she typically was "reserved, but connected."

PERSONAL CHARACTERISTICS
RELATED TO USE-OF-SELF PATTERNS

Along with the qualities mentioned above, many of the interviewees indicated that some of their own personal characteristics were a vital part of their professional way of relating to client families. How therapists deal with their own patterns of achieving success, being responsible, or being intimate frequently gives direction to their manner of using themselves in therapy. An example of how one therapist understands the interface between his personal and professional style is indicated in the following quote:

> I was a pretty intense person from the beginning. I was always trying to make sense of the world, always trying to find the way in which I connect. The foundation, now, to my way of being a therapist and what I believe is important in training is to learn about me and to be free to connect with other people.

Besides discussing the commonalities in personal and professional styles, many interviewees indicated that certain traits were simultaneously both a strength and a weakness in their professional work. An ultraresponsible therapist who had enjoyed professional success by taking charge of situations stated, "As this aspect of my style began to get out of hand in both my personal and professional life, I realized I was using too much of a good thing." The double-edged sword of a personal history of helping others through patience and tolerant acceptance is confirmed by another subject when she states: "My ability to be nurturing and to not give up on people is great; however, sometimes I go too far. Depending on the situation, I may have to balance it with prodding humor and provocativeness if there is going to be enough therapeutic tension for people to change."

Again, it is only after some personal and professional experience that therapists reported being better able to adjust to their own

idiosyncrasies within therapeutic relationships. Any personal characteristic can be useful or detrimental depending upon the circumstances. Using too much or too little of any personal trait, whether it
be nurturance, problem solving, detachment, responsibility, acceptance, and so on, can hinder a client. As well, it can inhibit the
development of therapist as a versatile clinician.

Dimensions Related to Use of Self

If the therapist's use of self is as much a technique as it is a
quality of relating, then it is important to begin looking at how
various therapists actually make use of this "prime instrument"
(Kramer, 1985). What and how thoughts, feelings, and actions are
incorporated into therapeutic style is critical to understanding and
facilitating the growth of therapists. The question, "How do you use
yourself within your therapeutic interactions?" elicited many responses on the theme of self-disclosure. In searching for patterns or
styles of sharing one's self with client families, several dimensions
emerged as important to the interviewees' comfort with and tendency to be self-disclosive.

One dimension continually referenced was verbal versus nonverbal disclosures of who the therapist was as a "real" person. Most
of the subjects felt that paralleling their own life with the client
family's life was a useful strategy. Although many used the technique of verbally sharing their commonalities with clients, a large
number of the subjects stated they did not always feel comfortable
with such verbal references. For example, Sydney and her husband
both worked out of their home. She believed that the personal
exposure emerging from her work environment allowed client families to visually see parallels between their own lives and that of the
therapist. Thus, Sydney believed that specific information about her
life was best left unsaid.

Many of the subjects suggested that they more freely shared
nonvisible parallels with clients. Examples of such parallels were
the therapist's struggles with being the oldest sibling, being a step-
parent, caring for an ill parent or a new baby, dealing with conflicting responsibilities, and personal or professional transitions. It is
interesting to note that few subjects mentioned interactional exam-

ples. Apparently, therapists are more likely to openly discuss individual parallels than relationship parallels.

Those who tended to talk of personal relationship examples began to delineate another important dimension. These subjects frequently discussed their comfort with relaying past versus present personal issues. Some, such as Mary, felt that sharing current situations was "too hard, emotionally." Most subjects agreed that sharing relevant past information was usually very effective without being too personally distressful.

If interviewees did not tend to share either past or present personal facts with their clients, they typically talked of several other ways of using themselves within therapeutic relationships. Some spoke of sharing their impressions, opinions, and/or feelings regarding the client's situation, whereas others stated that they frequently used movies, television programs, books, a friend's or another client's situations, and anecdotes to parallel and/or relate to client families. Rob stated that "it allows me to be more outrageous or intense in my emotional behavior when I've exposed fewer facts about myself."

Rob, as well as some other interviewees, indicated a comfort with sharing personal reactions to the therapeutic relationship itself. Again, some felt comfortable sharing themselves overtly, while others believed that they were able to convey these reactions nonverbally. The "freedom to share here-and-now emotions" such as tears and laughter, as well as talking directly about their response to the client and/or the process, was frequently referenced. Sydney, reiterating her comfort with showing rather than talking about herself, stated: "I try to feel what they feel with enough distance that there is a separateness as well. It means opening myself up to pain. . . . I try to provide nurturance and warmth through unspoken emotional arms."

Use-of-Self Styles

Based upon the dimensions detailed above, a continuum of self-disclosure styles was delineated:

> *Intimate interaction*—Tends to share self through verbal and nonverbal expressions of therapeutic reactions. References to present or past personal issues are likely.

Reactive response—Typically expresses both nonverbal and verbal feelings of emotional connectedness within therapeutic relationships, but generally does not verbalize personal life details or parallels.

Controlled response—Inclined to maintain a slight distance by limiting self-disclosures to past experiences, anecdotes, non-verbalized feelings, or literary parallels.

Reflective feedback—The exposure of self occurs through questioning or challenging families and by giving impressions. Seldom shares personal information or strong emotional reactions.

As can be seen from these four descriptions, the styles represent a three-dimensional continuum of self-disclosive behaviors. The first dimension relates to verbal versus nonverbal self-disclosure, while the second dimension represents present versus past disclosures. The third dimension links personal disclosure to other person or object references. The primary behaviors exemplified within each of the four styles typically include the entire continuum of possibilities within one or two of the three dimensions and only partial aspects of the other dimension(s). For example, operating within an intimate interaction style, a therapist self-discloses verbally and nonverbally about the present and the past. Other focused references, however, are infrequent when compared to personal self-disclosures. In contrast, when therapists use themselves in a controlled response style, they are more likely to verbally share other-oriented disclosures and past personal information than present personal feelings and facts with client families.

From the descriptions of styles detailed earlier, it is apparent that variations in ways to share oneself with client families are commonplace. Remembering that, depending on the context, therapists actually use a combination or variety of styles, it was surprising to discover that the interviewees tended more toward one style than the others. From their discussions, then, a present predominant style was indicated and thus attributed to each interviewee. To better understand the application of these four stylistic patterns, we will examine some of the quotes from subjects about their therapeutic use of self.

Intimate Interaction Style

The intimate interaction use-of-self style is the most self-disclosive of the four patterns. Many of the subjects indicating this style discussed their tendencies to be both verbally active and interactive with clients and to "not be just an expert operating, but a person trying to connect inside the family." Joan declared her reasoning for professional intimacy in this way:

> I just try to be me most of the time. I share my feelings, confront them, push to succeed, get connected, be funny, everything that's me as a human. Sometimes my cotherapist and I act out in front of the family. If we're fighting, I don't believe we should hide it—after all, maybe they can learn something from it. Also, most of them know what's going on with me. For example, recently I had a miscarriage and almost everybody knew it. That was okay; that's what was real in my life right then. Allowing families to give to me felt pretty good, too. For many of my families, allowing themselves to care that much and want to help is not such a bad thing.

As can be seen from this excerpt of Joan's interview, she verbally shared aspects of her personal life outside of therapy as well as her relationship with her cotherapist and the families themselves. Although she talked most vividly about using present examples, she is also willing to share past experiences if she believes they might be helpful to solving the family's dilemma.

Judith, a more strategically oriented therapist, clearly expresses her intimate interaction use-of-self style when she states:

> Since I try to limit my work with a family to ten sessions, I believe in using everything I can. I'm direct, up front, and goal oriented, so I use as many examples as I can. I share my own history, my beliefs, what's happening with my cotherapist right now, my movements, everything. Whatever it takes to build our relationship and yet, to get them moving so that they don't become dependent. I also tend to force emotions—sometimes by using my own and sometimes by just allowing the sadness or anger to come out.

As can be seen by the quotes detailed herein, the intimate interaction use-of-self style allows therapists to present and share a great deal of who they are as persons. The subjects describing this self-disclosive style did so for a variety of reasons, yet they all indicated a comfort with such openness in therapeutic relationships.

Reactive Response Style

The use-of-self style that employs expressing verbally and non-verbally one's connection with the client family's situation and feelings, yet not sharing much about one's own present personal life, is the reactive response style. Doug described how "sometimes I pull out an old picture of my parents or grandparents and use that to help them bring their families of origin into the therapy room," but he tended not to discuss his children even though he had pictures of them in his office. In opposition, he described how "when a client has had a significant impact on my life—either by their personal courage to change or their resourcefulness, I thank them for expanding my life. This type of sharing is real important to me." Although this self-disclosure is very intimate, Doug protects his personal life by not detailing specifically how he has been affected. Thus, his sharing is more other-focused than personal-focused.

Bryan detailed a use-of-self style very similar to Doug's. He stated, "I don't reveal much about myself. I keep the focus on therapy and the relationship right there. I do use my own emotional reactions—for information and for discussion." He continues by saying, "Depending upon the client, I may talk about how what they are doing or how their situation affects me. It depends upon whether they're ready to hear or not." To better understand the expectations of relationship inherent within a reactive response use-of-self style, three female family therapists who are also psychologists are quoted below.

Sydney stated, "I trust my intuition about self-disclosure. . . . [and] generally my intuition tells me not to share much personally. It's important that the clients not worry about my feelings." After establishing a family of her own and encountering a few critical experiences related to talking with her clients about her life, Sydney changed her use-of-self style. She stated, "I used to disclose more but now, with more experience, I disclose less. I need to keep a separation between my personal and my professional life." The cultural expectations of living in New England also seem to influence her decision about therapeutic relationships. She said, "Boston is a very traditional therapy place, so I always think about self-disclosures before I do one."

Andrea and Monique (both West Coast therapists) also indicate a reluctance to disclose much verbally. Andrea finds that by being "clear about my boundaries, I use myself in terms of allowing them to use me in any way they need to to work through something." She tries to be "careful about what I say, when I disclose" and instead to "just be present in a lot of other ways." Monique also talks of being present in other than verbal ways. She states:

> I give myself to my clients. I don't self-disclose much about the details of my life, but I do show my way of being—the way I respond, my empathy, my ability to share in their pain. I resonate in the "I-thou" connection. . . . There are times when there is something very sacred about being a therapist. Something about catching people in their deepest core. Just in the process of being together, something happens that may not have anything to do with therapy—almost a sacred communication. It's stronger than anything else that happens.

Therapists who have a reactive response use-of-self style obviously feel more comfortable sharing their person with clients than details of their personal lives. They appear to share very deeply on an emotional level and thus seem to need the distance provided by less detailed self-disclosures than found in therapists using an intimate interaction style.

Controlled Response Style

When therapists maintain a distance with clients by using disclosures from primarily nonpersonal or past situations, they are operating within a controlled response use-of-self style. The subjects indicating this style detailed a variety of methods and rationales that were consistent with their own characteristics. A few interviewees' statements exemplify these very personal patterns. Louise, for example, uses her familiar role of being the "funny family clown" and her cultural background when working with clients. Through the use of this role and her "cute British expressions," she can show herself rather than speak about herself. She feels that this allows her to be "not so close that I'm too revealed," but use things that "come natural and are pretty obvious." Rob, also, tends not to disclose details about his life but feels comfortable exposing parts of himself to clients. "Instead of disclosing facts," he says, "I tell lots of stories about people I know or the way I think about something. I show my 'crazies' as directly as I can 'cause I really enjoy having a good time and being as active as I can."

The freedom to be creative and active was one factor expressed as important to being less personally self-disclosive. Joe, like Rob, enjoys telling stories or anecdotes about himself and others. He describes his newfound creativity in this way: "I'm much more innovative now than I used to be and part of that is because I let my intuition take charge. I let myself go more easily if I haven't revealed too much detail about myself—it just makes me freer."

Sheila expresses another reason for not revealing many present details of her personal life with clients. She states:

> I have a sense of reserve to protect myself from getting hooked by my clients or their stuff. I will use some of my own family-of-origin work as an example, but of course, it's only those parts that I'm free with now. Most of the time, I'll use an example from somewhere else—like another client, an article I've read, a workshop I attended, a movie, or something else.

From reviewing these patterns of using more distant examples to parallel clients' lives, it appears that such a style provides opportunity in other ways of using themselves. These subjects indicated that they believed being personally revealed hindered their creative freedom. They enjoy being involved with their clients and tend to be either very playfully or intellectually challenging of themselves, the clients, and the therapeutic relationships.

Reflective Feedback Style

The use-of-self style exhibiting the smallest amount of personal self-disclosure is the reflective feedback style. Many of the subjects operating from this style believe, like David, that "something I work on before a case is to be less attached—you don't depend so much on outcome to determine whether or not you are a good therapist that way." He suggests that such detachment "frees you up to be more effective, challenge more, and use yourself more." Arlene, a recently trained therapist, concurs with David. Her focus is on "saying what is." By remaining somewhat aloof she believes she is more able to use herself in "the most important way—making the implicit explicit. It's most important to say what you see and I can do that better if I'm not self-disclosive and thus, more personally vulnerable."

Dean, however, suggests that this style of using himself does not always protect him from being vulnerable. It does allow him to remain focused on the client, though. He states:

> I model risk-taking behavior by asking direct questions and letting myself be wrong. If they say "wrong" then I can move out and back in again later. After I get a sense of their patterns I share my feelings about it—that's self-disclosure to me. . . . I just go with the flow and challenge people with my energy, my questions, and my observations, but I try to close off my relationships so that they don't interfere with my personal life.

Retaining personal distance in order to not "get hooked" or to deal with one's own achievement issues, of course, frequently establishes a particular role within the therapeutic relationship. For many strategic therapists, this is represented by one's position of power. For example, Greg talked of how being non-self-disclosive supports the role of the therapist as on top of the hierarchy. "Maintaining a top position cannot always be done if you're sharing lots of details about your own life," says Greg. "I want to be powerful in terms of helping 'cause I love therapy, love brainstorming, and love resolving things." Again, like Dean, Greg finds that sharing what he thinks is going on is definitely using himself. He enjoys "challenging them with a new way of looking at things—my way of seeing," and it "supports my desire to educate at the same time as I do therapy."

When therapists use themselves primarily in a reflective feedback style, they tend to only share their impressions of and goals for the client family. The personal distance made available by such a style apparently supports strong risk taking in other ways. As these statements suggest, to challenge people directly about the way they are behaving within their relationships is certainly another way of putting yourself on the line. For many therapists, the protective buffer of "not being known too intimately allows me to push further than I might otherwise feel comfortable going."

Since these comments would indicate that most therapists using a reflective feedback style came from a structural/strategic theoretical orientation, it is important to understand the patterns that were actually found across the comparison groupings. The next section, then, will review all the styles across all the critical groupings.

Use-of-Self Style Comparisons

Looking at self-disclosure styles across the demographic factors of training program attended, degree, marital status, and parenting status, it appeared that all styles were fairly equally represented. Specific differences were found when viewing these styles across therapeutic orientation, gender, birth order, and clinical experience.

In terms of theoretical orientation, male therapists working within a structural/strategic orientation indicated a high usage of the reflective feedback style. Therapists who identified themselves as following primarily Bowen family systems theory appeared to favor either the controlled response or the reactive response styles. Other than these two specific indications, it seems that the family therapy model followed did not determine the manner in which therapists used themselves therapeutically.

The most interesting difference was that while the majority of males (62 percent) were found to use the controlled response or reflective feedback style of self-disclosure, more females (65 percent) used the reactive response or intimate interaction styles. Only one man indicated that he responded primarily within the intimate interaction style and only one woman within the reflective feedback style. The woman, Arlene, a graduate student throughout her clinical years since family therapy training, stated that her style was changing to include more direct intimacy.

When looking at self-disclosure tendencies across the therapists' birth order, two interesting consistencies were found. First, although most birth order positions were found in each of the four styles, all but one of the subjects within the intimate interaction style were firstborn. Second, subjects who were the last born in their family of origin were typically less likely to reveal personal details than therapists of other birth order positions.

Finally, several differences were found when these styles were related to the therapists' clinical experience. One of the most interesting results was that the reflective feedback style was used primarily by therapists who were less than thirty-five years of age, whereas almost 50 percent of the therapists over the age of forty-six used a controlled response style. Therapists between the ages of thirty-five and forty-five were fairly evenly distributed across all the styles other than reflective feedback. Since many of the mature-stage therapists entered the family therapy field later in life, these results might be slightly misleading unless we look specifically at the subjects' years of clinical experience.

All therapists with less than seven years experience indicated either a controlled response or reflective feedback style. Female therapists with less than six years experience indicated using a controlled response or reflective feedback style while those averaging eleven years experience described using an intimate interaction or reactive response style.

Critical Events Affecting Use-of-Self Styles

Although a major focus of the interview was to determine interface issues in therapists' professional and personal lives, it was still surprising to discover that personal transitions and/or tragedies were the circumstances most likely to induce therapeutic style changes. Numerous factors affect how these family therapists made clinical use of themselves as persons, but some specific life and death events within their own immediate family were typically mentioned as having the strongest impact on professional changes.

Having children, for example, pushed some therapists to withhold more of their energy from therapy so they could attend better to the pressures of their personal relationships. Several subjects also indicated that having children made them more understanding and patient with others as well as less critical and competitive with themselves. In addition, many subjects stated that being a parent gave them more freedom to self-disclose and to feel more comfort-able with their own idiosyncrasies. One subject stated, "Besides becoming more tolerant, understanding, and accepting, I'm less rigid and less idealistic. . . . My therapeutic style fluctuates more and I'm much more willing to share myself with people. It doesn't seem as dangerous now."

If the birth of children can change a clinician's sense of danger or the "life and death voltages" (DeWitt and Shadley, 1981) inherent in family therapy, the death of a parent is particularly significant to changes in a therapist's use-of-self style. As might be expected, therapists experiencing these personal losses became much more interested in building a client family's relationship than solving their problems. Terry mentioned that after losing his grandmother and mother, he began to feel like the problem-solving focus really missed the boat. He felt that "people need to be connected!"

Besides focusing on the emotional connection between family members, interviewees also noticed that their own ability or interest in being emotionally intimate with clients increased. Many of these therapists found themselves more willing to share their personal reactions in sessions and to push for intensity in clients' therapeutic work. Finally, subjects talked of how the experience of loss caused them to reevaluate their priorities. Annie, for one, stated, "I've felt a need to take better care of myself. I do not have the energy to change others 'cause I can't stay as detached as I used to. . . . Now I'm more intimate, more confident, and more exhausted."

Interviewed therapists mentioned that other factors affected the way in which they used themselves, but no other factors were discussed as frequently or by as broad a range of subjects.

SUMMARY

In searching for similarities and differences in various family thera-pists' use of self, this investigation discovered more commonalities within the field than has been indicated by previous school-specific research. For example, connection, encouragement, and respect were invariably mentioned as critical to forming trusting interactions with client families, along with the well-known relationship aspects of em-pathy, warmth, humor, and genuineness. Therapists, no matter what their orientation, believed that an assortment of these therapeutic qualities were conducive to effective use of self. They also agreed that since the personal and professional selves interweave, self-awareness is very important to being a competent family therapist.

From this study's small sample of a cross-section of clinicians in the mid-1980s, theoretical orientation appears to be only one of several critical factors contributing to a therapist's use of self. Gender, amount of clinical experience, birth order, and significant life events also play an important role in therapeutic style. The most outstanding result of this study is that gender, rather than theoretical orientation, is most clearly connected to the various ways in which these clinicians make use of themselves in their therapeutic relationships. No matter what label they used to describe their orientation, female interviewees indicated that they frequently used personal life examples and/or present feelings with client families. Males, on the other hand, tended to focus on other people's feelings and situations when relating to or paralleling their clients' experiences. These gender differences were particularly notable when structural/strategic blend-oriented therapists were compared. Not only did female therapists within this orientation value the quality of genuineness more highly than their male counterparts, but they were much more likely to use an openly revealing self-disclosure style.

When gender was combined with professional experience level, the controlled response use-of-self style was most frequently found with the experienced male therapists (no matter the orientation), and the reactive response style was used by the most experienced female therapists.

Differences in how male and female family therapists' styles changed with added experience also became more evident when these two components were combined. Just as age affected men's tendencies to become more personally intimate, added experience appeared to allow them to become slightly more disclosive professionally. Less experienced females, apparently affected by the strong male voice in family therapy training programs, tended to share very little about their personal selves—even if it fit their personal intimacy style. As their clinical experience increased and they found a more "feminine style" of doing therapy, female therapists became much more openly self-disclosive. The most experienced female therapists, however, stated that they were more likely to make an emotional connection than a verbal one. One advanced therapist's statement, "I use me more now, but in some ways that is less" represents a reaction to this shift in use of self.

Although family therapists may initially be attracted to therapeutic styles that are symmetrical to their personal styles, they are "constantly evolving, changing mortals" (DeWitt and Shadley, 1981), who develop new skills and interests along their career-growth paths. The personal life events of becoming a parent or losing a significant loved one were most frequently mentioned as having a strong influence on changes in one's professional direction and therapeutic style. This result is particularly important because it is probably one of the least-discussed factors in training programs.

The interrelated issues of personal styles, training experiences, and developmental factors affecting use-of-self styles clarify the truth of Siddhartha's search in the growth of family therapists. As they discover themselves, they no longer need to seek a teacher. Monique states, in a different way, how this works for her (and perhaps, how it ultimately works for others):

> Once something is integrated, it becomes a part of myself and there really isn't any separation between the skill or technique and me. Maybe the use of self is the way that I transform this approach, technique, or skill into my way of being. . . . It includes everything that is the core of me. The part of myself that sort of blends with the universal.

REFERENCES

Alexander, J., Barton, C., Schiavo, R., and Parsons, B. (1976). Systems-behavioral intervention with families of delinquents: Therapist characteristics, family behavior and outcome. *Journal of Counseling and Clinical Psychology*, 44(4), 656-664.

Catherall, D.R. and Pinsoff, W.M. (1987). The impact of the therapist's personal family life on the ability to establish viable therapeutic alliances in family and marital therapy. *Journal of Psychotherapy and the Family*, 3(2), 135-160.

DeWitt, W.M. and Shadley, M.L. (1981). *A kaleidoscope of family systems: A trainee manual*. Reno, NV. Unpublished manuscript.

Dreyfus, H.L. and Dreyfus, S.E. (1986). *Mind over machine*. New York: Free Press.

Falicov, C. (1998). Commentary on Hoffman: From rigid borderlines to fertile borderlands: Reconfiguring family therapy. *Journal of Marital and Family Therapy*, 24(2), 157-164.

Goldner, V. (1985). Feminism and family therapy. *Family Process*, 24(1), 31-47.

Guerin, P.J. and Hubbard, I.M. (1987). Impact of therapist's personal family system and clinical work. *Journal of Psychotherapy and the Family*, 3(2), 47-60.

Gurman, A.S. and Kniskern, D.P. (1978). Research on marital and family therapy: Progress, perspective, and prospect. In S. Garfield and A. Bergin (Eds.), *Handbook of psychotherapy and behavior change*. New York: Wiley.

Hare-Mustin, R. (1987). The problem of gender in family therapy theory. *Family Process*, 26(1), 15-27.

Hesse, H. (1951). *Siddhartha* (trans. Hilda Rosner). New York: New Directions. (Original work published 1922).

Hoffman, L. (1998). Setting aside the model in family therapy. *Journal of Marital and Family Therapy*, 24(2), 145-156.

Knudson-Martin, C. (1994). The female voice: Applications to Bowen's family systems theory. *Journal of Marital and Family Therapy*, 20(1), 35-46.

Kopp, S. (1972). *If you meet the Buddha on the road, kill him*. Palo Alto, CA: Science and Behavior Books.

Kramer, J. (1985). *Family interfaces: Transgenerational patterns*. New York: Brunner/Mazel.

Naden, M., Rasmussen, K., Morrissette, P., and Johns, K. (1997). Sources of influence and topic areas in family therapy: Trends in three major journals. *Journal of Marital and Family Therapy*, 23(4), 389-398.

Neill, J.R. and Kniskern, D.P. (Eds.) (1982). *From psyche to system: The evolving therapy of Carl Whitaker*. New York: Guildford Press.

Satir, V. (1987). The therapist story. *Journal of Psychotherapy and the Family*, 3 (1), 17-26.

Shadley, M.L. (1987). The interweaving self: A systemic exploration of the patterns connecting family therapists' families of origin, training experiences, and professional use of self styles. Doctoral dissertation, Saybrook Institute. *Dissertation Abstracts International*, 48-09B, p. 2795.

Sprenkle, D. and Bailey, C.E. (1996). Editor's report. *Journal of Marital and Family Therapy*, 22(1), 155-160.

Wilcoxon, S.A., Walker, M.R., and Hovestadt, A.J. (1989). Counselor effectiveness and family of origin experiences: A significant relationship. *Counseling and Values*, 33(3), 225-229.

Chapter 10

Differential Use of Self by Therapists Following Their Own Trauma Experiences

Judith F. Bula

INTRODUCTION

Trauma is a universal experience. It is no respecter of rich or poor, of profession or occupation, of country of origin or family of origin, of talent or personal purpose. "In short, anyone can be traumatized, from the most well-adjusted to the most troubled" (Everstine and Everstine, 1993, p. 7). And when the one experiencing the trauma is the therapist, the professional helper, the social worker, the clinician, what then?

> Traumatic events call into question basic human relationships. They breach the attachments of family, friendship, love, and community. *They shatter the construction of the self that is formed and sustained in relation to others.* They undermine the belief systems that give meaning to human experience. . . . Traumatic events have primary effects not only on the psychological structures of the self but also on the systems of attachment and meaning that link individual and community. [Emphasis added] (Herman, 1992, p. 51)

How does a therapist use herself or himself differently as a professional helper when that self, upon which so much of the work depends, has just been shattered? Responses to trauma do vary from individual to individual. Some describe the shock, the denial, perhaps the flashbacks or mental confusion. Others speak about the need for withdrawal, for more structure, or for time to grieve the losses associated with a traumatic experience. Still others describe a "waking up to reality" or "getting unstuck." Some take on self-blame, possibly from a need to make sense out of what has happened or perhaps from the frequency of the message in a society that believes the individual has the ability to control what happens to him or her: "If only I had done something differently, this would not have happened to me." These responses, according to some researchers and authors (Everstine and Everstine, 1993) are natural, even healing, responses to unnatural, often devastating events. Do helping professionals who have been surrounded for years with literature on "post-traumatic *disorder*" and who work daily with trauma survivors really believe that the posttrauma experience is a response, with the purpose of healing, and not a disorder? Is there any change in these beliefs when they experience their own traumatic events?

After twenty-seven years as a social worker observing clients, as well as colleagues, who were experiencing a wide variety of traumatic experiences, and as a social work educator and supervisor supporting students and university colleagues who were facing various traumatic situations, and continuing my own study, research, and learning in the area of trauma and trauma recovery, it was not until facing a series of traumas myself several years ago that the sense of importance in communicating some of these observations and their documentation emerged. Literature on trauma and recovery in general is abundant at this time, but what continues to be more rare is a focus on the helping professionals' use of self when called upon to face their own trauma responses while simultaneously helping others through the same process.

For some helping professionals, it is exactly the experience of trauma that has led them to the choice of a helping profession. Through the belief that they can help others who are experiencing what they have been through, we witness the powerful contributions made to our professions by those whose credibility has been shaped from their own experience. They have been there and are using their experiences in that highest of all points of growth according to Alfred Adler, that of social interest, of "the innate aptitude through which the individual becomes responsive to reality, which is primarily the social situation" (in Ansbacher and Ansbacher, 1956, p. 133). This, the capacity to help others who face tragedies similar to their own, is a significant step in trauma recovery for many: those "who recover most successfully are those who discover some meaning in their experience that transcends the limits of personal tragedy," commonly found "by joining with others in social action" (Herman, 1992, p. 73).

Helping professionals also experience trauma when we have full practices, when we are teaching in universities, when we are raising children, when we are presenting at conferences, when we are preparing workshops, when we are writing policies, when we are conducting research interviews. Helping professionals experience trauma while holding the hands of victims of battering, while leading bereavement groups or divorce groups, while assuring the safety of a suicidal client, while talking with family members in the emergency room, while feeding the homeless, while talking about death with those who are dying, while listening to the horrors of ritual abuse and incest. Helping professionals are very likely, at some point in time, to be helping others with trauma at the same time they are recovering from traumatic events in their own lives. The following initial research questions emerged: What are the responses of helping professionals when they experience their own traumatic events? What choices do they make about use of self as they continue to help others?

Supporting literature for such an inquiry is provided in the earlier edition of this volume. Shadley's (1987) finding in her study to "determine interface issues within therapists' professional and personal lives" found it "surprising to discover that personal transitions and/or tragedies were the most likely circumstances to induce therapeutic style changes" (p. 134). Also, Miller and Baldwin's (1987) contribution in that same edition on the implications of the wounded-healer paradigm serves as a historical, philosophical, and mythological basis for looking at personal and professional shifts in the helping person's perspectives following her or his own woundedness. This present work can confirm, build on, and add to this earlier work by these authors.

In addition to the initial research questions stated above, several related questions arise: Does having "head knowledge" about trauma have an impact on how one experiences the stages of recovery? How does one decide whether to continue working, to stop working temporarily or permanently, or possibly even to change professions? What are the experiences of clinicians as they weigh the decision about telling clients about the trauma that has invaded their own lives? When is this particular use of self beneficial to clients and when may it not be in the best interest of the client's work? How does the journey through trauma and the posttrauma period of time increase or decrease the effectiveness of therapists and other helping professionals? These questions were used to form an interview guide as fifteen generous, perceptive, and wise individuals told their stories.

METHOD

In approaching this inquiry, the necessity of hearing the voices of the individual people was paramount. This resulted in the decision to use the qualitative research method of narrative analysis as the selected approach for gathering and analyzing data. Narrative analysis is concerned with "lives and lived experience"; "the emphasis . . . is upon the study of lives from the narrator's experience" (Manning and Cullum-Swan, 1994, p. 465). "These stories are seen as real" and the "narrative analysis typically takes the perspective of the teller, rather than that of the society" (p. 465). "This approach views texts as symbolic action, or means to frame a situation, define it, grant it meaning, and mobilize appropriate responses to it" (p. 465). To assure an information-rich description of the narrative that emphasizes the telling of the story, the researcher calls on various skills: purposeful questioning, reflections, probing aimed at introducing new ideas, elucidating parts of the story not previously emphasized (White, 1993, 1994), listening for other possible meanings, questioning underlying assumptions and beliefs, building on strengths and coping patterns, and tracking influential factors in the context of the story (Robbins, Chatterjee, and Canda, 1998, p. 314).

"There are no rules for sample size in qualitative inquiry. . . . The validity, meaningfulness, and insights generated from qualitative inquiry have more to do with the information-richness of the cases selected and the observational/analytical capabilities of the researcher than with sample size" (Patton, 1990, pp. 184-185). Twenty-eight potential participants were identified among colleagues as well as in the context of my supervision practice over a five-year period of time. After screening for availability, information richness, and maximum variation, fifteen sample members were selected and agreed to be interviewed. Twelve interviews were done face-to-face and audio recorded. Three of the participants had moved to other areas of the country, so their interviews were conducted by telephone with simultaneous note-taking plus immediate follow-up with field notes done by the researcher. Member checks, for which the participants are asked for their feedback for accuracy on the transcribed data, were conducted with all fifteen sample members.

All data were coded and analyzed to determine predominant themes and patterns, as well as seminal individual contributions, about the participants' experiences, the meaning they had given to the various events described, and the processing that had followed. This last area focused on the perceived impact of their trauma on their subsequent use of self in the professional role as therapist or other helping professional.

Sample members include social workers, psychologists, psychiatrists, one marriage and family therapist, and one physician with a specialty in family medicine. Ages range from twenty-four to sixty-two. Thirteen resided in the eastern part of the United States at the time of the interviews, one was in California, and one in Illinois. Thirteen indicated a middle-class socioeconomic status; two an upper-class SES. Nine of the sample are female and six are male. Ethnocultural backgrounds included African American, French Canadian, Hungarian, American Indian, Cuban, Irish, and Euro-American. All had received at least a bachelor's degree, eight participants held a master's, one had an MD, and three had received a PhD.

Sample members described a variety of trauma situations: a diagnosis of cancer, the suicidal attempt of a child, a car accident, the death of a child, a partner's diagnosis of HIV positive, divorce (2), a runaway child, an accusation of malpractice, the onset of multiple sclerosis, the death of a spouse, acknowledging an addiction to alcohol, violence in the marital relationship, a fire in the home, and rape. Because the retelling of the story can sometimes retraumatize the person, most sample members were selected for this study only if they were at least one year beyond the traumatic incident. The one exception to this requirement was the person who was experiencing the onset of multiple sclerosis. In a discussion with him, we agreed that an earlier interview would serve his needs much better. He was interviewed eight months after learning his diagnosis.

FINDINGS

It is not possible, given the limitations of space, to report on all of the data gathered and analyzed, nor would that serve the intended focus here. For purposes of this chapter, specific segments of the interviews have been selected because of their relevance to the research questions. Another criterion used in selecting the data for presentation here was the significance of the contribution in providing as full a description as possible of the experience of the participants' differential uses of self following their own trauma. Following the restatement of each research question, a brief description of each person (identified by a randomly assigned letter) is given. The "voice" of that participant, her or his response, is presented as an extract. Names within quotations have been disguised. The discussion within each section elucidates themes and patterns as well as connections with theory and literature.

Three major themes emerge from the data reported here: disconnection, use of self in redefining connections with clients, and the "new integration" (Satir, 1983) as a result of giving meaning to the experience and its aftermath.

DISCONNECTION

Research question: What was your response to (the traumatic event experienced)?

Dr. M is a fifty-four-year-old Euro-American psychologist with a specialization in eating disorders. The traumatic event he had experienced was an accusation of malpractice:

> The hardest was seeing myself become many of the qualities I dislike in others, blaming others for my predicament, spending

time with both the "fight and flight" ways of coping, getting immobilized, wanting to disconnect from everyone, especially anyone associated with this profession, I guess . . . seeing many of my Shadow parts enter my life all at once. Fear led the way and then came all those things that are the product of fear—need for control, lack of eye contact, feeling judgmental, rigid expectations [pause] of myself and of others, needing more order and routine in my day, playing it safe. I hated recognizing all these things in my behaviors.

J, now forty-six, was forty-three at the time she learned she had cancer. Her Euro-American heritage and her professional identity as a marriage and family therapist both played a role in how she defined her experience. She had these observations about her response:

At first, I tried to believe that they had gotten my test results mixed up with someone else's. Talk about denial . . . it doesn't get much better . . . or worse? . . . than that. Then I think I went into shock. I remember feeling my heart pounding and I wanted to have a conversation with it. Something like, "You just keep on going now, do you understand? If we can both just keep on doing what we're doing, maybe this will work out OK." During this time, I felt so disconnected from everything. I could see people looking at me and moving their lips, but I had no comprehension of what they were saying to me. This lack of connecting really seemed huge when my rose garden, which before brought me one of my greatest joys, was simply there. . . . "Oh, there are some roses," but I was completely indifferent about how they were doing. This was an enormous change for me.

H was facing the aftermath of his wife's death. He is a forty-four-year-old psychiatrist of Hungarian descent:

The exhaustion of grieving was profound so I tried to make an extra effort to listen to what my body needed in terms of rest. Some nights I would fall asleep while trying to eat my dinner. For about a year and a half, I lost my evenings, needing to go to bed around 8:00. I often thought about single parents with children, probably because I was working with several of them at the time. I wondered how they do it. It seemed possible that, under such circumstances, they would never be able to rest and would never be able to recover from such exhaustion. Of course, what I was probably fearing then was that I, too, would never be able to recover from how exhausted I was feeling.

B is a twenty-seven-year-old male African-American social worker whose partner had been diagnosed HIV positive:

> How did I respond? Structure. After the initial shock, I got very structured about everything . . . morning ritual, evening ritual, what had to be done on certain days. This is in contrast to a normally really laid-back guy. Like, man, I would see what I was doing and I'd say, "Where is this coming from?" It wasn't too tough to figure that one out. [Laugh] It was only my whole life that was falling apart, or at least that's the way it felt. But at least I could get the coffee made in the morning and that told me maybe I was coping after all.

L is a forty-eight-year-old social worker who describes her cultural heritage as European American. Her experiences with an emotionally and verbally abusive husband had resulted in L fearing for her own safety. After twenty-two years of marriage, she sought a divorce, which had been finalized fifteen months before her interview:

> At one point, I remembered the phrase "one day at a time" and realized I was coping by just concentrating on one ten-minute segment at a time. That's all I could emotionally handle at the time, but it got me through.

N returned home from work on a Wednesday afternoon to discover several firetrucks in her front yard. Her home had been partially destroyed by the flames. She is a fifty-eight-year-old Euro-American social worker:

> I had to keep working and I did want to continue seeing my clients but I knew I was experiencing the numbing. There was

a certain energy gone from my voice and I was sure this translated into a dullness in my eyes. I lost clients during that period of time. I can't blame them. I wouldn't have wanted to go to me either while that was going on.

Listening to these words, a common theme throughout is that of disconnection. Disconnection from the self one had known, disconnection from those things which brought joy and satisfaction, from relied-upon energy levels, from the sense of time, from people. Regarding the sense of time, the Everstines (Everstine and Everstine, 1993) have written, "A trauma victim's perception of time is virtually never accurate" (p. 17). And, while reflecting on the decreased energy, one participant described it this way: "It's like someone just pulled the plug."

Helping professionals, because of the demanding requirements of their training, have typically completed long hours of work on the self. If one assumes that this work has resulted in a relatively clear idea about what it means to be connected with self, the recognition of a disconnection from that self may be felt as a shock, as disorienting and confusing, yet at the same time such an awareness of self and the realities of trauma may also function as strengths to help gain a perspective on the events and their larger meaning. This possibility is explored further in a later section.

Shame, doubt, and fear are also expressed as part of the emotional world of the trauma survivors who have been quoted here:

> Shame is a response to helplessness, the violation of bodily integrity, and the indignity suffered in the eyes of another person (Lewis, 1971). Doubt reflects the inability to maintain one's own separate point of view while remaining in connection with others. In the aftermath of traumatic events, survivors doubt both others and themselves. Things are no longer what they seem (Herman, 1992, p. 53).

It was also interesting to note the number of phrases which seemed to convey the "need to fix it" in the above responses, even though the researcher asked for responses to the event in a general sense. "Just keep on going," "listening to my body," "I got very structured," and "concentrating on one ten-minute segment at a time" are all indicators of how the coping begins to happen even in the first moments immediately following the event. In fact, when the traumatic event extends over a period of time, such as rape or incest or during war, victims describe an awareness of coping behaviors that are present while the trauma experience is ongoing (Herman, 1992).

Even though the responses to traumatic events by helping professionals do not vary from the responses of others (Everstine and Everstine, 1993; Herman, 1992; van der Kolk, McFarlane, and Weisaeth, 1996; Waites, 1993), what does become evident as a variation from the data collected is the differing terminology with which these professional helpers describe their experiences with trauma. From their training, they have access to words that help them name the feeling or the process occurring around them and within them. This can have both an "upside" and a "downside," as the next group of findings will illustrate. These findings were the result of asking the participants about this knowledge they had gained academically and professionally and what, if any, impact it had on their recovery from traumatic events.

Research question: Do you think having the "head knowledge" about trauma and the recovery process had any impact on your own experience during and after (the traumatic event)?

A is a twenty-four-year-old male Euro-American social worker who had suffered a head injury in a car accident:

> It might have if I had had the chance to use my head, but it was my head that suffered the injury, so it wasn't good for much of anything at that time. What I needed was information about recovery from head injury, but I was looking at a bit of a Catch 22 here. The nature of my head injury was such that I was, at first anyway, only able to take in information for about two or three minutes before I started feeling exhausted and confused. And I could only do this in the morning. So, I usually got just enough of the facts to make me more anxious about how long I would be this way. Would it be forever? That thought alone caused me to get very depressed a couple of times during those early weeks. After that I did begin to see the progress, slowly, but it was there.

F is forty and she had been through and was still feeling the "fallout," as she called it, of her divorce after twenty years of marriage. Her ethnocultural background is French Canadian and she has been a psychiatrist for the past ten years:

> Oh, yes. Most definitely. My whole perspective shifted follow-
> ing my divorce. Some days it felt like I had gone back to coping
> like I had as a teenager. It was so embarrassing. Or I would start
> sentences thinking I was using my old, clear-thinking, articulate
> self, only to discover halfway through the sentence that I could
> not remember where I was going with the whole thought. It was
> so confusing and when it happened I would feel completely
> powerless. I was so disconnected with what was going on that I
> couldn't even pull myself together enough to apologize for my
> confusion. I would somehow stumble through but found I could
> not hear what I had just said, or what I did hear did not seem to
> make sense. That one really scared my kids a couple of times,
> too. If I had not known that these behaviors were part of what
> happens following a traumatic experience, I probably would
> have thought I was losing my mind. That "head knowledge"
> also helped me find some words to try to explain to the kids
> what was going on with me as well as with them.

D, a thirty-six-year-old female Native American social worker, was walking to her car after work one evening and was forced, at knifepoint, into a car with three strange men. She was blindfolded, taken to a motel, and was raped repeatedly for two hours before the men left her there:

> Hmmmm, well, let's see, that knowledge has served different
> purposes at different points in this whole thing. Right after the
> rape, I think it was my knowledge that helped me stay in my
> head as a way of denying, and a way of coping, with the horror
> of that night. But when the emotional part took over, literally
> took over my whole life, then that knowledge piece was no-
> where. I guess I had to go through that. There's no way to
> think your way out of a flashback. You just have to ride it
> through. Now, say, in the last few months, the emotional part
> of the memories are not running my life as much as before and

it is my head knowledge, as you call it, that is helping me see the steps I'm going through, it reminds me I'm not alone, and it is helping me to find a way to speak out more now, too.

These words of A, F, and D show the variety of responses as well as the differential uses of professional knowledge in the face of a trauma and the subsequent behaviors. Their responses basically represent the positions of "no," "yes," and "it depends on the place in the process." This variety is a helpful reminder that one cannot simply assume that having knowledge about an experience is going to serve as a resource in living one's way through that experience. In fact, as in D's observation, the intellectual knowledge can actually serve to disconnect from the too-painful feelings of the moment.

According to van der Kolk, McFarlane, and Weisaeth (1996), there are three ways in which knowledge, or information, may be distorted by people who have suffered a recent or as yet unresolved trauma:

> First, they overinterpret current stimuli as reminders of the trauma; minor stimuli come to have the power to activate intrusive recollections of the trauma. Second, they suffer from generalized hyperarousal and difficulty in distinguishing between what is relevant and what is not. Third, after dissociating at the moment of the trauma, many traumatized individuals continue to use dissociation as a way of dealing both with trauma-related intrusions and with other ongoing stressful life experiences. (p. 305)

From a practice standpoint, therapists who work with other therapists who have just suffered trauma can take this helpful information and avoid an easy assumption. Since the client possesses the information about how to respond to trauma, it could easily be assumed that the client will automatically respond to the trauma according to that information. To do so would be to ignore the potential distortions of overinterpretation, hyperarousal, and dissociation as identified by van der Kolk, McFarlane, and Weisaeth.

Similarly, from the standpoint of the therapist's use of self in working with clients following therapist trauma, an awareness of the tendency to use these same distortions in the processing of information can be extremely helpful. It is possible that a client's trauma could reactivate the therapist's trauma. If the therapist response at these moments is one of overinterpretation, hyperarousal, or dissociation, the therapeutic environment for the client's work will be placed greatly at risk. An awareness of the risk can offer the therapist a choice point even though, as argued previously, knowledge does not necessarily determine behavior.

This and a variety of other choices are faced by therapists following their own traumas. The data reported in the next section include responses about three of those choices: whether to continue working after the trauma, whether clients were told about the therapist's trauma, and whether it is more helpful to tell clients about therapist trauma.

USE OF SELF IN REDEFINING
CONNECTIONS WITH CLIENTS

Research question: What choices did you make about whether to continue your work following (the traumatic event experienced)?

K is a forty-eight-year-old family practice physician. As far back as he can remember, alcohol has been a presence, "with a capital P," at all of the celebrations in his Irish family. K believes he had a severe alcohol problem by the time he was nineteen, but he only began facing his addiction to alcohol two years ago, after a blackout that resulted in a trip to the emergency room:

> I stopped my practice immediately. Seeing the look on the face of my friend . . . he was on call in the ER the night I was brought in . . . [beginning to cry] . . . that was my wake-up call. I got into this treatment program the next week. I still have my license and I do want to return to practice sometime. Keeping my license depends on what happens here and on never going back to drinking. I'm hopeful, but I did feel a lot of stress on the job, and I have to find some other ways to deal with that before I get out of here.

E had enjoyed a successful psychology practice with adolescents for over fifteen years when he received his diagnosis of multiple sclerosis at the age of forty. He is part Latino and part Euro-American:

My clients and colleagues were all very supportive. Most of them had noticed the changes in me. There was some relief just knowing what it was, so I could tell them and we didn't have to guess anymore. I asked my doctor if I should plan to stop working. She said something about how important it was to decrease the stress in my life. Her recommendation was to plan on a gradual transition, she said, something like spreading it out over three months or so. When I asked her when I should start this transition process, it came as a real shock when she said, "As soon as possible, E___." Three and a half months later, my professional life, as I had known it up to then, came to an end.

As an oncological social worker, O, sixty-two, had led bereavement groups for many years. She had spoken of the vigil she maintained at the bedside of her son, who had died of leukemia. Her response to this question:

I did take a funeral leave for three weeks with my husband. For the first ten days, all I did was sleep. Then the doer part of me kicked back into gear and I got busy, or at least tried to. But, right in the middle of something, it would hit me. He really is gone. It took a long time for that to sink in. I did ask for, and was given, another three weeks of leave from the mental health center. That turned out to be an important time because, since it was far enough away from the event of his death and the services, I could take some of the solitary time I needed to begin my own letting go and grieving. It was only a beginning, but I believe it gave me enough of a foundation that I could go on with my work then and still let the feelings come up as they needed to from that point on.

Again, it is possible to see the variety of choices emerging here. The three illustrations used here reveal two of the four themes that were observed among all of the participants. The four themes are: choosing to stop work temporarily, seeing the trauma as situational and requiring transition time for healing, grieving, or treatment before returning to work; needing to stop all work permanently due to the serious and imminent terminal nature of an illness; leaving the profession and choosing another form of work; and, finally, choosing to continue working while recovering from the trauma. In each of the responses, an awareness of including self, other, and context can be seen and was also confirmed in the data from the next two research questions as well. This is not surprising in light of the fact that these questions, in particular, ask the participants to consider what they (Self) will do with their clients (Other) regarding their professionally defined work together (Context). The importance of these Self-Other-Context responses will be discussed at greater length following the data received from the next two research questions.

Research question: Did you tell your clients about what you were going through?

G, a forty-three-year-old female African-American psychologist, was awakened late at night one Saturday in August by the sound of police knocking on her door. Her teenage daughter, whose boyfriend had just broken up with her, had been rescued from the railing of a highway overpass where she had been planning to jump into oncoming traffic:

> No. I chose not to do that. It was something about protecting our family's right to privacy. Some things that are private, I have shared with my clients. But not this.

(Participant E):

> Yes, I felt they needed to know about it, about the MS, that is. Well, I was needing to say goodbye to all of them, too, so they needed to know why.

P faced her second divorce at the age of forty-four. Many members of her most important support groups, her family and her Lakota tribe, lived far away during the most difficult stages of the separation and eventual proceedings for the divorce. Her social work colleagues became her primary support at that time:

> Yes, I did tell my clients. Ours is a pretty small community and I wanted them to hear it from me rather than from someone

else. With my family clients, I told the parents separately and asked them to decide if they wanted to tell their kids or not. I did tell my women's group. Several of them have been through divorces themselves, but I assured them that I have a terrific support network and they didn't have to take care of me. I did let my clients know that I was still just as available to them as always, and I allowed some time with all of them to let them talk about any concerns they had for their own work. I thought some would choose not to continue but they all hung in there.

(Participant H):

If I had to cancel an appointment with them, I told them about T____'s death but if there was no change in the schedule for the client, then I did not tell them. Most of them heard about it, though, and were really kind and generous. I did get a feeling sometimes that they were watching me to see how I would handle my grief.

(Participant A):

I had to. What I didn't like about it, though, was that I had to do it by letter. I just didn't have the strength and I couldn't even carry on a conversation for longer than a minute or two without being completely drained. I don't know what I would have done without V____, my colleague. He called all my clients right after the [car] accident and talked with each one as long as they needed. He had offered to take my clients for me while I was recovering and told them all about this arrange-ment. Then he helped me put together the letter that went out to all of them.

(Participant M):

I wish I would have had the choice but the media got hold of it and it [the accusation of malpractice] was in the local newspa-pers and even as far away as F____. It happened very quickly and I didn't have the chance to talk with my clients personally before it hit the papers. Some clients called right away, so I spoke with them. Some just called to cancel their appointments. I did send a letter which, basically, explained the situation and that I would be continuing to see clients.

Research question: From your experience, is it more helpful to tell clients when you have experienced a traumatic event yourself, or is it more helpful not to tell them?
(Participant J):

> This is dictated by the situation mostly. I think that both the nature of the situation and the needs of the client are key factors in this decision. It is not necessary to leave the client guessing when it is obvious that something major has entered the therapist's life. Yet, at the same time, the helper must always weigh the client's capacity to cope if the contact with the therapist is threatened. If it is decided to tell the client, then some careful thought needs to be given about how to tell *each* client, according to his or her needs.

(Participant G):

> Well, you know, a lot of my clients seem to have huge issues with abandonment. With those clients, if I needed to be away for awhile, I would definitely tell them about my own trauma . . . maybe not all the details . . . sort of in a general way. I could reassure them that I would be back. I would try to connect it in some way to what the client is working on in his or her own therapy.

(Participant N):

> Most of my elderly patients in the skilled nursing care unit don't really have the mental capacity to track such a thing as my life experiences. There are a couple who would probably want to know. But the others . . . it would just be out of their range of consciousness. So, what I did do was to let several family members know, those who might be looking for me when they come in, and I told them that they could talk with W___, my supervisor, until I got back.

(Participant E):

> This is one of those use-of-self moments. My mentor used to also refer to something like this as a choice point. One thing that I try to keep in mind as a guide is to ask myself, "What is in the best interest of the client?" If it will help my client in some way to tell him or her about my own struggles or if it might hurt them in some way if I do not tell them, then, yes, I will give some brief factual information about what is happening. The boundary, though, is that the clients in no way feel they have to take care of me. That they know, without any doubt, that they are still the focus of our work together.

Given these last two bodies of data, about whether clients were told and, second, whether telling or not telling would be more helpful, how are these professional helpers using themselves as they care about their clients while also facing their own trauma? In every contribution made by these individuals, concerns are voiced that include wise and honest relationships with self and yet reach beyond the self to others and to the context. One is reminded of the words of Virginia Satir's teachings (Satir et al., 1991). Satir recognized that when Self, Other, and Context were are all being honored, congruence was present:

> Choosing congruence means choosing to be ourselves, to relate to and contact others, and to connect with people directly. We wish to respond from a position of caring for ourselves, for other people, and with an awareness of the present context. (Satir et al., 1991, p. 66)

It is from this stance of congruence that each of the participants made choices about his or her use of self in response to client, work, and family needs while facing the aftermath of their various traumatic experiences.

Self

A deep awareness of self is a necessary preparation for the conscious use of self. In the sharing of these particular stories, that awareness included not only the awareness of self but the awareness of the traumatized self and the subsequent changes in perception, focus, and capacity to function in a way that resembled the pretrauma state. These individuals spoke of the need for privacy, the acknowledgement of imminent endings, the importance of their support networks, and their vulnerability and sense of helplessness. These awarenesses are far beyond their professional roles and reach the commonality of the human experience, the universality of trauma. Frequently, there was the recognition that the clients, with their traumas, had been guides to the therapists who were simultaneously facing their own traumas. One person (J) described this awareness by saying, "My clients were my teachers, my models, in coping and perseverance."

This awareness of the traumatized self requires that the therapist consider ethical issues which are involved. Standard 4.05(a) of the Revised Social Work Code of Ethics states, "Social workers should not allow their own personal problems, psychological distress, legal problems, substance abuse or mental health difficulties to interfere with their professional judgment and performance or to jeopardize the best interests of people for whom they have a responsibility" (Rothman, 1998, p. 305). Situations that are cited as possible causes of such problems and distress read like the list of the traumas given by the participants of this study: situational job stressors; personal stressors such as the illness or death of loved ones or marital problems; physical or mental illness; or substance abuse.

Therapists experiencing trauma are, therefore, responsible for seeking their own therapy or counseling when that may be necessary. To seek help, the helping professional must confront the temptation to avoid that assistance. "Chances are, if you can't accept help, you can't really give it" (Dass and Gorman, 1985, p. 86). People in the helping professions "often fall prey to the myth that they are supposed to be invulnerable and able to handle everything, and so they may be reluctant to reach out to others and admit that they need help" (Smith, 1998). Other reasons cited for avoiding help when it is necessary are:

> fearing exposure of confidential information; concern about the cost of treatment; denial about the seriousness of the prob-

lem; and believing they should be able to solve their own problems. (Thorenson, Nathan, Skorina, and Kilbury as cited in Smith, 1998, p. 6)

As colleagues, we may be in a position to support co-workers who face some of these situations. We may find ourselves in the position of helping a traumatized colleague find another helping professional who can be of assistance during these posttrauma periods of time.

Other

Without exception, the responses to the last three research questions included consideration of the others in the person's life. Clients were mentioned, of course, since the questions are worded to include them. But family members, support networks, friends, peers, and colleagues were also mentioned. From the initial sense of disconnection, by nature of having to face one's experience of the trauma alone no matter how many people may be around at the time, coping with the trauma moves to a different place and the connecting and/or reconnecting with others.

Participants spoke of protecting family rights, of connecting with the clients' similar experiences, and of considering how the information about the therapist's trauma might have an impact, favorably or otherwise, on the client's work. Some were aware that being a role model for their clients had not changed during this time of crisis and was, in some way, even more of a factor in the client's observational learning. Now the therapists (those who continued seeing clients) had the opportunity to serve as models of how to make meaning of crisis and to move through it in ways that could bring resolution and further growth. The clients' capacity for coping, their varying needs for reassurance about the therapist's availability, and their cognitive capabilities were all factored into decisions made about how much and what kinds of information to share with them.

Context

Two major contexts are part of the participants' reflections on how they use themselves following their own trauma: family (or other primary relationships) and work. For eight of the participants, the trauma they were facing was directly connected with a family member or partner. For one participant, the trauma was directly related to the work situation. Family trauma and workplace trauma have been addressed in recent literature (Everstine and Everstine, 1993; Herman, 1992; van der Kolk, McFarlane, and Weisaeth, 1996; Waites, 1993) but a helping professional's differential responses to family and workplace following trauma has been only rarely addressed (Shadley, 1987):

> . . . the personal life events of becoming a parent or losing a significant loved one was more frequently mentioned as having a strong influence on changes in one's professional direction and therapeutic style. It appeared from the interviews that these major transitions and/or tragedies were likely to compel therapists into closer and more intimate contact with their client families. (p. 136)

The participants for this research gave words to the importance of family-of-origin dynamics and the role they played in the present crisis. They noticed how their friends and colleagues provided the support, guidance, and nurturing needed during recovery. The significance of support of spouses or partners was acknowledged. Several commented on their awareness of the boundary between work and family and the decision making that was necessary to keep that boundary clear and flexible for both clients and colleagues as well as family members. One participant (E) referred to his clients as "an extended family of sorts" when thinking about telling them about his diagnosis. It was also observed that the nature and degree of information given to clients and colleagues was a variation, more general and without as much detail, of that to which the family or close friends would have access.

Reflecting on these observations and perceptions which have come from the words of the participants, it is evident that in the midst of the experiences themselves, there is no real separation of the Self, the Other, and the Context. These can simply be helpful distinctions to shape a discussion. In the powerful life experience of an overwhelming and traumatic event, these three are part of a whole which, in turn, is an integral part of the posttrauma experience. Even though awareness may be drawn toward one or the other at certain times, the others are still present and included in the essence of the experience itself.

As the inquiry and the data gathering moved to the next level of meaning making, the words of the participants did portray this sense of an essence, a core meaning that gave purpose and direction to the necessary steps of moving on into the future and beyond the immediacy of the emotional impact of the trauma itself.

MEANING MAKING: A NEW INTEGRATION

Research question: Has this experience of trauma changed your effectiveness as a (therapist, social worker, psychiatrist, psychologist, physician, etc.) in any way?

C is a thirty-two-year-old mother of two, Euro-American in her ethnic and cultural background. She has had a psychiatric practice with adolescents for the past fifteen years. Her thirteen-year-old daughter had run away from home and was missing for ten days.

> I have been deeply changed by this experience. There is no doubt about that. It has changed who I am as a person so, yes, it has also changed who I am and how I act in my practice with my patients and their families. I believe I was effective before, but it was a different kind of effectiveness. The other way was an effectiveness that came from my academic learning and from the internship and residency experiences, more from the intellectual side. Now I have been taught another kind of effectiveness. That earlier effectiveness, in my late twenties and early thirties, I had to work hard and often struggle to remember and retain it. This learning, from my daughter's being missing, I will never forget, no matter how hard I might try.

(Participant M):

> I realized an increase in empathy for my clients who struggle with these same things. I also recall being struck with a sense of awe one day. With the intense levels of fear and distress I had heard from clients over the years, what incredible courage

it takes just to head out into the world each day. I had missed the magnitude of this until I experienced it following my own trauma.

James Cole (1997) has also indicated this empathic recognition of the other's experience, through an experience of one's own, as an essential element in arriving at a true behavior change which is the result of a deep shift in perception. This is the level of behavior change that restructures one's ways of perceiving and believing. It is beyond the level of change that simply explores new techniques or interventions, even though this may happen as a result of the deeper change.

(Participant B):

> I remember reading somewhere that when we want to gain knowledge, our actions focus on taking in, and when we want to gain wisdom, our actions focus on letting go. I have had to let go of so much in the past year, of my partner as I had known him, of our hopes and dreams together, even of who I was in the relationship with him before his diagnosis of HIV. All that has changed. Yet, somehow, I know I will be better for this, a better human being I mean. Never again will I take the preciousness and the temporariness . . . is that a word? . . . of life for granted. Every . . . underline that please . . . *every* relationship is temporary. If I take just this one awareness with me into my practice, the connections I make with people will have a whole new quality to them.

One rendition of the wisdom B is recalling can be found in Benjamin Hoff's (1981) interpretation:

> Along the way to knowledge,
> Many things are accumulated.
> Along the way to wisdom,
> Many things are discarded. (p. 43)

(Participant L):

> Yes, I believe I will be a much better listener and I won't have to come up with an answer to fix everything. This experience

has made very clear to me just how complex trauma situations are. There is the complexity of the individual people involved. Then there is the complexity of the dynamics in the relationship. Then there is all the stuff that goes on around them, the family, the community, even some of the policies that are out there to help women, people, who are in abusive situations. Even statistics have played a role in not making this a pretty picture. Those bumper stickers you see, the ones that say "Believe the children, believe the women, stop the violence" or something like that . . . they are right. I will now know that anyone who asks the question, "Why doesn't she just leave?" is someone whose ignorance is showing. They don't have a clue about the domestic violence situation. And, at the same time, these are the people who need more information. One way I may be seeing a change in my effectiveness as a social worker will be to serve as a public speaker about these issues. But, whether or not I do that, I know I will be a better listener with all of my clients.

The ability to listen may be the most essential skill to develop on a continual basis in the process of helping others. Too often it is easy to take the importance of listening for granted or to allow the busyness and fast pace of our lives to interfere with all that is needed to create a helpful listening environment. Yet, thankfully, our clients typically have ways of letting us know when they have not felt heard. L has found herself using the experience of her own trauma recovery in a type of self-evaluation leading to further development of her capacity to listen, to listen more deeply, sensitively, and carefully. One author, considering the importance of listening in the helping process, has expressed it this way:

> As we learn to listen with a quiet mind, there is so much we hear. . . . We hear our skills and needs, our subtle intentionalities, our limits, our innate generosity. In other people we hear what help they really require, what license they are actually giving us to help, what potential there is for change. We can hear their strengths and their pain. We hear what support is available, what obstacles must be reckoned with. The more deeply we listen, the more we attune ourselves to the roots of

suffering and the means to help alleviate it. It is through listening that wisdom, skill, and opportunity find form in an act that truly helps. But more than all these, the very act of listening can dissolve distance between us and others as well. (Dass and Gorman, 1985, pp. 111-112)

(Participant H):

Yes, I believe I will be more effective . . . in many different ways. But, you know, there is one that comes to mind first as I think about this question. I think I will stop wasting time dancing around people's pain from now on. It's not only that I think that is what is most helpful for clients or patients, but now I'm not afraid of going there myself. I can't imagine going through anything that would be more painful than what I experienced two years ago with T_____'s death, but I made it through. Not only did I make it through all that but, in some strange way, I feel I'm a better person now for having gone through it. I hope I can communicate to my clients that they don't have to face their pain alone, that we can go right into the middle of it together, and that there is a way to come out of it on the other side, forever changed but somehow OK, even stronger, and certainly capable of going on with one's life.

At one time or another, every helping professional must face her or his relationship with suffering. This is what we sign up for, perhaps without thinking about it quite that directly, when we choose our respective professions. "Nobody teaches us to face suffering in this society. We never talk about it until we get hit in the face" (Dass and Gorman, 1985, p. 52). H's words above remind us that we not only must face our own suffering but, to be helpful to others, we also need to have a perspective on suffering which allows for growth, which allows that suffering to be a teacher for us to move on into the next phase of living better equipped to face that which lies ahead.

So we have to find tranquillity even in the midst of trauma. . . . We look anew at how each situation can teach us, how it can help us evolve in our ability to confront and help alleviate suffering. We can be students working on ourselves to become more effective instruments of compassion. . . . Opening to our pain, exploring the roots of our suffering, at best with guidance and support, can always increase our opportunity for well-being. But this process also can be of immeasurable value in our efforts to be of service to others. As our understanding of our own suffering deepens, we become available at deeper levels to those we would care for. (Dass and Gorman, 1985, pp. 67, 72, 83)

(Participant D):

Yes, I do believe I will be more sensitive as I work with my clients. I know one thing is for sure. I will never use the term "post-traumatic stress disorder" again to describe this process. (JB: Why is that?) Why is that? Well, because I now know this is not a disorder. There is a natural healing process our psyches have to go through following experiences like that. Mine was the rape, but I think it is true for other trauma as well. The behaviors, the shock, the numbing out, the confusion, the exhaustion, all of it can certainly look like a disorder to someone who doesn't really know what's going on. But, once you've been there yourself, you know that person is doing the best she can given the circumstances of what she is dealing with. To call it a disorder, to me, makes the matter much worse for recovery. If I have to think of myself as "disordered" I get a label that gives me no direction for how to improve myself. If I call it a process, then at least I can have some hope that things are moving along. Does this make sense?

In fact, this makes a great deal of sense and D is not the only one who has been considering these different, more strengths-oriented, ways of looking at the aftermath of the trauma experience. The Everstines, in their book called *The Trauma Response* (Everstine and Everstine, 1993), have made significant efforts to encourage helping professionals to move beyond the disease model as a way of defining the posttrauma experience:

By looking away from the pathological aspects of a symptom or set of symptoms, we can see that *trauma is by no means a "disorder"* in the way that the term is used to refer to a break-down of the personality. By contrast, the *symptom* can be viewed as an element of a response pattern whose purpose is not to prolong or exaggerate or destroy, but rather to heal. (p. 11)

When the reaction to trauma is envisaged as part of a restor-ative process and not as abnormal behavior, a new incentive to helping the victim recover is gained. In any sphere of psychother-apy, it is a simpler task to aid a natural process than to cure a disorder. (p. 14)

Without exception, all fifteen participants agreed that significant changes to self had occurred in a personal sense, as well as in a professional sense, from their passage through a traumatic event and its aftermath. After at least one year's time, many were already observing the different ways in which that "new" self was being used in professional practice and in other relationships. The themes from the quotes include: a wholeness of experience beyond only an intellectual approach to helping others; increased empathic depth; the importance of knowing what happens when letting go of that which is most important to one's life and well-being; an increased depth and sensitivity in abilities of listening and hearing others; being more comfortable with the lessons to be learned from pain; and the transition from seeing the posttrauma period as pathological to seeing it as a natural and restorative, healing, process.

CONCLUSION

Trauma is "a fact of life, it is not a question of having it or not, but what to do with it" (Everstine and Everstine, 1993, p. 216). Fifteen participants, all of whom are professional helpers them-selves, were asked exactly this: What have you done with the trau-mas you have faced and what choices have you made about your uses of self as you walked your way through to recovery? They have spoken of disconnection, new definitions of what connecting means, and new integration. They have offered individual and unique meanings for their experiences, which allow them to move on into the next stages of their lives with a greater sense of their own wholeness and the wholeness of life itself.

It was not unusual to also hear words of doubt among the participants about whether they would still be able to go on as helpers of others in distress. Could they really use their traumas as resources to strengthen their work as helpers or would they ever be able to get beyond that time of feeling totally overwhelmed and confused? Self-doubt was a reality through every phase of recovery for the participants, yet it was very interesting to note that, side-by-side with the doubt of self was also a reliance upon the self to get through the experience. These individuals had developed a strong sense of self before facing the trauma in their lives. Because of this, the self within could both face the disintegration that comes with a traumatic experience at the same time that the fundamental, historical structure of the self could remain intact and serve as a ballast through the storm. They have shown that there is not necessarily a singular use of self as one moves through a posttrauma experience, but multiple uses of different parts of that self. In the magnificent sculpture that represents each life, certain corners and edges may disintegrate or be chiseled away by painful experiences, but the overall integrity of the sculpture itself can remain intact. We take with us the scars, the tangible evidence, from those experiences. This means taking on new shapes, new forms, new wrinkles, new colors, new ways of perceiving when we face trauma and move on. In this sense, then, we are once again reminded that in every ending, there is also a beginning, perhaps hidden at first but which slowly emerges with time.

REFERENCES

Ansbacher, H. and Ansbacher, R. (Eds.) (1956). *The individual psychology of Alfred Adler.* New York: Basic Books.

Borysenko, J. (1996). *A woman's book of life: The biology, psychology, and spirituality of the feminine life cycle.* New York: Riverhead Books.

Cole, J. (1997). The triad model: A powerful, safe process for reducing subtle prejudicial behavior. Presentation given at the Seventh Annual Conference of the National Association for Multicultural Education, Albuquerque, NM, October 28.

Dass, R. and Gorman, P. (1985). *How can I help? Stories and reflections on service.* New York: Alfred A. Knopf.

Everstine, D. and Everstine, L. (1993). *The trauma response: Treatment for emotional injury.* New York: W.W. Norton.

Herman, J. (1992). *Trauma and recovery: The aftermath of violence from domestic abuse to political terror.* New York: Basic Books.

Hoff, B. (1981). *The way to life.* New York: Weatherhill.

Lewis, H.B. (1971). *Shame and guilt in neurosis.* New York: International Universities Press.

Manning, P. and Cullum-Swan, B. (1994). Narrative, content, and semiotic analysis. In N. Denzin and Y. Lincoln (Eds.), *Handbook of qualitative research* (pp. 463-477). Thousand Oaks, CA: Sage.

Miller, G. and Baldwin, D. (1987). Implications of the wounded-healer paradigm for the use of the self in therapy. In M. Baldwin and V. Satir (Eds.), *The use of self in therapy* (pp. 139-151). Binghamton, NY: The Haworth Press.

Patton, M. (1990). *Qualitative evaluation and research methods.* Newbury Park, CA: Sage.

Robbins, S., Chatterjee, P., and Canda, E. (Eds.) (1998). *Human behavior theory: A critical perspective for social work.* Boston: Allyn and Bacon.

Rothman, J.C. (1998). *From the front lines: Student cases in social work ethics* (pp. 285-309). Boston: Allyn and Bacon.

Satir, V. (1983). Process Community Presentation. Crested Butte, CO.

Satir, V., Banmen, J., Gerber, J., and Gomori, M. (1991). *The Satir model: Family therapy and beyond.* Palo Alto, CA: Science and Behavior Books.

Shadley, M. (1987). Are all therapists alike? Use of self in family therapy: A multidimensional perspective. In M. Baldwin and V. Satir (Eds.), *The use of self in therapy* (pp. 127-137). Binghamton, NY: The Haworth Press.

Smith, D. (1998). Social worker impairment: Exposing the demons within. *Colorado Social Worker,* July/August, p. 6.

van der Kolk, B., McFarlane, A., and Weisaeth, L. (Eds.) (1996). *Traumatic stress: The effects of overwhelming experience on mind, body, and society.* New York: Guilford.

Waites, E. (1993). *Trauma and survival: Post-traumatic and dissociative disorders in women.* New York: W.W. Norton.

White, M. (1993). Commentary: The histories of the present. In S. Gilligan and R. Proce (Eds.), *Therapeutic conversations* (pp. 121-135). New York: Norton.

White, M. (1994). Narrative theory workshop. Austin, TX.

Chapter 11

Implications of the Wounded-Healer Paradigm for the Use of Self in Therapy

Grant D. Miller
DeWitt C. Baldwin Jr.

INTRODUCTION

The therapeutic encounter has the capacity to activate greater power and complexity than can be accounted for by the mere physical presence of the therapist in individual, family, and group therapy. Some of this mysterious power clearly is a function of role and charisma. From time immemorial, the healer[1] has achieved a place in society by means of special knowledge, training, and skills not ordinarily available to other members of society. Additional personal qualities probably function to motivate certain persons to become healers and to generate the charismatic power frequently attributed to this role and to such persons. At the same time, an important contribution to the equation comes from the patient,[1] whose pain, suffering, and need create a readiness to ascribe such power to another person in the hope and expectation of help. The nature of these hopes and expectations, as well as the corresponding role of the healer in a particular society or period of history, has varied widely along a continuum from activity to passivity.

It is not the purpose of this article to prescribe the role and behavior of the healer. However, we clearly assume and favor a positive, trusting relationship in which the healer genuinely interacts with a person in need, conveys warmth and empathy in a nonpossessive fashion, and attempts to grasp the meaning of the other person's life and experience in an effort to create an environment of safety and acceptance (Yalom, 1980). It is our view that the healer must not only create such an environment, but must be and act in such a way as to release and enhance the inherent healing powers of the patient.

How does this view relate to the use of the *self** in therapy? We propose that the nature of the helping relationship embodies the basic polarities inherent in the paradigm of the wounded-healer.[2] These polarities ultimately relate to the vulnerability and healing power present in both healer and patient. The wounded-healer paradigm presented here emphasizes the potential of the healer's vulnerable or wounded side to release such power in the therapeutic relationship. This chapter, then, will examine the paradigm of the wounded-healer in historical perspective, present a conceptual and diagrammatic model of the helping relationship, and finally, spell out the implications of this paradigm for the use of self in therapy.

POLARITIES

Fascination with the polarities of life is as old as recorded time. In their earliest statements, humans refer to the contradictions of life and death, light and dark, and health and illness. In fact, the myths of many cultures refer to deities in terms of such qualities. The Babylonian dog goddess was called Gula as death and Labartu as healing. In India, Kali was both the goddess of the pox and the healer.

In the *Symposium* (Plato, 1951), Aristophanes recounts an ancient myth that represented the earliest human beings as possessing four arms and four legs, with one head and two faces, each looking in opposite directions. These beings supposedly possessed such qualities and intelligence that they caused fear and envy in the gods, resulting in the head and body being cut in half to reduce their power. Since then, the severed parts have endeavored to reunite in order to know, even for a moment, the ecstasy of reunification and

---

*Whenever the term *self* is first employed in a chapter as part of the concept of the use of self in therapy, it is italicized to call attention to its special use.

wholeness. Indeed, the attempt to balance polarities lies at the heart of most of our efforts to understand our place in the cosmos (Meyerhoff, 1976).

THE MYTH OF THE WOUNDED-HEALER

In the context of polarity, the concept of the wounded-healer takes on a powerful meaning for the helping professions. Indeed, the paradox of one who heals and yet remains wounded lies at the heart of the mystery of healing. As with polarities, there is a long history of the concept of the wounded-healer, which is stated clearly in the myth of Asclepius and Chiron (Graves, 1955). Asclepius is born of the union of the god Apollo and the mortal woman Coronis. During her pregnancy, Coronis is killed by Apollo's sister, Artemis, when it is discovered that Coronis has been unfaithful to Apollo. While Coronis is on the funeral pyre, Apollo snatches Asclepius from her womb, and gives him to the centaur healer, Chiron, to raise. Paradoxically, Chiron suffers from an incurable wound originally caused by the poisoned arrows of Hercules. Thus, Chiron is a healer who is in need of healing. Kerenyi (1959, pp. 96-97) comments, "All in all, Chiron, the wounded divine physician, seems to be the most contradictory figure in all Greek mythology. Although he is a Greek god, he suffers an incurable wound. Moreover, his nature combines the animal and Apollonian, for despite his horse's body, mark of the fecund and destructive creatures of nature that centaurs are otherwise known to be, he instructs heroes in medicine and music." Under Chiron's tutelage, Asclepius becomes the Greek god of healing.

The image of the wounded-healer is found again in the medieval myth of Parsifal. In the account of Chrétien de Troyes, the Fisher King, despite possessing the Holy Grail, which grants all things to all persons, suffers interminably from an incurable wound (Johnson, 1974). The Fisher King is unable to avail himself of a cure for his own wound, but instead must wait until the liberation of the Holy Grail.

Equally rooted in our past is the tradition of the shaman, the primitive healer who, in most societies, is not only doctor but priest (Harner, 1980; Meyerhoff, 1976). The shaman is able to have direct contact with the gods and spirits, experiences heaven, hell, and the world, and stands at the junction of the opposing forces of life and death. Shamans enter into and take on the wounds and illnesses of their people, transcending these by their force and power. In many ways, the shaman is a wounded-healer in the fullest sense.

RECENT INTEREST
IN THE WOUNDED-HEALER PARADIGM

More recently, interest in the paradigm of the wounded-healer has experienced a revival among Jung and his followers, perhaps because of their interest in polarities, mythology, and archetypes. Jung (1951) refers to the wounded-healer paradox when he states, "Only the wounded doctor can heal," while Guggenbuhl-Craig (1978) maintains that a healer-patient archetype exists and is activated each time a person becomes ill. In his view, each patient has an inner healer. However, when the intrapsychic or inner healer does not act to heal the patient, the sick person may seek an external healer. Not only does the patient have a hidden inner healer, but the healer has a hidden inner patient, and healer and patient frequently cast mutual projections upon each other based on their hidden parts. "Real cure can only take place if the patient gets in touch with and receives help from his 'inner healer.' And this can only happen if the projections . . . are withdrawn" (p. 128). Thus, the healer must be aware of and be in touch with his or her own wounded side, if these projections are to be withdrawn. If the projections remain, both healer and patient attempt to manipulate each other to conform to their inner needs.

A MODEL FOR VIEWING
THE HEALING PROCESS

Figure 11.1 is a diagrammatic representation of Groesbeck's thesis, with numbered arrows representing both positive and negative interactions affecting the healing relationship. Examples are included here to provide clarification.

In Arrow 1, the patient becomes wounded by one or more problems faced in human existence. The discomfort and pain experienced

FIGURE 11.1. Diagram of the Wounded-Healer Paradigm

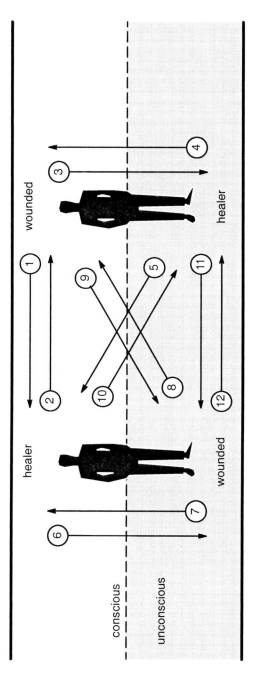

Source: Adapted from Groesbeck, 1975.

247

by the wounded patient stimulates a conscious search for help. A large number of factors are typically considered in choosing a particular healer, but many of these contribute little to healing. For example, an individual or family may seek therapy from a well-known and charismatic psychotherapist, but unless certain ingredients to be listed below are present in the therapeutic relationship, healing may not occur.

The healer, with his or her professional training, licenses, and experience, consciously and objectively deals with the wounds of the patient (Arrow 2). The presence of the wound in the patient causes an emotional and/or physical imbalance that activates the wounded-healer polarity in the patient (Arrow 3) and a strong wish to be healed and return to health. Like metal shavings drawn to a magnet, attention to the discomfort of the wound bars the patient from conscious awareness of the healer within himself (Arrow 4). The inner healer polarity of the patient, then, is disregarded and is projected onto or identified within the outer professional healer (Arrow 5).

Although all patients project their inner healer onto the professional healer to a certain degree, certain individuals do this to an extreme. Dependent individuals emphasize the importance of the professional healer through passively relinquishing their responsibility. Occasionally, flattery is used to maintain such a relationship, which not only inhibits healing, but tends to reinforce the projections of the professional healer.

The approach of a wounded individual for treatment also activates the wounded-healer polarity within the helper (Arrow 6). If the wounded pole is not experienced or integrated by the healer (Arrow 7), the wound is likely to be solely identified in or projected onto the patient (Arrow 8). Projection of healer wounds onto the patient (Arrow 8) is largely unconscious and is likely to occur in a number of circumstances, especially if both helper and patient have something in common and consciously or unconsciously identify with each other. In such a case, treatment may be compromised through loss of professional objectivity.

Excessive sympathy for the patient may also arise in this situation, resulting in a collusion with the patient. Egan (1997, p. 78) cautions that sympathy may be a block to effective listening and future treatment: "If I sympathize with my client as she tells me how awful her husband is, I take sides without knowing what the complete story is. Helpers should not become accomplices in letting client self-pity drive out problem-managing action."

The following case example illustrates other problems that may occur (Arrow 8). During the first year of an internal medicine residency, a resident whose father was an alcoholic was observed to deal harshly with patients having alcohol-related physical problems. He was overheard saying, "You chose to drink, which eventually led to this problem; so don't expect me to prescribe much pain medication." In this case, anger toward the resident's alcoholic father was inappropriately displaced and projected onto the alcoholic patient.

Both of the authors have suffered chronic illnesses and are literally wounded, perhaps partially explaining our mutual interest in the wounded-healer paradigm. One author has had diabetes for over *forty* years. As a diabetic physician approached for care by a diabetic patient, this author must be aware of a bewildering number of feelings (Arrow 8). Otherwise he may demand inappropriately strict diabetic control, or too little control, depending on his unconscious needs to deny his own wound. The other author, a hemophiliac, has had difficulty mastering the biochemical mechanisms of blood coagulation. If wounds are left unconscious or poorly integrated into conscious awareness (Arrow 7), the quality of patient care (Arrow 2) may be adversely affected.

The helper's inner wound projections (Arrow 8) may occur frequently in briefer and less introspective therapies conducted by healers of all professions. Within the psychologically oriented healing disciplines, however, projections seem less acceptable since greater self-understanding is expected. As suggested by the above case examples, strong emotions can be the stimulus for self-reflection and uncovering of wounds. If the helper can remain open to and learn from the strong feelings created by the patient's wounds, greater awareness and integration of his or her own wounds may be realized.

Patient wounds are occasionally identified in their helpers (Arrow 9), whether actually present or not. For example, a male member of a small therapy group expressed concern over how the facilitator must be troubled by his crooked teeth. It was later shared by the group member that he was frequently worried about his physical appearance to the extent that meeting new people created great anxiety.

The conscious and direct support by the helper of the patient's inner healer is a positive interaction facilitating the integration and increased awareness of the inner healer of the patient (Arrow 10). For example, a family having a recurrent problem may be reminded of past effective problem-solving approaches used to remedy the problem and encouraged to focus on their healing family resources.

In another example, a woman patient with agoraphobia and secondary alcoholism was being successfully treated for agoraphobia, although her life-threatening alcohol abuse continued. In a direct and caring manner, the therapist refused to continue treatment for the agoraphobia unless the patient responsibly used her inner healing forces to discontinue drinking.

The mystery of the healing process deepens when the interactions of the patient-healer and wounded-helper poles are considered (Arrows 11 and 12). The helper takes on the wounds of the patient (Arrow 1) and begins experiencing his or her own wounded polarity (Arrow 7), increasing an awareness of his or her own vulnerability. The helper's wounded pole activates and helps actualize the patient's healer pole, a step necessary for true healing (Arrow 12). Both patient and healer experience themselves more fully through greater awareness of their human potential to be both wounded and healed. This occurs both intrapersonally and interpersonally, ending in a greater sense of balance and wholeness for both individuals as polarities of each are consciously experienced.

Unconscious interactions between patient and helper (Arrows 11 and 12) are also potentially harmful. As suggested by Langs (1985), patients may be more aware of the healer's wounds (Arrow 9) than the healer himself (Arrow 6). This awareness is rapidly repressed and the patient unknowingly becomes the healer (Arrow 11) in a role reversal that inappropriately benefits the professional healer and blocks progress for the patient. Langs conducted in-depth interviews with patients who had been in psychotherapy and discovered that many are unconsciously abused or manipulated to meet the needs of the professional healer. In such situations, neither patient nor professional are healed, even though the latter's needs may be briefly met.

However, when the patient experiences true healing, it often serves to heal the wounded pole of the professional healer (Arrow 11). In this case, there is mutual healing for both. This interaction will be addressed later in relation to professional burnout.

CRITICAL ELEMENTS IN THE HEALING PROCESS

Listening

While teaching medical students and residents for many years, the authors have noticed how these young developing professionals are consistently able to describe an image of an ideal physician that includes the ability to listen and the presence of a high level of technical knowledge and skill. Due to the consistency and universality of their responses, it is tempting to attribute this to a genetic trait or a healer archetype. However, it is more likely that during the first three years of life, their emotional or physical pain was relieved by a listening significant other, in most cases the mother. The mother no doubt acts as a training template for listening and nurturing that is incorporated into self and later described in the image of the ideal physician or healer. Empirical support for this notion is provided by Schore's (1994) work on affect regulation and the origin of self.

Since most people have had the benefit of such a training template, it is likely that everyone possesses an image of an ideal healer who listens and is skillful. When wounded (Arrow 1), patients search for healers matching their image of an ideal physician or healer. If either listening or skill is lacking significantly in the chosen healer, all manner of problems may arise, including the patient being late to appointments, distrust, failing to comply with treatment, prolonged healing times, complications to treatment, failing to pay treatment fees, and considering the healer a "bad doctor." In short, the greater the difference between the ideal image and actuality, the less likely the patient will heal.

Adequate training and professional licensure ensure a certain measure of technical knowledge and skill no matter what our mental health discipline. The ability to really listen to and empathize with another is more difficult to train and to assess, but it is the most important tool we have in helping others. Patients must be heard in order to heal.

What factors must be considered to improve the effectiveness of our listening? Certainly a common language is basic to understanding and knowing another person (Chomsky, 1972). Yet even with a similar language, an understanding of patients' gender, race, early childhood experiences, religion, values, age-related developmental tasks, and socioeconomic status are important in hearing another (Comas-Diaz and Jacobsen, 1991; Kochman, 1991).

To know ourselves is to know and heal our patients. If the medicine resident mentioned earlier had been in touch with his anger toward patients having alcoholism as a result of growing up with an alcoholic father, he might have been more helpful in dealing with his patient.

Mohl and Warrick McLaughlin (1997) state that we discern meaning in that which we hear through filters of our own cultural backgrounds, life experiences, feelings, the day's events, physical sense of ourselves, sex roles, religious meanings, and intrapsychic conflicts. Our filters can serve as blocks or as magnifiers if certain elements of what is being said resonate with something within us. These writers go on to say that when the filters block, we refer to it as countertransference or insensitivity; when they magnify, we call it empathy or sensitivity.

Mohl and Warrick McLaughlin (1997) also point out that being intellectually grounded in a theoretical listening perspective may structure listening and help serve patients' healing. For example, a healer grounded in patient-centered theory will give control of the content of the interview to the patient and provide noncontingent positive regard and empathy (Rogers, 1951). A cognitive-behaviorist focuses attention on hidden assumptions and distortions, behavioral contingencies, and listens as a benign expert (Corey, 1996). A self-psychologist listens for how the patient developed a sense of self from others and provides empathetic mirroring and affirmation in the process (Kohut, 1991). A healer schooled in family systems theory focuses attention on the complex forces influencing each member of a family and attempts to be a noninvasive and neutral facilitator who encourages balance in the family system (Corey, 1996). In short, in addition to the importance of knowing self and what it is to be a human being, theoretical grounding is extremely important to listening and subsequent healing.

What factors must be kept in mind that might block effective listening? Lack of consciousness regarding the above factors seems obvious, but other current distractions from being with and hearing patients need comment. The DSM-IV (American Psychiatric Association, 1994) has been extremely helpful in establishing diagnoses, conducting research, communicating with fellow professionals, and in reimbursement for services. Tremendous recent advances have been made in all areas of psychology and medicine. However, we have concerns that making diagnoses may become an end in itself. Careful listening to important existential issues may be minimized or ignored when these issues may be the major cause of illness.

Similar avoidance, distraction, and irritation may result from the pressures of managed care where time and number of visits become the focus of healer attention. Healers are pressured to focus briefly on crisis symptoms and less on root causes of patients' complaints.

The role of listening in the history of psychological healing was addressed by Jackson (1992), who studied philosophical, religious, and medical sources from antiquity to the present. He noted that we are in an era of incredible advances in molecular biology and warned that while seeing more, we are at high risk of hearing less, since hearing is generally more difficult than seeing. To be effective healers, we must both hear and see.

Wholeness

In considering the healing process, it is useful to consider the origins of the word *heal*, which derives from the Anglo-Saxon word *hal*, meaning whole. To heal, *haelen*, is to make whole (*Webster's New Twentieth-Century Dictionary*, Second Edition, 1979). In general, factors facilitating healing also facilitate a sense of wholeness through the recognition and acceptance of all of one's parts and polarities. Gestalt therapy makes such integration a specific goal of therapy (Perls, Hefferline, and Goodman, 1951). Thus, healing and wholeness should be considered together.

Due to the constant distractions and demands of existence, a sense of wholeness in life is necessarily short-lived and elusive, even though one may expend much time and energy seeking it. A feeling or sense of wholeness often occurs with discovery of hidden parts of oneself, for example, finding an opposite pole leading to a greater sense of understanding and balance; the feeling of unity with another in sexual intercourse; the very transient sense of absurdity in a joke; the feeling of completeness when one experiences the dignity of a dying individual; and the sense of joy found in birth or a religious experience.

The authors believe that effective psychotherapy should contribute to healing and a greater sense of wholeness. Yalom (1980) and Gabbard (1994) have examined altruistic common denominators of effective psychotherapy as reflected in outcome research. Yalom states that the effective therapist genuinely interacts with the patient, conveys warmth and empathy in a nonpossessive fashion, and grasps the meaning of the patient's life and experience. Gabbard clearly shows from a number of empirical studies arising from several mental health disciplines that empathy and a therapeutic alliance are the critical elements in producing positive change in the practice of psychotherapy. These qualities create an environment of such safety and acceptance that the patient can reveal those parts of the self that are usually hidden and that cause imbalance and illness. Through therapy the patient learns to interact with all of his or her parts and becomes able to experience wholeness more frequently.

Conscious Inner Attention

Although these altruistic qualities are laudable and must be present to facilitate healing, therapists must also learn to consciously attend to their inner selves, if they are to truly attend to the inner selves of their patients. Needleman (1985, p. 84) believes this ability to be the secret of Freud's insight and creativity. He writes, "Freud had unconsciously discovered within himself the existence of a level and quality of human attention hitherto unsuspected and unrecognized by modern science, and found that this force of attention had not only served to balance Freud's own intellectual and emotional functions, thereby enabling him to be compassionate and insightful in the presence of his patients, but also that this force of attention itself 'radiated' to his patients a really effective healing influence, both in the sense of tangible healing energy and in the sense of calling forth in them the arising of their own self-mobilizing power of inner attention." As with Freud, it is through conscious inner attention that the therapist most effectively heals patients.

Conscious inner attention may be learned in psychotherapy or analysis, during which unconscious elements emerge for examination. The practice of examining one's hidden self in the presence of another soon becomes integrated and a part of the conscious inner attention useful to the effective healer. In Figure 11.1, all of the arrows arising from the healer's unconscious represent hidden conflicts that potentially clash with the patient's needs. The effective healer is aware of these conflicts in a way that promotes patient healing rather than detracting from it.

Vulnerability

We believe that conscious inner attention to one's wounds and conflicts leads to a sense of vulnerability. This, in turn, makes possible the unconscious connection between the healer's wound and the patient's healer (Arrows 11 and 12). As stated by Knight (1985), "the true healer cannot stand outside of the healing experience as a disinterested observer, but must be ready to have his or her own wounds activated and reactivated, but contained within and not projected." Through an encounter with the vulnerable healer, the patient finds more than temporary relief or alleviation of symptoms. Rather, the patient is able to go beyond fears and resistances and discover the full meaning of his or her illness through a genuine understanding of the self. Weizsacker, as quoted by Jaspers (1964), states, "Only when the doctor has been deeply touched by the illness, infected by it, excited, frightened, shaken, only when it has been transferred to him, continues in him and is referred to himself by his own consciousness, only then and to that extent can he deal with it successfully" (p. 27). The genuine wounded-healer accepts his or her own wound along with that of the patient and finds therein an illumination that enables him or her to transcend the experience, while remaining forever both patient and healer.

Conscious attention to one's vulnerability may be augmented by the presence of a serious physical illness, particularly one that is chronic and unrelenting in nature. The literally wounded helper with such an illness is forced to attend to his or her own vulnerability and is likely to more humbly interact with the patient. The literally wounded helper is also likely to show greater empathy and understanding with the patient, since they share in common their woundedness.

Of greater significance, however, is the possibility that a literal wound in the helper may contribute to the helper's own wholeness. After being afflicted by severe rheumatoid arthritis, Kreinheder (1980, p. 15) writes, "When you become ill, it is as if you have been chosen or elected, not as one to be limited and crippled, but as one to be healed. The disease always carries its own cure and also the cure for your whole personality. If you take it as your own and you stay with this new experience, with the pain and the fear and all the accompanying images, you will be healed to a wholeness far beyond your previous so-called health." In regard to the healing role, Kreinheder continues, "If you are going to be a healer, then you have to get into a relationship. There is a person before you, and you and that other person are there to relate. That means touching each other, touching the places in each other that are close and tender where the sensitivity is, where the wounds are, and where the turmoil is. That's intimacy. When you get this close, there is love. And when love comes, the healing comes. The therapist is an expert in the art of achieving intimacy. When you touch each other intimately and with good will, then there is healing" (p. 17).

However, Rippere and Williams (1985) discuss the tendency for many professional healers to wear a "protective mask" to keep patients at a distance. They claim patients respond positively to the "elusive quality of empathy" when healers remove their professional armor and reveal their vulnerability. The crucial factor of vulnerability, known for millennia, is frequently overlooked in the glitter of contemporary helper technology.

The contributions of Martin Buber (1970) in regard to the facilitation of healing cannot be overstated. He characterizes the common form of human interaction as "I-It," in which subject deals with object. This simple "I-It" relationship is unfortunately all too typical of many healer-patient interactions (Arrows 1 and 2). Buber decries this relationship as superficial and basically meaningless. In contrast, he describes the "I-Thou" relationship, in which each person is both subject and object and is able to recognize the totality of the other in this common experience. He believes that the greatest thing one human being can do for another is to confirm the deepest thing within. Sometimes the deepest things within healers are their wounds.

Healers who relate openly and totally with patients model the I-Thou relationship, which contributes to patient as well as healer wholeness. Also, when healers pay attention to their own inner selves, they can receive and follow clues provided by strong emotions, find the source of their personal wounds and experience their own vulnerability. Healers may, at times, share this information with patients if such sharing is in the best interest of the patient. If in doubt, it is best not to share personal information. As Frieda Fromm-Reichmann (1950) instructed, it is most important for us "to be able to listen and to gather information from another person in this other person's own right, without reacting along the lines of one's own problems and experiences." However, whether the process is shared or not, the humility and insight gained through self-awareness is very important.

RELATED CONSIDERATIONS

Interest in the Healing Professions

In considering the motivation for entering the healing professions, one wonders if a sense of woundedness is not a major factor. Jung (1946) states, "The doctor knows, or at least he should know that he did not choose this career by chance" (p. 177). Adler (1956) also claims, "To be wounded means also to have the healing power activated in us; or might we possibly say that without being wounded, one would never meet just this healing power? Might we even go as far as to say that the very purpose of the wound is to make us aware of the healing power in us" (pp. 18-19). Striking confirmation of these statements exists in the past history of substance abuse counselors, a large percentage of whom have themselves been addicted. Their effectiveness in dealing with addicts may relate to the awareness of their own wounds.

Professional Burnout

As healers consciously attend to their own vulnerability and deal with the pain of their patients, they become receivers (Figure 11.1, Arrow 11). In other words, the healing encounter generates a flow of energy between patient and doctor, and this may be a sustaining source for true healers. Healers who cannot avail themselves of this profound source are more likely to experience loss of professional energy and effectiveness. Brokenness and vulnerability by themselves may rob a healer of psychic energy and contribute to burnout. The act of affirming common human brokenness and vulnerability can bring life-giving energy and healing to both healer and patient.

It is hypothesized that burnout will probably be greater in professionals using more problem-oriented or technique-oriented approaches, such as cognitive-behavioral approaches used by many psychologists, and medication-oriented or somatic treatment prescribed by psychiatrists. With these approaches, an "I-It" interaction is more likely to exist in which the professional does not always attend to the wounds of patients or admit vulnerability. It is also hypothesized that healers using such approaches may over time discover a need to move toward other treatment modalities that allow the wounded aspects of themselves to be discovered and integrated.

Creativity

It was clearly implied above that wholeness is closely associated with creativity. Indeed, moments of great psychic energy and joy appear to arise from acts of other- or self-discovery and integration that provide a feeling of transcendence over the mundane finitude of our daily lives. These are the moments when polarities are reconciled and united and when wounds are healed. Such experiences of deep communion and understanding with ourselves or with others constitute a wellspring of truly creative insight and energy. We believe that the use of self in therapy can result in such experiences of growth and creativity. As with the ancient mythological figures, who accomplished miracles despite their suffering, the wounded-healer remains creative and strong. Creativity is constantly renewed despite, or perhaps because of, the wounded-healer's vulnerability.

Neumann (1959) may have had this in mind when he pointed out that "the creative man is always close to the abyss of sickness" (p. 186). In addition to facilitating healing, pain and suffering may be an effective stimulus for the creative process.

Teaching and Parenting

The wounded-healer paradigm may be adapted to explain highly effective teachers and better than "good enough" parents. The authors hypothesize that effective teachers are consciously aware of their own continuing "learnerhood" and prepare their lectures and seminars with greater sensitivity to the needs of their students in terms of accurately assessing levels of existing mastery, styles of learning, and how far their students may be pushed to learn new material. Effective teachers also are able to activate the unconscious "teacher" within students. Similarly, good parents are aware of their "inner child" and are likely to be more sensitive to the developmental needs of their children. They are also more likely to appropriately activate and reinforce the adult aspects of their children.

SUMMARY

In this chapter, we have attempted to unravel the timeless mystery of healing. We have seen how wounded patients deny their inner healers as they search for and are treated by professional healers. We have also considered how less effective professional healers are often role bound, and deny or repress their own wounds while attempting to heal. Factors facilitating healing have been examined, including listening and the importance of conscious inner attention to and acceptance of one's own vulnerability.

From all these considerations, it appears that therapists' acceptance of their own wounds through conscious awareness of their vulnerability contributes to a sense of wholeness, which in turn enables patients to do the same and, thus, empower their own healers.

NOTES

1. In preparing this chapter, the authors frequently chose to name the acting individuals healer and patient. Despite the medical association of these words,

this paradigm is useful for anyone involved in the helping professions, including counselors, social workers, family therapists, and psychologists. "Patient" was used rather than "client" since most patients are more obviously wounded and this is not necessarily the case with clients. A heavy emphasis on the overt interaction between patient and helper (Figure 11.1, Arrows 1 and 2) without awareness or consideration of helper woundedness may contribute to an inferior, dependent, or dehumanizing position for the patient. Some helping professionals use the word "client" to remedy this situation. With the wounded-healer concept presented here, both helper and patient must humbly and mutually enter into the interaction for successful healing to take place.

2. The authors purposely hyphenated the words "wounded-healer" even though literature references frequently do not. If left unhyphenated, the word "wounded" is subordinate and the wounded-healer polarity becomes less balanced. The unhyphenated approach may also contribute to the erroneous conclusion that we are discussing a professional having personal problems, such as the "impaired physician."

REFERENCES

Adler, G. (1956). Notes regarding the dynamics of the self. In *Dynamic aspects of the psyche*. New York: Analytical Psychology Club.

American Psychiatric Association. (1994). *Diagnostic and statistical manual of mental disorders*, Fourth edition. Washington, DC: American Psychiatric Association.

Buber, M. (1970). *I and thou*. New York: Scribners.

Chomsky, N. (1972). *Language and mind*. New York: Harcourt Brace Jovanovich.

Comas-Diaz, L. and Jacobsen, F. (1991). Ethnocultural transference and countertransference in the therapeutic diad. *American Journal of Orthopsychiatry* 61(3): 392-402.

Corey, G. (1996). *Theory and practice of counseling and psychotherapy*, Fifth edition. Pacific Grove, CA: Brooks/Cole Publishing Company.

Egan, G. (1997). *The skilled helper: A problem-management approach to helping*, Sixth edition. Pacific Grove, CA: Brooks/Cole Publishing Company.

Fromm-Reichmann, F. (1950). *Principles of intensive psychotherapy*. Chicago: University of Chicago Press.

Gabbard, G.O. (1994). *Psychodynamic psychiatry in clinical practice*, Second edition. Washington, DC: American Psychiatric Press.

Graves, R. (1955). *The Greek myths*, Volume 1. New York: Penguin.

Groesbeck, C.J. (1975). The archetypal image of the wounded healer. *Journal of Analytical Psychology*, 20(2), 122-145.

Guggenbuhl-Craig, A. (1985). *Power in the helping professions*. Dallas, TX: Spring.

Harner, M. (1980). *The way of the shaman: A guide to power and healing*. San Francisco: Harper and Row.

Jackson, S. (1992). The listening healer in the history of psychological healing. *American Journal of Psychiatry,* 149(12): 1623-1632.

Jaspers, K. (1964). *The nature of psychotherapy: A critical appraisal.* Chicago: University of Chicago Press.

Johnson, R.A. (1974). *He: Understanding masculine psychology.* New York: Harper and Row.

Jung, C. (1946). Psychology of the transference. In Read, H., Fordham, M., and Adler, G. (Eds.), *Practice of psychotherapy, collected works.* Bollingen 20, Volume 16 (pp. 133-338). New York: Pantheon Books.

Jung, C. (1951). Fundamental quesitons of psychotherapy. In Read, H., Fordham, M., and Adler, G. (Eds.), *Practice of psychotherapy, collected works.* Bollingen 20, Volume 16 (pp. 111-125). New York: Pantheon Books.

Kerenyi, C. (1959). *Asklepios, archetypal image of the physician's existence.* Translated by Ralph Manheim (Bollingen Series LXV). Princeton, NJ: Princeton University Press.

Knight, J.A. (1985). Religio-psychological dimensions of wounded healer. Presented at the annual meeting of the American Psychiatric Association, Dallas, Texas, May 20.

Kochman, T. (1991). *Black and white styles in conflict.* Chicago: University of Chicago Press.

Kohut, H. (1991). *The search for the self: Selected writings of Heinz Kohut 1978-1981.* Madison, CT: International Universities Press.

Kreinheder, A. (1980). The healing power of illness. *Psychological Perspectives,* Spring 11(1): 9-18.

Langs, R. (1985). *Madness and cure.* New York: New Concept Press.

Meyerhoff, B.G. (1976). Balancing between worlds: The shaman's calling. *Parabola,* 1(2), 6-13.

Mohl, P.C. and Warrick McLaughlin, G.D. (1997). Listening to the patient. In Tasman, A., Kay, J., and Lieberman, J.A. (Eds.), *Psychiatry,* Volume 1 (pp. 3-18). Philadelphia: W.B. Saunders.

Needleman, J. (1985). *The way of the physician.* New York: Harper and Row.

Neumann, E. (1959). *Art and the creative unconscious.* Bollingen Series LXI. New York: Pantheon Books.

Plato (1951). *The symposium.* Translated by W. Hamilton. New York: Penguin.

Perls, F., Hefferline, R.F., and Goodman, P. (1951). *Gestalt therapy: Excitement and growth in the human personality.* New York: Dell.

Rippere, V. and Williams, R. (1985). *Wounded healers.* Chichester: John Wiley and Sons.

Rogers, C. (1951). *Client-centered therapy.* Boston: Houghton-Mifflin.

Schore, A.N. (1994). *Affect regulation and the origin of the self: The neurobiology of emotional development.* Hillsdale, NJ: Laurence Erlbaum Associates.

Webster's New Twentieth Century Unabridged Dictionary, Second Edition (1979). New York: Simon and Shuster.

Yalom, I.D. (1980). *Existential psychotherapy.* New York: Basic Books.

Chapter 12

The Self in Family Therapy: A Field Guide

David V. Keith

Through its several doorways, many enter the psychotherapy profession in an effort to deepen their connection with the Self. Too often, professional training patterns take over and the Self is obscured or put to sleep.

To illustrate, first-year medical students join me in family interviews. I am frequently impressed by their deadly accurate, though unschooled, observations of family dynamics. When they return two years later in their psychiatric rotation, I am again impressed by how distorted the vision of these same students has become. The distorting lens is a theoretical construct (chemical imbalance) or identification with a new worldview (science clarifies all experience).

What happens to this Self (whatever It is) with which we seek to deepen our connection? Too often a professional image is erected and the Self is suffocated by education, blinded by theory, and burdened by its own intelligence. It enters a dormant stage, sometimes forever, sometimes reemerging in a midlife crisis, in the experience of having a child, in facing death or one of its symbolic equivalents.

We psychotherapists live with patterns of passive acceptance of patient and community demands, which, if not countered, lead to self-destruction or paralysis. Psychotherapy patterns turn into "schools" which escape passivity by turning to models with prescribed behavioral sequences, or by seeking validation in science with a database from which inevitable conclusions may be derived (Keith and Whitaker, 1978).

All of these models (model = myth without divine characters) inhibit spontaneous behavior by therapists with the implied threat of damage to patients. The structure that develops as a protective cage for the Self of the therapist comes to dominate and frustrate the therapist. Although the patients of the imprisoned therapist remain undamaged, many continue to have a problem. They can make social changes, but do not gain personal spontaneity.

If the therapist cannot be a Self, neither can the patient. It is my recurring belief that if the therapist remains in a professional role, the patient is unable to leave the complementary role. The model for the role-dominated patient is the good child, socially adapted but without imagination.

There is a well-worn, but illustrative, joke about an old psychiatrist and a young psychiatrist getting on the elevator at the end of a day's work. The old psychiatrist is fresh-looking, immaculately groomed, with a carnation in his lapel. The young psychiatrist is disheveled and tired looking. He says to his older colleague, "How do you listen to this stuff all day, and come out looking so fresh?" Says the old psychiatrist, "Who listens?" The old psychiatrist is all professional role, and each day is a carbon copy of the one preceding.

The problem for the therapist is how to make a Houdini-like escape from the chains of professional image and survive. That is where the person of the therapist comes in, because, for better or for worse, the dynamics of therapy are in the person of the therapist (Whitaker and Malone, 1953). And while the Self cannot be "known" in an assured, left-brained, take-a-final-examination way, it needs to be familiar so that the mature professional therapist can guide it.

It is important to note that the author works as a family therapist. Therefore, the focus is on the *interpersonal* components of health and pathology. Likewise, implicit in this chapter is that this personal Self is best known in relation to other selves, for our purposes here, cotherapists and patients. These ideas do not translate automatically into individual therapy patterns. The personal Self is much more suspect in working with individuals. The presence of the family and the cotherapist allows more freedom and security for patients and therapists. An exception would occur when a cotherapy team works with an individual.

In the midst of writing, my wife, Noel, and I visited an art museum. We were standing back admiring one of Jackson Pollock's giant paintings. "See if you can find any form in that canvas," said Noel. I could not. "Now, fix on a dot, and see if you can hold it." I could not. The dynamic, fluid quality of Pollock's work did not offer any specific form nor would it allow the eye to rest. It demanded movement. Noel said, "That's the way your chapter comes across. It is interesting, but it is sometimes difficult to . . ." That story is a guide to your involvement with this chapter. The suggestion that my thinking was patternless and confused was a little hurtful, but I enjoyed the comparison to Jackson Pollock.

This personal Self of the therapist is, in fact, a community of selves. The mayor of this community is the professional self. It has a professional degree, does diagnostic interviews, maintains technical proficiency, reads professional journals, and takes few chances. The subject of this chapter is a more obscure Self, the personal Self; the one who would rather be on the floor building a Lego spaceship with the four-year-old than writing this paper.

This personal Self with its capital "S" is something we experience obliquely, understand with our peripheral vision, and see through a glass but darkly. It sneaks up on us. It is unintentional. It did not decide to become a Self. It did not decide to be conceived. It began with an orgastic communion of Selves, and is best known by its appearance in interpersonal experience. It also appears in dream experience, unexpectedly and often inscrutably.

This elusive Self with its capital "S" is something I have forever wanted to know. But "know" is the wrong word. In my fifth decade "familiar" rings more true. I am familiar with my Self to the point of being both pleased and pained with its familiar unpredictability. In dreams it appears as a giant in a miniature world, as a lover, as a woman, and as a barefisted warrior. Sometimes the Self is helpless and fleeing, sometimes it is confused and often partially dressed. Oddly, its occasional appearances in therapy metaphorically mirror the dream appearances.

This Self is crazy and creative. Often, it is too playful for its own good. And it strains to speak or to appear with eccentric overtones. Its intuitive accuracy sometimes surprises. This Self has no firm image. It is that furtive schizophrenic, both chronic and acute, fragmented and out of focus. It forgets to return certain phone calls, and negatively hallucinates most administrative responsibilities. It has a certain Christlike quality, hungry to change the world, too often thinking of death as just another dream possibility from which it will awaken. In its hunger for love and other variations of human contact, it is impetuous and frequently shows poor judgment. Its simultaneous arrogance and humility leads to silence. Flickers of rage appear at the edges. Haunted by dependency, it looks furtively backward at the ghost of failure.

But this Self is not just a me. It is an amalgam of endless fragments from those deeply loved. I am most apt to find It in relation to someone else. I often wonder, am I really a me or just a complicated sum of my relationships? "Did I just say that, or was it one of those fragments speaking out of turn?"

During a difficult period in a struggle I was having with a family, the father remarked, speaking of psychotherapy, "I can never understand how they get intelligent people to do this kind of work." There are times when I feel the same way. But what he could not see, and what I often forget, is the seductive quality that therapy with families has. Nor could he see how often I am able to leave my therapist's chair and become a patient with the deep pleasure of contacting another Self in those indescribable moments of bilateral therapeutic experience.

SOME FEATURES OF THE PERSONAL SELF

This is a preliminary exploration on a series of notes kept over the past eight years; a view of the Self from a therapist's sketch-book, if you will. For all I know there may be no such thing. The Self that may be spoken of is not the true Self. It may be only like the unicorn, a mythical beast. Or like the adult, it may exist only as a theoretical construct. What is crucial is its availability in relation to the other.

The Self appears by surprise. When it appears, the professional self decides whether to recognize It. Although there are those moments when It either bursts or sneaks in, circumventing protocol. It is there during an awkward moment in therapy; one that we wished had not happened. But then a therapeutic shift is noticed at the next interview. Sometimes in the evening, at home, my family hears me groan or sees me shake my head. It usually means that I am having a flashback to a family therapy session and something I said or failed to say. It probably also means that the Self found its way into the session. Those flashbacks happen rarely, if at all, in relation to sessions with individuals.

For better or for worse, this Self is:

- Against the culture. It is the part of us that is not socially adapted.
- Creative or crazy or spontaneous and unpredictable.
- Often ridiculous or silly.
- Largely unconscious.
- Potentially dangerous to me as well as to the other. It is not convinced that death really means anything.
- Often ridiculous.
- Inconsistent.
- Not anesthetized by "born-again" enthusiasm, but struggles with the pain of growing until death comes.

THE SELF AS IT APPEARS IN THERAPY

The following are some manifestations of the Self as it appears in therapy. What is coming into focus is that the therapist's personal Self appears only in relation to the patient's personal Self:

- Power
- Integrity
- Sense of my absurdity and the use of humor
- Freedom for anger and creative hatred
- Metaphorical reality
- Residue of outside experiences
- Freedom to advance or retreat from any position (Whitaker, 1976)
- Development of peer relationships (cotherapy)
- Capacity to be freely loving

Power

Bateson has protested the use of physics concepts, such as power, for describing human relationships (Keeney, 1983, p. 125). I am always uneasy in disagreeing with Bateson, but the etymology of power has to do with human behavior, which is inescapably cyber-netic, meaning "to be able" (Partridge, 1958). In therapy, I link power with the freedom to use my professional image or to be myself, at my initiative. I consider it a limited freedom.

In the beginning of therapy, power has to do with the freedom to set the structure for the therapy. Who will be there, and when and where will we meet? In the first interview, power has to do with how the information will be presented. This component is managed by the professional self.

At the second interview the professional self continues to domi-nate. Power is used to stay out. "What do you want from me? Are you certain you want to be here? Maybe we should quit now." There is a serious question about who shall provide motivation for family change, the therapist or the family's desperation. Palazzoli-Selvini (1985) asks, "Why do patients make it so hard for us to help them?" Too often the professional assumes that because they made an ap-pointment, they want to be in therapy. Often, they come in only to see what is needed. Before the next step is taken, they need to sign the operative permit. The professional often urges that therapy con-tinue. They make it hard for us to help them because we take away the family's responsibility for itself. The Self of the patient with its intuition warns of hidden danger.

There is a good example of this problem in the way that child psychiatry is sometimes practiced. Too often, child psychiatrists believe that they can parent better than the real parents. The child psychiatry version of family therapy has the quality of child psy-chiatry training for the parents. Parents learn to be professional. As I think of family therapy it offers an opportunity for the family to have the therapeutically valuable, regressive experience of patient-hood.

As caring increases, power diminishes or equalizes in the rela-tionship context (Keith, 1981). At this point it is not possible to push families around. The fluctuating dance of therapy begins as the therapist moves in and out, close in with caring and attention, then distant and indifferent. Now the power of the therapist resides in the capacity to change himself or herself, the power to join and the power to separate. The mode is similar to parenting, where the mother has the freedom to shift generational level as needed. She may sometimes be parental. "Before you go ride your bike you are going to clean your room." At other times she is a peer. "Let's make rhubarb pie and surprise Dad." Or she may be a generation down. "Do you think I'm being unfair?" Power is manifested in the capacity to move between generations rather than moving in response to the other's demand.

Integrity

Technical proficiency is the professional precursor of integrity. Integrity colors decision making and can bring us into conflict with the community. As experience accumulates, the demands on the professional self may be in conflict with the demands of the personal self. An example would be a psychiatrist who grows uncomfortable with the use of psychotropic medication and the community expectations for a psychiatrist.

Integrity of the Self refuses to become any image that is offered. The doctor part of me is a role function. I am not a physician; I work as a physician.

Integrity does not permit the Self to presume to know what the Other thinks. Likewise, it does not permit Other to think it knows what Self thinks.

Integrity refuses to be all-knowing and is comfortable with the knowledge that all human problems do not have answers.

Sense of My Absurdity and the Use of Humor

I like humor and find it useful in working with families. It is always spontaneous, and with adults it is the most available form of play therapy. Psychotherapy takes place in the overlap of two areas of playing, that of the therapist and that of the patient (Winnicott, 1971).

Humor can have a sadistic and distancing quality, but what is hidden is the way it introduces sudden moments of intimacy and peer relationship. Humor by itself is not sadistic; it is the *person* who is sadistic. Humor by itself is not distancing; it is the person who is distancing. There are times after an interview that has had a feeling of fun and intimacy, when I will feel vaguely depressed. It must be because of the loneliness that follows closeness. So in that sense, humor makes us aware of the distance in our relationships or of the sadistic components that lie beneath that thin veneer of social protocol.

Humor distorts reality and allows us to see another way, exploding the bonds of logic or social propriety. For example, when the thirteen-year-old son was rude to the forty-five-year-old therapist, the father scolded him, saying that he "should show more respect to Dr. . . ." He could not remember the doctor's name. "Just call me 'Butch,' " said the therapist.

Humor acts as a wonderful enzyme for making the symptom interpersonal. Telling a joke, using double entendre, or a gentle tease is an ambiguous invitation to be personal. Shared humor is a self-to-self experience.

Humor is a way to be insulting without being annihilating. The therapeutic relationship may induce an anesthetized infantalism in the patient if the therapist is too supportive. Gentle insults induce individuation with concomitant self-responsibility.

The following case sample illustrates. The Fakes were referred by the pediatrician because their previously angelic daughter, age fourteen, had evidenced mild disobedience. The father was passive and lethargic. The mother was neurotic and hyperactive. She mentioned being on a medication that she referred to as her "sleeping dope." The cotherapists took it to be a reference to her husband.

By the way, how many family therapists does it take to change a lightbulb? Forget the lightbulb, let's rewire the house.

Did you hear about the Norwegian who loved his wife so much he almost told her?

Humor is like any spice. It must be infused in right proportion so as to improve the taste. Beware using humor to depersonalize therapeutic experience. A symptom may be the therapist's anxiety mounting before adding the humor. In fact, anxiety in the therapist may be a specific contradiction to using humor. Finally, humor can turn into an empty runaway, nonsense with no affective implications.

Freedom for Anger and Creative Hatred

If you have not been hated by your therapist, you have been cheated (Winnicot, 1949). Anger and hatred are ways to be more deeply interpersonal. To extrapolate from Winnicot, if there is no hatred there is no marriage. And are our children cheated when we fail to hate them?

In this era of self-understanding and conscious efforts at parenting, we learn we should not come down to our children's level. That is, we should not be as hateful toward them as they are to us. Yet, if we seal ourselves off they are cheated and burdened by the illusion that anger and hatred are personally inappropriate. Therapists are like parents. When the therapist comes down to their level, both grow from it when the generation gap is reestablished.

Case Example

Working with Mrs. L, a chronic mental patient, and her grown daughter over a period of a year was both frustrating and satisfying. As she left the life of a chronic mental patient and became more self-owning, she began a pattern of admiring her therapist in a way which he found increasingly aggravating. His frustration mounted one day as she went on and on about him, until he exploded, "Will you shut up! Just shut up!" She was insulted and left, saying she would not return. After she left, the therapist was remorseful, but felt it best that the situation be allowed to take its own course. Mrs. L returned three weeks later. In effect she had ended therapy and now restarted. She said that while she had been initially insulted it occurred to her that her esteemed doctor might be having a nervous breakdown. If he, an esteemed doctor, was having a nervous breakdown, it somehow made her history more human.

Metaphorical Reality

This is the most creative component of any therapy. It is that jointly unconscious poetry that moves in and out of awareness. It is found in our verbal slips, in the adjective which we hear ourselves using with this particular family, or in visual images stimulated by their presence.

Children live constantly in this reality. I am suspicious of families and therapists who think they do more "work" by leaving the children home. The children's presence enriches the metaphorical atmosphere of therapy, which increases the likelihood of the whole person being affected by the experience.

John Sonne's (1973) concept of the Metaphorolytic family has been useful to me. This is a family that allows experience to have only one level of meaning. This is the kind of family that does not know how to play, the kind of family that is cornered by its own normality.

Case Sample

The Drs. H., a psychologist and an economist, struggled in their marriage. Both were paralyzed by their professional images. She became extensively self-mutilating and he increasingly distant and work-preoccupied. Their four-year-old daughter was present in the interviews, which the therapists videotaped. The H's asked to see a videotaped interview, but watched only a short segment, complaining that the noise their daughter created as she played made it impossible to hear the adult conversation. When the therapist looked at the tape, the daughter was playing a game with dolls. Her "noise" was the doll crying, "Help, Mama. Mama help. Somebody help her." The recording of her play was the most crucial subtext of the interview, giving voice to her mother's anguish. But the parents, in their effort to be more realistic (metaphorolytic) about the problem, heard only nonmetaphorical noise.

Residue of Outside Experience

The psychotherapy koan, "the dynamics of therapy are in the person of the therapist" (Whitaker and Malone, 1953), suggests that the therapist's outside living dynamics feed the therapy situation. If outside living is dead, is the therapist's effectiveness diminished? There are those times when the therapist is disrupted by events in personal life: a child is ill, the therapist's marriage is disrupted. These real-life troubles may alter functioning, but not necessarily in a detrimental way. Often while technical proficiency diminishes, the person is more present.

At a time when we were preparing to move to another city, I began to think of moving as a symbolic death. It was impressive how often death became an issue in the families I was working with.

In reviewing my psychotherapeutic work with schizophrenics I developed a list of schizophrenic patients with whom I had had profound experiences. I was impressed to discover that each one corresponded with periods of personal emotional arousal. Four were time-related to the birth of our children and another to a time when I was a psychotherapy patient.

The Freedom to Advance or Retreat from Any Position

The Self is not paralyzed by reason or consistency. It changes hypotheses so that any problem can be seen from a different perspective. It is available to see unexpected change in a family. The freedom to be inconsistent is another doorway to creativity for the family. At one point in the interview the Self may empathically support the scapegoat's effort to change the family, then later tease the scapegoat for being a boor. No family becomes a fixed theoretical construct.

The Development of Peer Relationships

The split image (therapist/person) is most available in an experienced cotherapy connection that permits creative craziness in the therapy interview without metaprocessing.

Likewise, the Self of the patients is more present when their family is present.

The Capacity to Be Freely Loving

Developing the capacity to be freely loving is a primary goal of psychotherapy. It emerges with experience, lies out beyond the realm of technique, and requires the balanced functioning of the professional and the personal selves.

Of interest to me as I work on the concept of the Self in the therapist is how often my experience as a patient returns. I recall hearing our therapist say that he loved me, but I did not believe it for a long time. When I did I ended being a patient. Our patients need to know that we love them. In that way they can begin to give up being patients.

SUMMARY

This personal Self speaks in half-truths and innuendo. Thus most of what is included here is only partially true and should not be translated directly into the reader's experience.

The professional self, a social role, provides the structure for the personal Self to make appearances in family therapy. This Self does not show up as a free-standing entity, but rather as part of a joint experience with the Self that lies behind the patient Self, another social role. The therapist's Self appears as an invitation to the patient's Self to appear. An important result of the communion of selves is in the joy of acknowledging another Self, but satisfied with the fact that they are separate. In successful therapy they end as peers.

And the Self lived ever after, however, not always happily.

REFERENCES

Keeney, B.P. (1983). *Aesthetics of change*. New York: Guilford Press.

Keith, D.V. (1981). Power: Physical or mental? A response. *Pilgrimage*, 9, 32-33.

Keith, D.V. and Whitaker, C.A. (1978). Struggling with the impotence impasse: Absurdity and acting in. *Journal of Marital and Family Counseling*, January, 69-77.

Palazzoli-Selvini, M. (1985). Towards a general model of psychotic family games. Address presented at the Forty-Third Annual Conference, American Association of Marital and Family Therapists, New York, October.

Partridge, E. (1958). *Origins, a short etymological dictionary of modern English*. New York: Macmillan Publishing Company, Inc.

Sonne, J. (1973). *A primer for family therapists*. Moorestown, NJ: The Thursday Press.

Whitaker, C.A. (1976). The hindrance of theory in clinical work. In P. Guerin (Ed.), *Family therapy: Theory and practice* (pp. 154-164). New York: Gardner Press.

Whitaker, C.A. and Malone, T.P. (1953). *The roots of psychotherapy*. New York: Blakiston Press.

Winnicot, D.W. (1949). Hate in the countertransference. *International Journal of Psychoanalysis*, 30, 69-74.

Winnicott, D.W. (1971). *Playing and reality*. New York: Basic Books.

Chapter 13

I Look for I:
The Self of the Therapist—Part II

David V. Keith

A BRIDGE OVER NONLOGICAL WATERS

This second essay, "I Look for I," probably should have been written before "A Field Guide." This essay (1999) is more fundamental; the first (1987) is an application. But I had to write the one that should have been second in order to get to the one that should have been written first. Both are mildly nonlogical. In an academic context this thinking would be inadmissible. In a clinical context a thought disorder could be suggested. Think of these essays as a combination of playful and serious. There is a lack of clarity, because in both cases I am trying to understand something by writing about it. I am not smarter than either essay. I have shifted some things in the way I think about the abstract, fluid reality of the I, Self, and the social self. In the first paper, I said I (the Self) am the sum of my relationships. I think now that there is an "I" which is more than the sum of its relationships. In the first chapter I wrote as an observer of this Self. In this chapter I am attempting to give "I" a voice. Perhaps there is a system, a community of selves. "I" is in the center, usually overshadowed, yet the root of our uniqueness. The professional self is not the mayor; it has prominence only in a certain context. The professional self is not much fun as a husband. And the professional self can neither dance nor play music. Finally, in this second essay, I talk about the implications of the "I" in the way we think about psychotherapy.

* * *

The mask is magic, character is not innate: a man's character is his daemon, his tutelar spirit; received in a dream. His character is his destiny, which is to act out his dream. (Brown, 1966)

"The other One, the one called . . . [Dave Keith] is the one things happen to. . . . I am destined to perish, definitively and only some instant of myself can survive in him. . . . Thus my life is a flight and I lose everything and everything belongs to oblivion or to him" (Borges, 1962). In that other essay from 1987, he referred to the Self, with the capital S. I am that Self. I am I. Jacob Needleman (1982) says the essential philosophical question (with the ever-elusive answer) is "Who am I?" I, of course, am simply I. I am who Dave refers to as his Self. I don't *know* myself, I *am* myself. For Dave, I am unknown, and unknowable. I am his daemon, his tutelar spirit, his destiny. When you look for the I in you, you enter a labyrinth constructed of mirrors, encoded messages, and other pseudo-objective deceptions. To engage in the search requires that you be an impeccable observer. There are many distractions. Some of them are cultural pathologies. I am uncertain as to whether Paxil, Xanax, or Trilafon enhances impeccability. By attending to the labyrinth of the unknown, you encounter the depths of people and the world. When you attend to theories, you may see only what the theory invites you to see, because theories have no depth and little dimension. A good clinician is an impeccable observer. A therapist is a combination of clinician and healer.

I am behind intuition. I am behind poetry. But I have little to do with fixing the world. I have little to do with research or theory building. Money means nothing; it is one of those lies Dave must live with.

I love complexity and seeing through it to dynamic ordering. Dave does as well. He refers to it as the "aesthetics of experience," but he gets overexcited, and he doesn't explain it very clearly. He would probably sound less naive, more articulate, if he paid less attention to me. I don't know why that is. My monologue is deteriorating. I don't even know which of us is writing this. I will back out and turn it over to Dave.

* * *

I am Dave, and I am also I. But I is elusive. I am still fascinated by the idea of an I, of the daemon received in a dream, which does not change, but which unfolds. Then there is a social self, that actor, who is always changing and adapting, who does and who is known by others. The difference is not clear, and it is best defined playfully, or by metaphor, as in poetry. The question about I and the social self are more vivid when raised to consciousness in therapy, but also in any intimate relationship with another: marriage, parenting, teaching, or healing. The question is important in intimate relationship with myself: artistic work, being alone. The question comes up in encounters with Death or its symbolic equivalents: illness, failure. And it comes up in encounters with madness: confusion, depression.

You see, in the labyrinth categories are not clearly distinguished. But keep this in mind; avoiding madness may be the maddest way of being mad (Brown, 1991). Or said differently, there is a danger in avoiding the confusion of the labyrinth, of failing to be aware of what we don't know we don't know.

THIS SELF IN PSYCHOTHERAPY

As before, I am writing as a family therapist. The professional world I know best is a sort of crossroads: family therapy, psychiatry (child and general), and medicine; a deep belief in psychotherapy as a pattern for healing. Family therapy began, in part, as an effort to increase the scope of conventional psychiatric practices, to enhance healing. Although the common sense of some would suggest otherwise, I believe the Self is most available in the multipersonal context of the family. The Self is activated and nourished by ambiguity and by intimacy. The affect in family relationships, which are biological and therefore eternal, makes the I more available. But our social selves become anxious at the spontaneity and unstructured, idiosyncratic qualities of the Self. The Self appears to undermine social values and structure. But I believe it maintains a life-enhancing tension. In my opinion, psychotherapy is a fundamentally countercultural process. Counseling is a process for social adaptation.

Family therapy, particularly, began as a movement that questioned conventional patterns of living and healing. But as the movement gained popularity, it became a culture-supporting institution. It was a movement that wanted recognition from the mass culture, so it sold itself to the mass culture. But in the world of business, the customer is always right, and the customer did not want the whole thing—it took only selected components. Mass culture said, "We will recognize you if you conform to the values we set forth, if you act like a science, and if you develop theories based on reason, and *please* teach people to conform, to mind their manners." And soon psychotherapy was an agency of the mass culture. It went from being an undefined something to being an overdefined something. The culture said, "You need to show results. You need to do something we can all understand." And soon, the concept of I/Self re-emerged as an attractively packaged, low-fat, artificially flavored, decaf something else. Not I.

The psychotherapy that is countercultural is not found in academic training programs or in academic journals. Psychotherapy, like most things that are worth knowing, cannot be taught. It must be learned. In this sense, psychotherapy is like music. It does not belong to anyone. It is a process that comes through the therapist, as music comes through the musician.

A DEVELOPMENTAL SCHEMA FOR DISTINGUISHING AMONG PSYCHOTHERAPIES

I want to use a homemade developmental schema to distinguish between a psychotherapy that acknowledges and nurtures, attends to I, and a psychotherapy that operates as a cultural agent in support of social adaptation (Keith, 1996). I am drawing this distinction for the sake of illumination. I would like to review an idea that evolved out of conversations with Carl Whitaker (personal communication, 1991), and comes from *Keith's Catalogue of Flawed Explanations* (Keith, in press).

I am an adult playing the duplicitous social word games of adulthood. Calling them "games" is not to trivialize them. For example, I am not a physician, I am a person who was trained to play the game of physician. Psychotherapy is one of the games. I play some of these games with passion, energy, and dedication. Some, I play with awkwardness and pain; some, because of shyness or ineptitude, I avoid completely. In my role as parent, I teach my children to play these games of social adaptation. Being a good player is crucial to survival and to healthy, satisfying living. Writing is an interesting game. As I work on this essay, I find myself alternating between two levels of consciousness. Most of the time, I am writing with you, the audience, in mind. In the perpetual television of my fantasy, I see you as critical and disapproving, but gradually shifting to understand me. But there are other moments when I become truly Self-absorbed. You fade from awareness, and I am using the writing to explore, to push some edge of growth in understanding the idea of I-ness.

However, as I indicated in the other chapter, there is another component to me. I am more than a tricky social game player. I am a printout of earlier programming by my family. The software at my core, installed in the dream period of infancy, developed in my family living during my preverbal infancy years when I was the victim of the world of my family, the world of adults. I have virtually no memory of this time or these experiences. When I arrived in the adult world, I had no memory or veto power. I lacked the ability to think about what was happening to me. My self-esteem comes from this period, out of my being loved by them. It was also in that period that I was irreparably wounded by what they were unable to do for me out of their anxiety, their fear, out of their sense of inadequacy. The programs installed at that point have been or can be little altered. During this period, I was emerging, but there was no individuation.

The chronic undifferentiated schizophrenic in all of us can be found here. Likewise, those problems called chemical imbalances, or character defect are related to these programs, which are virtually inaccessible to reason-based language.

Then, when I reached two years, I became something of a problem. I began to individuate. I learned to say "no." And it was not clear if my demands were based on need for food or on need to dominate my world and my adult servant/tyrants. By two and a half, three, I began to be programmed for adulthood. I then started to learn these duplicitous games. I learned different ways to say "no." I learned to protect my innocence through self-justification. Particles of memory began to appear. By the time I was three the training was in full swing. I learned not to bite just because I was upset. I learned to be polite. I learned duplicity in the name of adaptation.

Today most psychotherapy is done in the realm of social adaptation, teaching us how to get along in the world. But the psychotherapy that the mass culture is not very interested in, and I am fascinated by, attends to the software that makes up the Self. I do not think of this software as changeable, but the therapy aims at gaining more access to it, making more of the Self accessible. It helps get more access to the Self. Experience does this.

MY COMPUTER AS A MODEL
FOR ME GAINING ACCESS TO MYSELF

I have a computer that came with an abundance of software programs installed. I have become expert in using the word processor program. Then I had to figure out how to use e-mail in order to correspond with some friends. When I need to learn something new, I begin with hesitancy, anticipating the inevitable series of frustrations. Those mistakes lead to learning, and in the end, I know more of my computer. In the same way, experience leads us to more knowledge of the Self with the capital "S." Experience produces demands and frustrations and ultimately learning (by the way, experience also produces injury that may block learning). As time goes on, experience accumulates, and pushes learning about the Self. Psychotherapy can be the experience that leads to learning about Self, but more often, psychotherapy is a catalyst for change. Or therapy becomes a template for how to get something out of our own experiences with a meaningful other person.

It may be helpful to know that this way of thinking is stimulated by our experiences in working with families with schizophrenia and serious psychosomatic illness. The way these ideas translate into schizophrenia is that instead of a genetically based chemical imbalance, we think of schizophrenia as a desperate, forced immersion in I. Support is needed to make it back to the surface. However, in the immersion, damage may occur that is irreversible. What does that mean about psychotherapy with schizophrenia? For me, it means the therapist forces the family together and neutralizes the schizophrenic's desperate rampage to bring about change. The family's attempt to be therapeutic to its own member is interrupted. We make all family members acknowledge their own pain and turn them toward the labyrinth of themselves. The process, when it works, moves the schizophrenic person out of the pivotal position in the family.

It is difficult to attend to these processes. Deeper symbiotic/symbolic connection with patients is involved. The process pressures the Self of all who are involved. (The process almost routinely provokes disturbing symptoms in the therapist.) The Self of the therapist can become temporarily disoriented. The experience challenges identity and competence and leads to questioning the very meaning of the Self. And, as I noted above, it is much more likely to succeed in the presence of the family.

I have been paying attention to I; the searching is a clumsy, but crucial, counterbalance to mass culture. Psychotherapy emerges as a means to restore the I, but it is taken over by the culture, neutralized. Remembering I, looking for I is to enter a labyrinth of darkness, deception, and meaninglessness. But it is exactly in this descent into meaninglessness, without panic, but with the impeccable eyes of the searcher, that the meaning of life and relationships is deepened. It is humbling to write in this way. I hope I said something interesting, if not helpful to you.

THE END

REFERENCES

Borges, J.L. (1962). Borges and I. In *Labyrinths, selected stories and other writings* (J.E. Irby, Trans.). New York: New Directions Publishing Corporation.

Brown, N.O. (1966). *Love's body* (p. 92). New York: Random House.

Brown, N.O. (1991). *Apocalypse and/or metamorphosis* (p. 2). Berkeley: The University of California Press.

Keith, D.V. (In press). *Keith's catalogue of flawed explanations.*

Keith, D.V. (1996). The growing edge in psychotherapy: Healing and play. Lecture presented at The Growing Edge, a Tribute to the Ideas and Work of Carl Whitaker. Rome, Italy.

Needleman, J. (1982). *The heart of philosophy.* San Francisco: Harper and Row.

Whitaker, C.A. (1989). *Midnight musings of a family therapist* (M. Ryan, Ed.). New York: W.W. Norton and Co.

Epilogue

What are the implications of a belief that the self of the therapist is central to the therapeutic process? One important conclusion is that it needs to be a major focus of attention from both a clinical and training standpoint. Mauksch, in a personal communication, suggested that if the self is considered an essential resource, it deserves to be looked upon from the perspective of a technological model of resources management. The use of this precious resource, then, warrants and deserves the application of skills, care, and maintenance. When one contemplates the expenditure of efforts, thought, and time that go into learning how to use a computer, it is ludicrous to think of the scant attention paid to this most complex instrument, the self.

A major consideration is the protection of the client. Since the self has a potential for negative as well as positive impact, our first guide should be Hippocrates' dictum "to do no harm." There are unfortunately many examples of therapeutic relationships that have been grossly misused in the service of the therapist's own uncontained needs. Young therapists especially need guidance in positive use of self, because their fear of having a negative impact on the client through misuse of self means that they may hold themselves back from sharing their humanness, for fear of making a mistake. As Aponte and Winter point out in Chapter 7, being a family therapist demands enormous personal self-knowledge and discipline since the patient's difficulties can so often resonate with those of the therapist.

The development of the self of the therapist must be a continuous and ongoing process. Although the foregoing statement seems obvious, it is easy to fall into a routine of daily life and work that denies the time and energy necessary for the nurture of the self. The consequences of such a neglect are unfortunate because an alive and vibrant self is a source of energy and creativity that is of benefit to the therapeutic encounter as well as to the well-being of the therapist.

Index

Page numbers followed by the letter "f" indicate figures; those followed by the letter "t" indicate tables.

Order Your Own Copy of *This Important Book for Your Personal Library!*

THE USE OF SELF IN THERAPY, SECOND EDITION

_____ in hardbound at $49.95 (ISBN: 0-7890-0744-4)

_____ in softbound at $24.95 (ISBN: 0-7890-0745-2)

COST OF BOOKS_____

OUTSIDE USA/CANADA/
MEXICO: ADD 20%_____

POSTAGE & HANDLING_____
(US: $3.00 for first book & $1.25
for each additional book)
Outside US: $4.75 for first book
& $1.75 for each additional book)

SUBTOTAL_____

IN CANADA: ADD 7% GST_____

STATE TAX_____
(NY, OH & MN residents, please
add appropriate local sales tax)

FINAL TOTAL_____
(If paying in Canadian funds,
convert using the current
exchange rate. UNESCO
coupons welcome.)

☐ **BILL ME LATER:** ($5 service charge will be added)
(Bill-me option is good on US/Canada/Mexico orders only;
not good to jobbers, wholesalers, or subscription agencies.)

☐ Check here if billing address is different from
shipping address and attach purchase order and
billing address information.

Signature_____

☐ **PAYMENT ENCLOSED:** $_____

☐ **PLEASE CHARGE TO MY CREDIT CARD.**

☐ Visa   ☐ MasterCard   ☐ AmEx   ☐ Discover
☐ Diner's Club

Account # _____

Exp. Date _____

Signature _____

Prices in US dollars and subject to change without notice.

NAME _____

INSTITUTION _____

ADDRESS _____

CITY _____

STATE/ZIP _____

COUNTRY _____ COUNTY (NY residents only) _____

TEL _____ FAX _____

E-MAIL_____
May we use your e-mail address for confirmations and other types of information? ☐ Yes   ☐ No

Order From Your Local Bookstore or Directly From
The Haworth Press, Inc.
10 Alice Street, Binghamton, New York 13904-1580 • USA
TELEPHONE: 1-800-HAWORTH (1-800-429-6784) / Outside US/Canada: (607) 722-5857
FAX: 1-800-895-0582 / Outside US/Canada: (607) 772-6362
E-mail: getinfo@haworthpressinc.com
PLEASE PHOTOCOPY THIS FORM FOR YOUR PERSONAL USE.

BOF96